Christina Latham-Koenig
Clive Oxenden
Mike Boyle

ENGLISH FILE

Intermediate Plus Student's Book

Paul Seligson and Clive Oxenden are the original co-authors of *English File 1* and *English File 2*

Contents

G pronouns
V working out meaning from context
P vowel sounds

What's your first name?

It's Caroline, but most people call me Caro.

1A Why did they call you that?

1 SPEAKING & LISTENING

a Work with a partner. Talk about your names.

- My **full name** is...
- I'm **named after**...
- Some people **call me**... **for short**.
- I have a **nickname**. It's...
- I hate it when people **call me**...

b 1 2 Listen to four people talking about their names. Write the names down, and tick (✓) the people who are happy with their names.

c Listen again and answer the questions for each person.

1 Why did their parents choose the name?
2 Do they have a nickname, or are they called something for short?
3 Do they like their name? Would they like to change it?

d Are *you* happy with your name? Would you like to change it?

2 PRONUNCIATION vowel sounds

a 1 3 Look at the first names in the chart. Listen and circle the name which doesn't have the sound in the sound picture.

1	Chris	Bill	Olivia	Brian
2 iː	Peter	Steve	Emily	Eve
3 æ	Alex	Adrian	Andrew	Ann
4 ɔː	Sean	George	Paula	Charlotte
5 e	Adele	Ben	Leo	Jessica
6 eɪ	Sam	Grace	James	Kate
7 əʊ	Tony	Joe	Robert	Sophie
8 aɪ	Ryan	Liam	Michael	Simon

b With a partner, decide if they are men's names, women's names, or both. Write **M, W,** or **B** in the box. Are any of them short for another name?

c ➤ **p.166 Sound Bank.** Look at the typical spellings of the sounds in **a**.

d Look at some common British surnames. How do you think they are pronounced?

Adams Evans Harrison Johnson Jones
Mason Murray Taylor Walker Wright

e 1 4 Listen and check.

3 READING & VOCABULARY working out meaning from context

a You're going to read an article about names. Before you read, look at the title of the article. In what ways do you think a name can help or hurt you?

b Read the article and write the headings in the correct paragraphs. There is one heading you don't need to use.

A Life expectancy
B Names and careers
C How people see you
D Popular names in history
E Success at school

c Read the article again. Answer the questions with a partner.

1 How do people see you differently if you're called Elizabeth, or Sophie, or Ann?
2 What kind of names might help you to get better results at school?
3 Why might someone called Ellie choose to be an electrician?
4 When you are applying for a job, is it an advantage or a disadvantage to have an unusual name?
5 What kind of initials should you have if you want to live longer?

Guessing the meaning of new words and phrases
When you are reading and find a word or phrase you don't know:
1 Decide if you think it's a noun, a verb, an adjective, etc.
2 Try to work out the meaning from the context (the other words around it).
3 If you still can't work out what it means, either ignore it and carry on reading, or use a dictionary to help you.

Is your name helping or hurting you?

Wendy Isabel Nichols

Most of us never think about our names. They're just names and they usually don't mean much – or do they? New research has come out which suggests that our names can affect everything from our emotional well-being to our career paths, and even how long we live.

1 ________________

A recent survey asked 6,000 people in the UK to rank common names for men and women in three categories: successful, lucky, and attractive. The results showed a strong preference for certain names. People called James and Elizabeth were seen as the most successful, Jack and Lucy were the luckiest, and Sophie and Ryan were the most attractive. Overall, it seems that the best name for men is James, which came near the top in all three categories. The least desirable ones were George and Ann, which ranked near the bottom in all categories.

2 ________________

The potential effects of your name go beyond perceptions. According to several studies, teachers give higher marks to children with attractive names. In the US, where grades are given on a scale from A (excellent) to D (poor), another study found that students with first names beginning with A or B received higher marks than students whose first names started with C or D.

3 ________________

Some experts also believe that people are attracted to jobs that sound like their names. One study found that people called Dennis and Denise are more likely to become dentists. There are hairdressers called Harry, artists called Art, and even a lawyer called Sue Yoo*. Even if your name and job don't match, your name could affect your job prospects. A study found that American employers were more likely to consider the CVs of applicants who have 'normal-sounding' names. Researchers also say that companies are more likely to promote people if their names sound successful.

4 ________________

It may seem incredible, but there is evidence that your name could affect how long you live. Researchers compared the death certificates of people with 'positive' initials (such as J.O.Y. or F.U.N.) and people with 'negative' ones (such as D.I.E. or S.A.D.). The results? People with positive initials live about four years longer than the average, while people with negative initials die about three years sooner.

So if you have an 'undesirable' name, should you change it to a new one? Most experts say no. For most people, having a positive attitude will help more than giving yourself a new name.

* The name Sue Yoo sounds like the phrase 'sue you', which means to make a claim against somebody in court.

Brian Adams Davies

d Look at the highlighted words or phrases in the article which are related to research. Try to work out what they mean, and how they are pronounced.

e Now match them with 1–9.

1 ________ *noun* people who study something carefully to discover new facts about it
2 ________ *noun* the facts that make you believe something is true
3 ________ *noun* an investigation of the opinions of a particular group of people
4 ________ *noun* the number you get when you add two or more numbers and then divide the total by the number of figures you added
5 ________ *noun* different levels or numbers used for measuring something
6 ________ *verb* to put in order according to quality, importance, etc.
7 ________ *adjective* probable or expected
8 ________ *adverb* generally
9 ________ *preposition* further than

f 1 5 Listen and check. Under<u>line</u> the stressed syllable.

g Do you think *your* name is helping or hurting you? Why?

4 SPEAKING

Do the questionnaire in groups.

Angelina Jolie and Brad Pitt with their children

WHAT'S IN A NAME?

- What are three first names you really like and three you don't like at all? Why do you like or dislike them?
- What are the advantages and disadvantages of...?
  - having a very common name
  - having a very old-fashioned name
  - having a very unusual name or a foreign name
  - being named after a celebrity or royalty
  - having the same first name as your father or mother
- Can you think of people who...
  - have a name that suits their appearance or personality? Why does it suit them?
  - have a name that doesn't suit them? Why doesn't it suit them?

5 1 6 SONG *Rio* ♫

6 LISTENING & SPEAKING

a Look at the brand names. How do you pronounce them? What do these companies make?

b 1 7 Listen to a radio programme about brand names. Which of the brands…?

1 is named after a Greek goddess ______
2 is named after the company's founder ______
3 has a name which means 'three stars' ______
4 is named after a very large number ______
5 has a name which means 'sound' plus 'boy' ______

c Listen again and answer the questions.

1 What do the 'I' and 'K' in IKEA stand for?
2 What did Samsung originally sell?
3 What was Nike's original name?
4 Why did Sony's founders choose its name?
5 What does the man say about the spelling of 'Google'?

d Look at the photos. What are the two products called? Do you know why?

e Work in pairs **A** and **B** and read about the two products. **B** ➤ **Communication** *How was it named?* *p.104.*

f **A** read about how the Kindle was named. Find answers to the questions below.

1 Who named the product?
2 What instructions did the company's founder give for choosing a name?
3 What does the name mean?
4 Why is the meaning appropriate?

How was the Kindle named?

There were ebook readers before the Amazon Kindle, but the Kindle was the first to become popular around the world. Since it first appeared in 2007, millions of Kindles have been sold, and in fact Amazon now sells more ebooks than paper books.

When it was time to give the Kindle a name, Amazon's founder, Jeff Bezos, asked Michael Cronan to try to think of one. Cronan, who was an American designer, also had a business that created names for companies and products. Bezos told him that he didn't want a high-tech name. Amazon's customers loved traditional paper books and Bezos didn't want to annoy them.

Cronan and his wife talked a lot about reading, and about the warm, comfortable feelings people get from it. A lot of different names were considered, but he finally chose 'kindle', which means 'to light a fire'. Cronan thought that this would remind people of the excitement they feel when they are enjoying their favourite book. The name was also inspired by a line from the French novelist Victor Hugo: 'to read is to light a fire'.

g Tell **B** about how the Kindle was named, using questions 1–4 to help you.

h Now **B** will tell you about how the iMac was named.

i Talk to a partner.

1 What are some well-known brand names from your country? Do you know where the names came from?
2 What's the name of the brand and model of your computer, car, or phone? Why do you think they were given those names?
3 Can you think of a product name which you think is very clever? Why? Do you know one which doesn't suit the product well?

7 GRAMMAR pronouns

a Look at the sentences from the texts in **6**. What do the pronouns in **bold** refer to?

1 *Bezos told* ***him*** *that* ***he*** *didn't want a high-tech name.*
2 *Amazon's customers loved traditional paper books and Bezos didn't want to annoy* ***them****.*
3 *Jobs asked Segall for a new name that had 'Mac' or 'Macintosh' in* ***it****.*
4 *A few days after coming up with the name, Segall went to Jobs and suggested* ***it*** *to* ***him****.*

b ➤ **p.132 Grammar Bank 1A.** Learn more about pronouns and practise them.

c 1 9))) Listen and change the word order in the sentence. Change the direct object to *it* or *them*.

))) *1 Give me the book.* — *Give it to me.*
))) *2 Give her the shoes.* — *Give them to her.*

d Think of a couple you know well (friends or family). Tell your partner about them and try to get all of the pronouns right. Give the information below, and anything else you know about them.

names jobs how they met pets children appearance personality

I'm going to tell you about my neighbours. ***His*** *name is Mario and* ***hers*** *is Sara.* ***She****'s a writer and* ***he****'s an accountant.* ***They*** *haven't got any children but* ***they*** *have a dog.* ***Its*** *name is Beppo...*

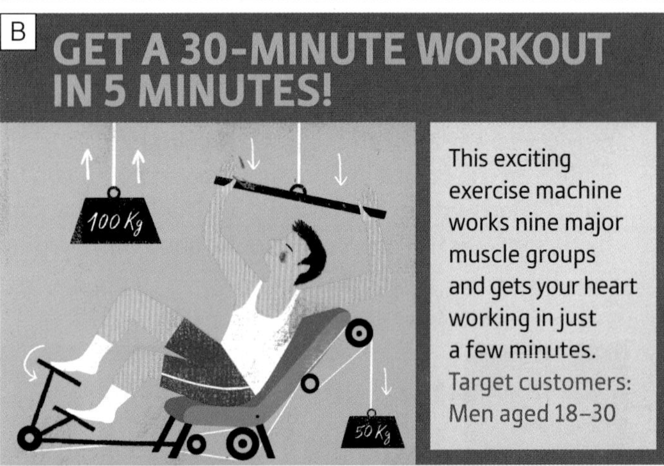

8 SPEAKING

a Read about three new products. Would you like to buy them? Why (not)?

b In pairs or groups, talk about what would make a good name for the products. Think about:

- the name's meaning, sound, and length
- things that the name could remind people of
- how you want people to feel about the product
- how easy the name would be to pronounce
- the names of similar products

c Make a list of possible names with your partner or group.

The car	The exercise machine	The translation app

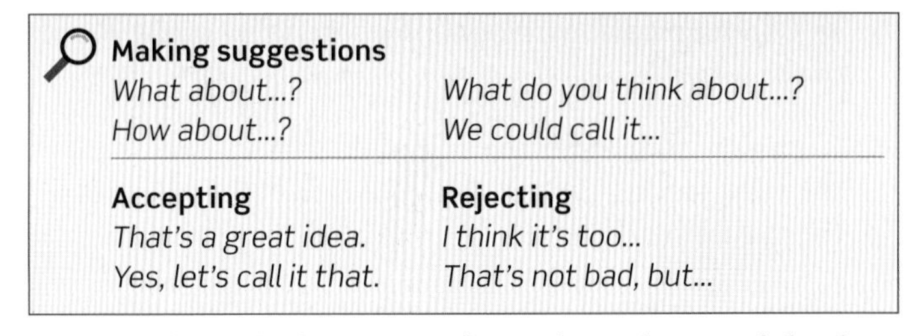

d Decide on the best name for each product, and think about the reasons why the names are right.

e Present your best name to another pair or group.

We suggest the name... for the car.
It's a perfect name because...

G adjectives
V adjective suffixes
P word stress

Are you getting the red shirt?

No, I prefer the green one. Green suits me better than red.

1B True colours

1 VOCABULARY adjective suffixes

a Take the colour personality test. Then compare your colour choices with a partner.

Colour personality test

What kind of person are you? Your preferences in colour may reveal the answer! Look at the colours quickly and write 1 on the colour that immediately attracts you the most. Then number the others 2–8. Don't think about fashion or whether the colour looks good on you, only on how they make you feel.

b ➤ **Communication** *Colour and personality p.104.* Read the results of the test.

c Complete some adjectives from the colour personality test with the right ending *-y, -ive, -less, -able, -ish.* How do people who have these qualities behave?

mood___ rest___ self___ sensit___ soci___

d ➤ **p.152 Vocabulary Bank** *Adjective suffixes.*

2 PRONUNCIATION word stress

Word stress on adjectives formed with suffixes
When an adjective is formed from a root word and a suffix, the stress is always on a syllable of the root word, e.g. *rely – reliable.* The stress does not change when a negative prefix is added, e.g. *unreliable.*

a Underline the stressed syllable in the bold adjectives in the questions below. Remember it will never be on the prefix or suffix.

1. Who is the most **glamorous** person you know? What makes him / her like that?
2. Are you very **possessive** of anything, e.g. your phone or your laptop? Why don't you like other people using it?
3. Were you a **rebellious** child or teenager? What kind of things did you do?
4. What are your most **comfortable** clothes? When do you wear them?
5. Do you think you are a **creative** person? Why (not)?
6. Have you ever been to a very **luxurious** hotel or restaurant? Where? Was it worth the money?
7. Have you ever felt **envious** of a brother or sister? Why (not)?
8. What's the most **impressive** monument or building you've ever visited? Why did you like it so much?
9. What kind of **unhealthy** food do you really like eating?
10. What do you think is a **suitable** present to take if somebody invites you for a meal in their house?

b 1 14)) Listen to the adjectives and check. Then listen again and repeat them.

c Work with a partner. **A** ask **B** questions 1–5. Then **B** ask **A** questions 6–10.

3 LISTENING & SPEAKING

a Look at the website and the photos below. What do you think colour analysis is? Do you know anyone who has tried it?

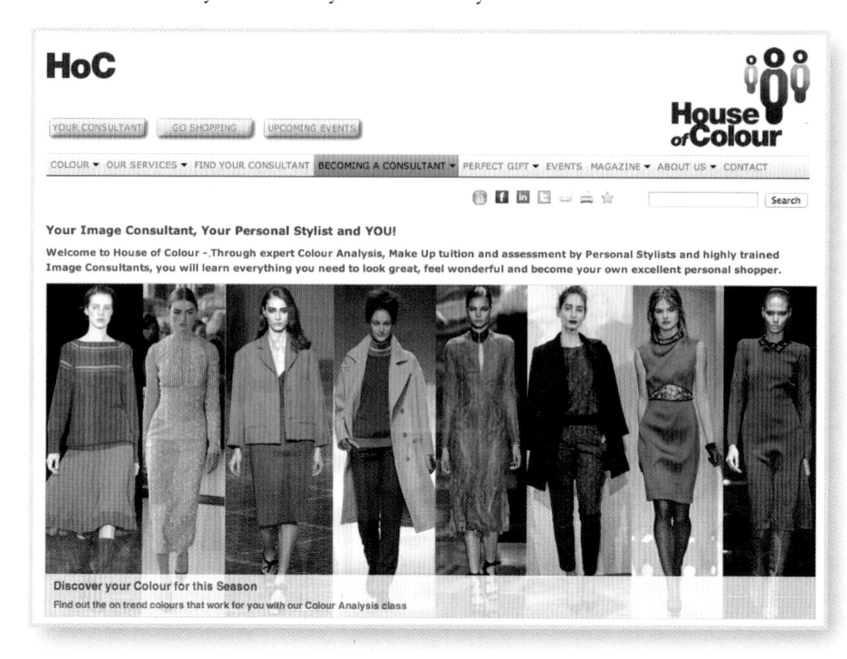

b 1.15 Listen to an interview with Wendy Woodward, a woman who tried colour analysis. Answer the questions.

1 Which photo shows Wendy after she did colour analysis?
2 Why did she do colour analysis?
3 How did she feel after she had done it?

c Listen again. Mark the statements **T** (true) or **F** (false).

> **Tip: True / False listening**
> - Read the questions before you listen.
> - Work on one question at a time.
> - Check your answers when you listen again.

1 A stylish colleague told Wendy about colour analysis.
2 Wendy went on her own to do colour analysis.
3 The colour analyst worked out her colours by making her try on a lot of different clothes.
4 Wendy learned that she was a 'winter' person.
5 Winter people should wear pale colours.
6 Wendy very rarely wears black nowadays.
7 Soon after the colour analysis she bought some cheap new clothes.
8 She exchanged clothes with her friends because they were different seasons.
9 People immediately told her that she looked more glamorous.
10 Wendy's mother and husband have also now done colour analysis.

d Listen again and correct the false statements in **c**.

e Talk to a partner.

1 Would *you* like to try colour analysis? Why (not)?
2 What colours do you prefer for these things? Why?
   - clothes (e.g. T-shirts, trousers, shoes, etc.)
   - cars
   - mobile phone cases
3 Do you know anyone who...?
   - wears one colour almost all the time
   - drives a bright red car
   - dyes his / her hair an unusual colour

   What are they like?
4 What kind of colours do these words remind you of? Can you explain why?

spring autumn
summer **winter**
angry relax money
love holiday

4 GRAMMAR adjectives

a Complete each sentence with a word from the list.

as in more most much ones than the

1 According to a paint company survey, the world's ________ popular colour is blue.
2 White meat is healthier ________ red meat.
3 Black tulips are much more expensive than pink ________.
4 The blue whale is the largest creature ________ the world.
5 Insurance for a red car can be a bit ________ expensive than for other colours.
6 White tigers are ________ less common than ordinary tigers.
7 Black tea isn't as good for you ________ green tea.
8 According to a survey, ________ most popular car colour in Europe is black.

b ➤ **p.133 Grammar Bank 1B.** Learn more about adjectives and practise them.

c Talk to a partner. Choose two topics or two questions from each section.

Compare them!
1 restaurant food and home-made food
2 being an only child and having lots of brothers and sisters
3 the English and people from your country
4 walking or running outdoors and going to the gym
5 studying in the morning and studying at night
6 going on holiday abroad and going on holiday in your country

I think restaurant food is better than my home-made food because I'm not a very good cook, but it's much more expensive and it usually isn't as healthy...

Extremes!
1 What is ______ place you've ever been to? (hot)
2 Which sportsperson from your country do you think is ______ role model? (positive)
3 Which is ______ restaurant in your town? (popular) Which is ______? (expensive)
4 Where are some places you often walk to? Which are ______ to and ______ from your home? (close, far)
5 Who is ______ person you know? (clever) Why do you think so?
6 Where are you ______: at home, at work, or somewhere else? Why? (stressed)

The hottest place I've ever been to was Rome in August. It was much too hot to go sightseeing...

5 READING

a Look at some names for colours from an online clothing website. What colours do you think they are? Would you use any similar words for colours in your language?

berry ivory melon mint
morning sky mushroom wine

b Look at four colours from a well-known UK paint company, Farrow & Ball. How would you describe the colours?

c With a partner, try to match the colours to their names.

Arsenic Cabbage White Dead Salmon
Monkey Puzzle

d Read the article about the paint names. Check your answers to **c**.

What colour is Dead Salmon?

There was a time when you could tell what colour something was by its name. Red, green, even lemon yellow or royal blue immediately told us what something would look like. But, as anyone who has recently bought clothes, a car, or even children's crayons has probably noticed, the trend for giving colours bizarre names is now everywhere, and the image they create in our mind does not necessarily correspond with the actual colour.

One company which may have taken this trend the furthest is the popular UK paint company Farrow & Ball. They sell a wide range of beautiful colours with very unusual names. It is easy to laugh at these names, but in fact many of them have stories behind them.

Dead Salmon Why did the company give this attractive brownish-pink colour such a depressing-sounding name? In fact, the name has been used for this colour for more than 200 years. According to Farrow & Ball, the name comes from an 1805 bill for the painting of the library of an old English country house. 'Dead' actually referred to the paint finish, in the way matt or gloss might today.

Arsenic The name of this pleasant greenish-blue colour may surprise people who associate the name with a poisonous chemical and think of it as a white powder. However, in the late 18th century, arsenic was used to create a colour called Paris Green, which was commonly used in paint and wallpaper. Many people became ill as a result of living in houses with Paris Green walls or wallpaper, including, it is said, Napoleon.

Monkey Puzzle This dark greyish-green colour is named after a kind of pine tree found in Chile and Argentina. The tree got its English name in the 1800s after examples were brought to London, and somebody commented that it would be very difficult to climb, even for a monkey.

Cabbage White This subtle shade of white, which has a slight blueish hint, also gets its name from nature. It is named after the Cabbage White butterfly, so-called because the caterpillars feed on cabbages.

e Read the article again. Then cover the text and look at the colour names in **c**. In pairs, say what you can remember about the origin of the names.

f Look at the highlighted adjective and noun phrases. With a partner, try to work out what they mean.

g Would you use any of these colours to paint a room in your house? Are unusual colour names a trend in your country as well?

6 SPEAKING & WRITING

a You're going to describe your favourite room in your house to a partner. Think about these things:

- why it's your favourite room
- the decoration and furnishing, e.g. walls, curtains, blinds, cushions
- the furniture
- paintings, posters
- what else is in the room

While you listen to your partner ask questions to help you imagine what the room is like.

b ➤ **p.113 Writing** *Describing a room.* Write a description of your favourite room.

Practical English A bad start

1 VIDEO JENNY IS BACK IN LONDON

a 1 19 Jenny works in New York for the magazine *New York 24seven*. She has just arrived in London. Watch or listen to her talking to Andrew. How does he help her? What problem does she have at the end?

b Watch or listen again. Mark the sentences **T** (true) or **F** (false). Correct the **F** sentences.

1 Jenny is in the UK for business and pleasure.
2 Andrew was on holiday in New York.
3 Jenny's husband (Rob) is working in San Francisco.
4 Andrew gives Jenny back her laptop.
5 He introduces himself, and says his surname is Paton.
6 Jenny's flight to London was delayed.

Why do you think a man was watching Jenny and Andrew? What do you think he is going to do?

2 VIDEO REPORTING LOST LUGGAGE

a 1 20 Watch or listen to Jenny reporting her missing suitcase. Answer the questions.

1 How long is Jenny staying in the UK?
2 What does her suitcase look like?
3 What's in it?
4 How long will it probably take for Jenny to get her case back?

b Watch or listen again. Complete the **You Hear** phrases in the dialogue on p.13.

c 1 21 Watch or listen and repeat some of the **You Say** phrases. Copy the rhythm and intonation.

d Practise the dialogue with a partner.

e In pairs, roleplay the dialogue.

A You are a passenger on flight BA1722 from San Francisco. You have just landed at London Heathrow Airport and your luggage hasn't arrived, so you go to Lost Luggage to report it. **B** works at the Lost Luggage counter. Use the **Useful language** to help you to describe your luggage.

B You work at the Lost Luggage counter at London Heathrow Airport. **A**'s luggage hasn't arrived. Take **A**'s details and give a reference number.

f Swap roles.

Useful language: describing luggage
Type of luggage: *suitcase / case; sports bag; backpack / rucksack*
Colour: *It's dark / light / greyish blue*, etc.
Material: *It's made of hard plastic / canvas / synthetic material*, etc.
Size: *It's small / medium size / large*
Extras: *It has four wheels / a logo / a label*, etc.

You Hear	You Say
Can I help you?	Yeah, my suitcase hasn't arrived.
________ flight were you on?	Flight RT163 from JFK.
I'll take your ________ and then I can issue you with a reference number. Can I have your name, please?	My name's Jenny Zielinski. That's Z-I-E-L-I-N-S-K-I.
And you're a ________ to the UK.	That's right.
How ________ are you staying for?	Ten days.
OK. How many ________ are you missing?	Just one – a suitcase.
Can you ________ it for me?	Well, it's kind of greyish blue... and hard plastic, I think.
And what ________ is it?	Oh, it's medium size, like this. And it has wheels.
Anything else?	Yeah, there's a small lock and a label with my name and phone number on it.
And what was ________ the suitcase?	Just about everything! Clothes, toiletries, all my personal belongings, really.
Can I have your ________ in the UK?	Just a minute. It's The Grange, Marsh Lane, Long Crendon, Oxfordshire.
And a ________ number?	Yes, it's 001 202 494 012.
And finally, can you ________ this?	Of course. Do you have any idea where it is? I mean, do you think it's still in New York?
It's possible. We're very ________ for the inconvenience. Here's your reference number. You can track the progress of your luggage ________, or just give us a call. But we should be able to get it back to you within 24 hours.	That'd be great. Thank you.

3 VIDEO AT HENRY'S HOUSE

a 1 22 Watch or listen to the rest of Jenny's day. What other problem does she have?

b Watch or listen again. Answer the questions.

1 What does Henry help Jenny with?
2 Is Rob having a good time in Alaska? Why (not)?
3 What is Jenny drinking?
4 Whose computer is she using?
5 Who is Luke?
6 When is Jenny going to see him? Why?
7 What is Henry going to lend Jenny?

Who is Selina Lavelle? Why do you think Grant (the man who was following them) is watching Henry's house?

c Look at the **Social English phrases**. Can you remember any of the missing words?

Social English phrases

Henry	(And) it's ________ to see you.
Jenny	It's ________ to see you too.
Henry	No, no, ________ me take that.
Henry	You've had a hard journey. ________ me.
Jenny	It's weird, ________ it?
Rob	I really ________ you.
Jenny	Oh no! That's ________.
Rob	It's not your ________, is it?
Rob	Oh ________! You'll look great in those, Jenny!

d 1 23 Watch or listen and complete the phrases.

e Watch or listen again and repeat the phrases. How do you say them in your language?

Can you...?

- [ ] explain why you are travelling to a place
- [ ] report lost luggage
- [ ] greet someone you haven't seen for some time
- [ ] sympathize with someone about a problem

G present tenses
V holidays
P /s/ and /z/

What time does your flight leave?

At 9.00. I'm getting the 7 o'clock train to the airport.

2A Pack and go!

1 VOCABULARY holidays

a Look at the X-ray pictures of a backpack and a suitcase at airport security. Can you identify the 12 items inside them? Which item(s)...?
1 do you have to take out of your bag when you go through security
2 are you not allowed to take through security

b ➤ p.153 **Vocabulary Bank** *Holidays.*

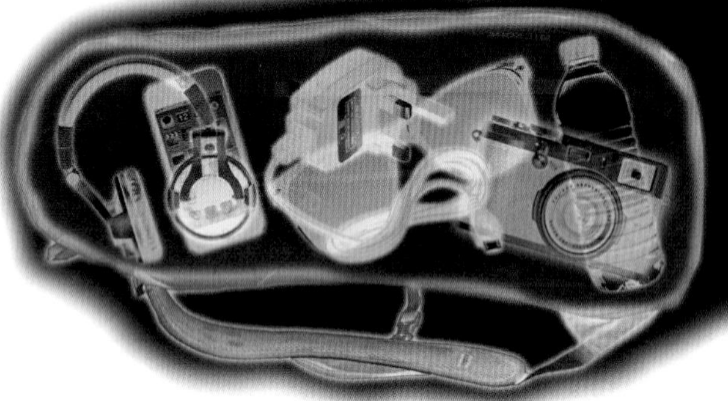

c Make a list of the ten most important things you make sure you take with you when you go on holiday.

d Compare with a partner. How many things are different?

e Read the introduction to an article. What do you think the top three things are that the British most often forget to pack?

Home | News | Sport | TV | Health | Science | Travel | Money

Britons spend £118 million replacing forgotten holiday items

By TRAVEL REPORTER

Forty-one per cent of Britons forget to pack at least one essential item when they go on holiday, according to a survey.

In total, almost 15 million important holiday items are left behind each year, and Britons spend £118 million buying these things again once they reach their destination.

Comment Print

Adapted from the Daily Mail

f 1 27 Listen to the top ten items in reverse order, and write them down. Did you guess the top three correctly?

g Have you or has anybody you know ever forgotten something really important when they went on holiday? What happened?

2 PRONUNCIATION /s/ and /z/

a Look at the word below. What sound do the pink letters have, S or zebra?

scissors

b 1 28 Listen and check. Practise saying it.

c 1 29 Listen and write the words in the correct column.

bags cruise flip flops holidays massage passport
pyjamas razor safari sunset swimsuit towels

S	zebra

d 1 30 Listen and check. Practise saying the words.

e ➤ p.167 **Sound Bank.** Look at the typical spellings of the sounds. In what position is *s* never pronounced /z/?

f Practise saying the phrases

some sunglasses
summer clothes
bags and cases
shoes and socks
striped pyjamas
see the sights

3 LISTENING

a 1.31 Listen to five airport security screeners. Match them with pictures A–E.

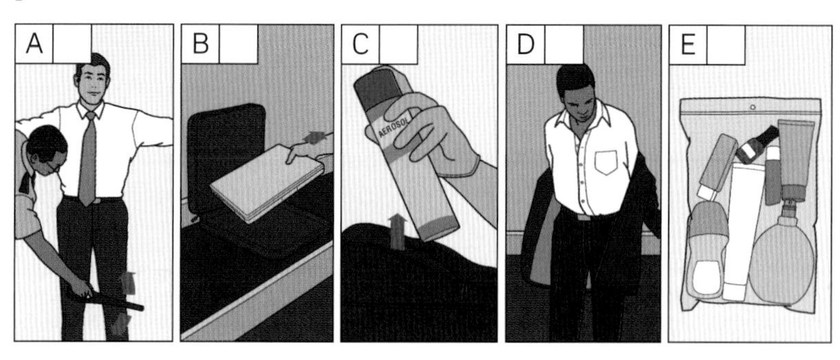

b 1.32 Listen to an interview with a US security screener. Does she feel mainly positive or mainly negative about her job?

c Listen again. Choose **a**, **b**, or **c**.

> **Tip: Multiple-choice listening**
> - Read the questions carefully before you listen.
> - Don't choose an option just because it has a word you heard in the recording. Make sure *all* of the information is correct.

1 She mentions taking away people's ____.
  a food and drink
  b scissors and razors
  c perfume and shampoo

2 When she has to take things away from passengers she ____.
  a enjoys it
  b feels bad about it
  c thinks it's just a routine part of her job

3 What she likes best about her job is ____.
  a meeting all sorts of different people
  b keeping the things that she takes away from passengers
  c being able to get free flights

4 Some of her colleagues get angry with people who ____.
  a are rude
  b are trying to hide things
  c are slow

5 She thinks some screeners can be unfriendly because ____.
  a they work long hours
  b the job is very repetitive
  c the rules are always changing

6 One thing that annoys her about passengers is that ____.
  a they complain about travelling
  b they get aggressive
  c they don't know the rules

7 Passengers are most polite to the security screeners ____.
  a early in the morning
  b in the afternoon
  c late at night

d Have you ever had a problem going through airport security? What happened? Was the screener friendly?

4 SPEAKING & WRITING

a Look at the page from a website. Read some of the ideas for cheap holidays. Discuss the questions with a partner.

1 What do you think are the pros and cons of each idea?
2 Do you know anyone who has done these things? Were they a success?

Want a cheap holiday? Try these ideas

1 Go couch-surfing. On websites like couchsurfing.org, local people will let you sleep on their sofa for free. It's not luxury travel, but you'll meet friendly locals and see how they really live.

2 Swap houses. Exchange houses with someone in the place you're going to visit. You stay in their place, and they stay in yours. Websites like homelink.org can arrange this for a small fee.

3 Save on travel costs. Book early for good offers with low-cost airlines. Use special services such as InterRail for travelling around Europe by train, or check out car-sharing websites like ridefinder.eu.

4 Eat street food. In many cities, even really expensive ones, you can find food which is both tasty and cheap at stalls in the street. For example, try crêpes in Paris, kebabs in Istanbul, and tacos in Mexico City. Most places have their own delicious speciality.

5 Try 'voluntourism'. These holidays combine volunteer work and tourism. Help in an orphanage, work on an organic farm, and more – all for free. You'll save money and have experiences you'd never find on a package holiday.

b With a partner, write short paragraphs on three more ideas for saving money on holiday. Give reasons why each one is a good idea.

If you travel off-season, you'll save money on train and plane tickets, hotel rooms, and even food.

c Show your three ideas to another pair. Which tips are the most useful?

5 GRAMMAR present tenses

a Caroline's going on holiday to Majorca. Circle the right verb form to complete her tweets. Tick (✓) if both forms are possible.

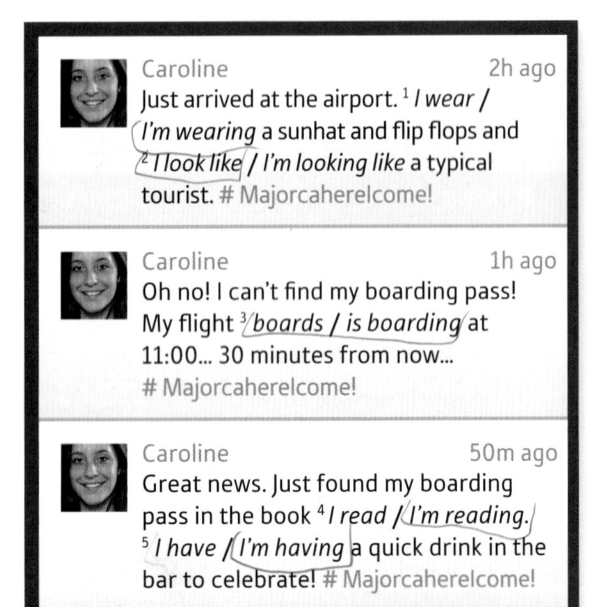

b Compare answers with a partner. Explain why you think each form is right.

c ➤ **p.134 Grammar Bank 2A.** Learn more about present tenses and practise them.

d ➤ **Communication** *Caroline's holiday plans* **A** *p.105*, **B** *p.106*.

e Make questions with the present simple or present continuous. Then ask and answer with a partner.

Holidays

- / you / prefer summer holidays or winter holidays? Why?
- / you / plan a holiday at the moment? Which places / you / think about? What / you / want to do there?

Weekends

- What / you / usually do at the weekend?
- What / you / do this weekend?

Today

- What time / this class / finish? Where / you / go after class today?
- What / you / do / this evening? Where / you / have dinner?

6 READING

a Think of some times when you have seen or met tourists from another country. Discuss the questions.

1 Where were the tourists from?
2 Where were they and what were they doing?
3 What was your impression of them?

b You are going to read an article about two tourism surveys. Before you read, discuss the questions with a partner. Choose answers from the nationalities in the list.

Which nationality or nationalities...?

the Americans the British the French the Germans
the Greeks the Italians the Japanese the Spanish

1 enjoy doing sport on holiday
2 love sunbathing
3 almost never sunbathe on holiday
4 drink more alcohol than usual on holiday
5 are the world's best tourists
6 are considered very polite
7 leave the worst tips
8 leave the most generous tips
9 make a lot of noise
10 dress well when they are on holiday

c Read the article once, and compare your answers to the findings in the surveys. How many did you guess correctly?

d Read the article again. Look at the highlighted words and phrases. With a partner, work out their meanings.

What different nationalities do on holiday...

A new survey of holidaymakers in Europe and the USA has found that the holiday you enjoy may depend on the country you come from.

Some holiday destinations were popular among all nationalities. The beach, for instance, was the undisputed leader among all destinations in the survey.

Activity holidays are also popular, for example, cycling, sailing, or trekking holidays. Even when their main aim is to relax, travellers said that they enjoyed seeing the sights and visiting places of interest in and around their holiday destination.

There are, however, country-specific differences:

- The Greeks are particularly keen on sport during their holidays, with 75% engaging in some kind of sporting activity.
- Sunbathing is extremely popular with the Germans. Almost 50% named it as their favourite holiday activity, especially on Spanish beaches – in fact 25% of high-income Germans are planning to go to Spain in the next 12 months. Going hiking and eating out in upmarket restaurants came second and third for Germans.
- Citing concerns about skin cancer, only one in ten Americans said sunbathing was something they would do on holiday. Eager to soak up the history and culture that they can't find at home, 46% of Americans prefer to go on tours of museums, historic buildings, and other places of interest.
- About 60% of UK travellers admitted drinking more while away than they would normally do, with 28% saying they had five or more alcoholic drinks every day.

Information from www.marketresearchworld.net, www.dailymail.co.uk, www.business-standard.com

... and what the locals think of them

Another survey, conducted by Expedia, an online travel company, has ranked the Japanese as the world's best tourists. The British and the Canadians rank second and third among the 27 nationalities in the survey. The survey also revealed that the French have the reputation for being the world's worst tourists.

Around 4,500 hoteliers across the globe gave their opinions on the best travellers overall, as well as on specific categories including politeness, generosity, behaviour, fashion sense, tidiness, and how much they complain.

The survey found that:

- The Japanese, British, Canadians, Germans, and Australians are considered the most polite tourists. The French were considered the most impolite.
- Hoteliers also found the French to be the most frugal and the meanest tippers. The biggest tippers were the Americans, followed by the British, the Germans, and the Japanese.
- The top three loudest nations were the Americans, the Italians, and the Spanish. The Japanese were ranked as the quietest.
- The Americans were at the bottom of the list for fashion sense, with the stylish Italians and French taking top prize.
- The Japanese, Germans, and British were considered the tidiest tourists. The Americans ranked at the bottom here as well.
- The Japanese were ranked as the least likely to complain, followed by the Canadians and the Swiss. The nationalities who complained the most were the Americans, the Germans, and the French.

e Talk to a partner.

1. What would you say are the favourite holiday destinations for people from your country? What do they like to do there?
2. How do you think people feel about tourists from your country in the categories from the survey (polite, generous, etc.)?

7 SPEAKING

a Choose two of the ideas below to talk about. Think about what you are going to say, and make notes.

a place I'd really like to go to for a holiday

a great winter holiday I once had

things I do differently when I'm on holiday (clothes, tipping, activities...)

a holiday I will always remember from my childhood

things tourists do that annoy me

a family holiday when everyone argued

a holiday when I had a lot of problems

a holiday when I did a lot of sport

b Work with a partner or in small groups. Talk about your topics, giving as much information as you can. Listen to the other student(s) and ask for more information.

Asking for more information

Ask questions about what people say to show interest and keep the conversation going.

Really? Why is / was that?
What will / did you do next?
What is / was it like?
Would you do it again?

8 WRITING

➤ **p.114 Writing** *Holiday tweets.* Write a series of holiday tweets.

9 1 37 SONG *Destination: Anywhere* ♫

G possessives
V shops and services
P 's; linking

Where did you get your bag?

At a small shop a friend of mine recommended.

2B Opening up or closing down?

1 VOCABULARY shops and services

a Look at the photos. Do you usually buy these things...?

- online
- in a small local shop
- in a supermarket, hypermarket, or department store
- in another way

b ➤ **p.154 Vocabulary Bank** *Shops and services.*

c Talk to a partner. What's the difference between...?

1 a DIY store and a hypermarket
2 a stationer's and a newsagent's
3 a dry cleaner's and a launderette
4 an estate agent's and a travel agent's
5 'the shop's closing' and 'the shop's closing down'

2 LISTENING & SPEAKING

a Look at the photos. Do you see similar sights in any areas of your town?

b Read the article about high streets in the UK. Why have they changed so much? What are some towns trying to do?

Can anyone save the British high street?

The high street was once the heart of communities across the UK. The butcher's, baker's, and greengrocer's were all there, run by locals who knew their customers by name.

But today one in seven high street shops has closed down, or has been replaced by a café or a beauty salon, as shoppers drive to out-of-town hypermarkets or malls, or buy online. The recession doesn't help either. In the worst-hit towns, more than one-third of the small high street shops have disappeared.

To try to save their high streets, some towns now offer free parking nearby. Others plan to have live music and theatre performances in the town centre, and others are encouraging small businesses to move into empty shop spaces and open 'pop-up shops' (quirky, interesting shops that close or change after a few weeks). The towns are hopeful, but are these efforts too little, too late?

c 1 40 Listen to four people talk about their local shopping street. Who is most optimistic about the situation of small shops?

d Listen again and complete the chart.

	Harry	Kate	Ken	Bea
1 Where do you live?				
2 What shops are there near you?				
3 What's happening to small shops in your area? Why? Do you think this is a good or bad thing?				

e Interview a partner with the questionnaire below.

My local shops

1. What kinds of shops are there near where you live?
2. Do you go to them much? If not, where do you buy things?
3. What shops have opened up or closed down near you? Are you pleased or sorry about it?
4. Are there any markets near you? Do you ever go to them? Do you have a favourite stall?
5. What chain stores are there near you? (H&M, Zara, etc.) Do you shop there? How do you feel about them? Are they in competition with local shops?
6. Are small shops in your country struggling? Do you think it's important to support them? Why (not)?

3 GRAMMAR possessives

a With a partner decide if the highlighted phrases are right (✓) or wrong (✗). Correct the wrong phrases.

1 Could you tell me where to find childrens' books?
2 What's Carlos's surname? I can never remember it.
3 I'm going to Marta's to study this afternoon.
4 Is this your new car's husband? It's lovely!
5 I mustn't forget it's the my mother's birthday tomorrow.
6 I'm sure you'll like Tony. He's a really old friend of mine.
7 I didn't like the film's beginning, but the end was good.
8 One day I'd love to have mine own flat.

b ➤ **p.135 Grammar Bank 2B.** Learn more about possessives and practise them.

4 PRONUNCIATION 's; linking

The pronunciation of 's
The 's, like the s added to plural nouns and the third person of verbs, can be pronounced in three different ways:
1 /s/ after the unvoiced sounds /k/, /p/, /f/, /t/, and /θ/
2 /z/ after voiced sounds (most other sounds)
3 /ɪz/ after /s/, /z/, /ʤ/, /ʃ/, and /ʧ/

a 1 44)) Read the information box. Then listen and repeat the phrases.

1 /s/	my parents' house	my wife's brother
2 /z/	my friend's car	the men's toilets
3 /ɪz/	Charles's flat	my niece's husband

b 1 45)) Listen to the phrases. Is the *'s* 1 /s/, 2 /z/, or 3 /ɪz/?

☐ Maria's mother	☐ Max's motorbike
☐ Philip's phone	☐ Mr Smith's salary
☐ Tom's train	☐ my neighbours' new dog
☐ my wife's work	☐ George's job

c Practise saying the phrases.

d 1 46)) Listen and repeat the sentences, linking the marked words. Do you know why they are linked?

1 What's the name‿of the shop?
2 Jane's‿an‿ex-colleague‿of‿ours.
3 Some friends‿of mine‿are coming for dinner this‿evening.
4 Is that‿all your‿own work?
5 He lives‿at the top‿of the hill.
6 We're having lunch‿at‿Anne's.
7 They make their‿own bread.

e Practise saying the following sentences with a partner. Do you agree?

1 Mother's Day and Father's Day are just commercial opportunities for shops to sell more.
2 A chemist's should be open 24 hours a day.
3 It's safer to eat meat bought from a butcher's or a market than from a supermarket.
4 There's no point in spending much on children's clothes and shoes because they don't last for long.
5 If you don't like your friend's partner, it's better not to say so.
6 There should be a law against a boss's children being employed in his or her company.

5 READING

a You're going to read about a UK shopping site, *NotOnTheHighStreet.com*. Why do you think the founders decided to call it that?

b Now read **About us** and check.

ABOUT US

Award-winning entrepreneurs Holly Tucker and Sophie Cornish founded the website NotOnTheHighStreet.com from a kitchen table. Two working mothers, they loved discovering handmade and beautiful objects for themselves and as gifts, the kind of things that were sold in quirky markets, craft fairs, or small boutiques. But finding these places took time.

So Sophie and Holly came up with an idea. What if there were one place which brought together unique and hard-to-find objects from all over the UK? From this idea, NotOnTheHighStreet.com was born. Launched with just 100 sellers, there are now thousands of talented and creative small businesses who sell here, with more joining every week. Each seller hand-makes their products, and sends them directly to the buyer. Happy shopping!

c Read about three of their sellers. Write the questions in the right place. There is one question you do not need.

A *What are your ambitions for the future?*
B *What sort of products do you make and sell?*
C *How does the place where you live influence your products?*
D *Do you also sell in shops or only from the website?*
E *How is your health now?*
F *Where did you start your company and where do you work now?*
G *When did you set up your business and why?*

d Read about the sellers again. Answer the questions with **KW**, **AB**, or **EC**.

Which seller...?

1 makes things that people specifically ask her for ☐
2 gives some of the money she makes to a good cause ☐
3 started her business after she moved house ☐
4 would like her business to be more international ☐
5 started working again after a period of not being able to ☐
6 creates products out of unwanted things ☐

e Look at the **highlighted** words related to crafts and work out their meanings.

f If you were able to buy one thing from one of the sellers, what would you buy? Who would you buy it for?

6 SPEAKING

Choose three of the topics and tell a partner about them. Give as much information as you can.

Talk about something you've bought which...

- was personalized for you
- you bought directly from the person who made it
- was a present for a friend or relative
- made you feel better
- was made locally
- you couldn't really afford, but you just had to have
- was eco-friendly
- you later had to take back to the shop

GIFTS HOME GARDEN PICTURES & PRINTS JEWELLERY FASHION BABY & CHILD PETS WEDDINGS SEE MORE FIND

SOME OF OUR SELLERS

KRESSE WESLING

1 ______ ?

My husband and I have built our entire business around 'upcycling' – recycling old materials to make something new. We take old fire hoses* and create belts, wallets, phone cases, and bags from them.

What inspired you to start your business?

Recycling has always been a passion of ours. As soon as I saw some of the London Fire Brigade's old hoses, I instantly fell in love with them. We now collect old hoses across the country and 50% of the profits go to the Fire Fighters Charity.

2  ?

It started in a single room where we lived in Brixton, London. Now we have a large workshop. We've recycled over 170 tonnes of hoses.

*hose = a long tube made of rubber used for putting water onto a fire, gardens, etc.

ABIGAIL BRYANS

Describe your product range. What makes it unique?

I make wooden signs with clever sayings. '*Champagne is the answer*' is one of my most popular signs. I also get many fantastic requests for personalized signs from customers.

3  ?

About ten years ago, I was on my own with three small children and no job. Over the years I had made small gifts like photo frames and sold them to friends, and it was a friend of mine who told me, 'Don't be frightened to fail'. Hearing those words inspired me to start the business. Now I'm working full-time at my kitchen table in south London.

4  ?

I would just love my designs to be sold around the world. I'd also love a little workshop so that I didn't have to work in my kitchen!

EDWINA COOPER

What inspired you to create your business?

I'd always enjoyed painting, but about ten years ago I had a stroke*. I couldn't speak or move my right hand, which I use to paint. The doctors said I'd never paint again, but I slowly got better. A few years later, a friend asked me to do an illustration for her business. She liked what I did and it inspired me to start painting again.

5 ______ ?

Much better. I'm fully recovered now and I'm selling my hand-painted cushions on NotOnTheHighStreet.com. I'm so happy that people like what I do.

6 ______ ?

My husband, son, and I moved to the Isle of Wight about seven years ago, which is when I started painting cushions at home. I'm inspired by the island, and my customers say my paintings make them feel like they're on the island with me.

*stroke = a sudden serious illness when a blood vessel (= tube) in the brain bursts or is blocked

1&2 Revise and Check

GRAMMAR

Circle a, b, or c.

1 I emailed ______ the photos.
a her b she c hers

2 What are ______ surnames?
a them b theirs c their

3 He made ______.
a for me coffee b coffee for me
c coffee to me

4 My sister ______.
a lent them to us b them lent to we
c lent to we them

5 The red shoes are nice, but I prefer those ______.
a blue one b blues ones c blue ones

6 He's ______ man I've ever met.
a the bossiest b the most bossy
c the more bossy

7 She's ______ in her new job than she was before.
a much more happy b more happier
c much happier

8 The film was ______ than the book.
a a bit better
b bit better
c a bit more better

9 ______ a word he says.
a I'm not believing b I don't believe
c I'm not believe

10 You look worried – what ______ about?
a are you thinking b you are thinking
c do you think

11 Where ______ on holiday this summer?
a do you go b are you going c you go

12 ______ our grandparents next weekend.
a We're visiting b We're visit c We visit

13 I love looking at other ______ family photos.
a people's b peoples' c people'

14 What's the ______ where you were born?
a village's name b village name
c name of the village

15 We grow all ______.
a the own vegetables b our own vegetables
c ours own vegetables

VOCABULARY

a Complete the sentences with an adjective made from the **bold** word.

1 My grandmother is extremely ______. **glamour**
2 Teenagers can be very ______. **mood**
3 Don't be so ______! **child**
4 She's very ______. She won't do anything stupid. **sense**
5 He's always been ______ – he loves painting. **create**
6 Their car's not really ______ for a family of four. **suit**
7 Our hotel room was ______. **luxury**
8 Work is very ______ at the moment. **stress**
9 It's a bit ______ to carry so much money. **risk**
10 Her Russian is very ______. **impress**

b Complete the words.

1 There are lots of mosquitoes – where's the **i**______ **r**______?
2 We're going on a **s**______ in Kenya – I hope we see elephants!
3 It's a **p**______ holiday, so everything's included.
4 He stayed in the sun for too long and he got **s**______.
5 It always takes me ages to **p**______ my bags.
6 I need a new **m**______ **c**______. The one in my camera is full.
7 Free **g**______ tours of the museum leave every hour.
8 I can't go swimming. I don't have my **s**______.

c Where can you buy these things? Write the name of the shop.

1 meat ______
2 a newspaper ______
3 bread ______
4 flowers ______
5 aspirins ______
6 a house ______
7 fish ______

PRONUNCIATION

a Circle the word with a different sound.

1	toothpaste	safari	expensive	baker's
2	sunbathe	butcher's	brush	fishmonger
3	raincoat	comb	memory	overall
4	possessive	clothes	bizarre	sights
5	delicious	envious	chemist's	healthy

b Underline the stressed syllable.

1 im|pul|sive
2 sight|see|ing
3 pro|fi|ta|ble
4 am|bi|tious
5 news|a|gent's

CAN YOU UNDERSTAND THIS TEXT?

a Read the article once. Do you agree that the kind of holiday you enjoy depends on your personality?

Make sure your holiday matches your personality

'Choosing the right holiday is more than just picking a place or experience that sounds fun or interesting,' says Arthur Hoffman of Expedia Asia Pacific. 'Travellers should think carefully about what they and their travel companions are like, and then research travel destinations,' he says. 'This will help ensure the right holiday for the right person and their personality.'

So here's some advice on what different personality types should look for when picking their next holiday.

Extrovert / introvert

Extroverts enjoy holiday experiences that provide high levels of excitement, novelty, risk-taking, and social interaction. [1] ______, restaurants, and crowded cafés rather than art galleries and temples or churches. They love action-packed holidays that never stop.

Introverts are the opposite: they like activities that promote reflection and intellectual or spiritual experiences.

Nervous / relaxed

Nervous individuals tend to prefer destinations, cultural activities, and food types that remind them of home or of past travel experiences. When travelling overseas, they often choose restaurants that serve food similar to their country of origin. Unusual experiences tend to worry them. [2] ______, they can find resorts or holiday experiences with high levels of socialising and activities stressful.

Relaxed people are just the opposite. They are OK with trips involving unknowns, and take new challenges in their stride.

Open / closed

Open people will rarely go back to the same destination unless they have fallen in love with the place and want to explore it further. They enjoy big cities that offer lots of variety, such as Mumbai, London, Paris, New York, or Sydney.

Closed people visit places they have fond memories of, such as their hometowns. [3] ______.

Conservative / eccentric

Conservative types will often take holidays that others will be impressed by within their immediate social circles. [4] ______ and showing them their latest holiday photos.

Eccentrics take holidays that might not win them much social approval, such as bird-watching in Siberia!

Careful / spontaneous

Careful people like to plan well in advance – way before a holiday even begins. They want to know the exact where, when, and why of their holiday, and often have a long list of must-sees. [5] ______ and will spend a lot of time researching on the internet and reading travel guides. They often record their holidays through photos, videos, travel diaries, or blogs.

Spontaneous people don't make plans and will go along with the flow.

b Read the article again and complete it with phrases A–F. There is one phrase you do not need.

A They tend to have strict time and money budgets
B They often go back to the same holiday destination again and again
C They tend to prefer busy, lively places
D They love telling others where they have been
E They often go on holiday with large groups of friends
F Although they prefer not to travel alone

VIDEO CAN YOU UNDERSTAND THESE PEOPLE?

1 47))) In the street Watch or listen to five people and answer the questions.

Diarmuid

Edisha

James

Sean

Elayne

1 Diarmuid's mother chose his name to help him to remember ______.
  a a person b a city c a country
2 Edisha's names were chosen by ______.
  a her father b her mother c her aunts
3 Two colours James says he likes, or used to like, are ______.
  a red and green b green and blue c red and blue
4 What Sean remembers about the holiday is ______.
  a watching the rain b playing in the rain
  c arguing in the rain
5 Elayne prefers to shop online because ______.
  a it's more convenient for her
  b she doesn't like all the people in the malls
  c she likes the choice you have online

CAN YOU SAY THIS IN ENGLISH?

Do the tasks with a partner. Tick (✓) the box if you can do them.

Can you...?

1 ☐ agree or disagree with this statement, and say why: *Our names can affect how successful we are in life.*
2 ☐ talk about what makes a successful brand name
3 ☐ compare how different nationalities behave on holiday
4 ☐ ask and answer these questions:
- What do you usually take on holiday? Have you ever forgotten anything important?
- What shops are there where you live? How are they changing? Where do you usually do your shopping?

VIDEO **Short films** A farmers' market
Watch and enjoy a film on iTutor.

G past simple, past continuous, or *used to*?
V stages of life
P *-ed* endings; sentence rhythm

What were you like as a teenager?

Very different! I used to have long hair, and I played in a rock group.

3A The generation gap

1 GRAMMAR past simple, past continuous, or *used to*?

a Look at the picture of a school playground. Which child or children do you think is / are...?

a tomboy a 'girly' girl a bookworm
a well-behaved child quarrelling
being naughty

b 2 2))) Listen and check. Do you identify with any of them? Which one? Why?

c Read the posts on a blog where people write about what they were like as children. Who thinks they have changed the most / the least?

d With a partner, circle the correct form of the highlighted verbs. Why is the other form not possible?

e ➤ **p.136 Grammar Bank 3A.** Learn more about the past simple, the past continuous, and *used to*, and practise them.

What kind of child were you... and have you changed?

Nick I'd say I was a pretty well-behaved child. I loved toy cars, and [1]*I was spending / I used to spend* hours lining them up to create traffic jams. I was an only child so I didn't have as much opportunity to be naughty as other kids! I think I'm still someone who avoids conflict but sadly I don't have as much of an imagination as I used to.

Laura I was a good mix between girly girl and tomboy. I loved playing outside – but I didn't like jeans, I liked pretty clothes. For example, I remember once when I climbed a really high tree but I couldn't get down, because [2]*I was wearing / I used to wear* a pink frilly dress and it got caught in the branches! In that sense I haven't changed much. I still love wearing pretty clothes and I still love going for walks in the country.

Sarah As a child [3]*I used to be / I was being* very shy. My dad was in the army so my family moved around a lot, a different school almost every year. I became a lot more confident after [4]*I started / I used to start* university. A lot of the people at uni didn't know anybody else, so it was easier to make friends. In fact nowadays many people see me as outgoing!

2 PRONUNCIATION & SPEAKING
-ed endings; sentence rhythm

a 2 5 Listen to the three different pronunciations of the *-ed* ending.

1 /t/ I used to be shy. I liked animals.

2 /d/ I've changed a lot. I enjoyed exams.

3 /ɪd/ I started school. It ended in tears.

b 2 6 Listen to some more regular past simple verbs. How is the *-ed* ending pronounced? Tick (✓) the right box.

	/t/	/d/	/ɪd/
1 I hated eating vegetables.			
2 We looked alike.			
3 I tried everything.			
4 We lived abroad.			
5 I hoped to pass.			
6 We decided to move.			

c Practise saying the sentences.

Past or present?
When the *-ed* ending is pronounced /t/ or /d/, it can often be difficult to hear whether a regular verb is in the past or present tense. Use the context to help you.

d 2 7 Listen to six more sentences. Are the verbs in the present or past? Write **Pr** or **Pa**.

1 ___ 2 ___ 3 ___ 4 ___ 5 ___ 6 ___

e 2 8 Listen to the rhythm of the conversation below. Then practise it with a partner. Copy the rhythm, and try to pronounce the *-ed* endings correctly.

A **When** was the **last time** you **stayed** at a **hotel**?

B **Last year**. We were **driving** to the **south** for a **holiday**, and we **stopped** at a **hotel** for the **night** on the **way**.

A Did you **use** to **go** to **hotels** when you were a **child**?

B **No**, we **used** to **spend** the **holidays** at my **grandparents'**. They **lived** in a **village** in the **country**.

f Talk to a partner.

Events in your life
Take it in turns to ask and answer the questions with the past simple form of the verb.

1 Where ___ you born? (be)
Where ___ you ___ when you ___ a child? (live, be)
2 How old ___ you when you ___ primary school? (be, start)
___ you ___ your first day? (enjoy) What ___ you ___? (do)
3 When ___ the first time you ___ abroad? (be, travel)
Where ___ you ___? (go)
4 When ___ the last time you ___ a meal for friends? (be, cook)
What ___ you ___? (make) ___ your friends ___ it? (like)
5 When ___ the last time you ___ relatives? (be, visit)
Who ___ you ___? (visit) What ___ you ___? (do)

Where were you born?

I was born in a small town called Morella.

When I was younger
Do you agree with these statements? If you do, explain why. If you don't, change them so that they're true for you.

When I was younger...
1 my town **used to have** better shops and services than it does today.
2 children **used to spend** more time playing outside than they do now.
3 people **used to cook** more, and eat out less.
4 the weather **didn't use to be** as changeable.
5 more young people **used to go** to university. Now they all want to get a job when they finish school.
6 people **didn't use to watch** so much TV.

I don't agree with 1. I think there used to be fewer good shops. We now have a new shopping mall outside the centre of town.

What was happening?
Add two more times and dates that you remember well to the list. Where were you then? What were you doing?

- at midnight on 31 December of last year
- at 9.00 last night
- at lunchtime on your last birthday
- ___
- ___

At midnight on 31 December of last year, I was at a friend's house. We were playing music and dancing...

3 VOCABULARY stages of life

a Which stage of life is each person in? Match the people and the photos.

- a baby
- a toddler
- a child
- a pre-teen
- a teenager
- in his / her early twenties (= 20–23)
- in his / her mid-thirties (= 34–36)
- in his / her late forties (= 47–49)
- a pensioner

middle-aged
The word *middle-aged* means different things to different people, but usually refers to a person in their forties or fifties.
I'm not sure how old he is, but he looks middle-aged.

b 2 9))) Listen and check.

c Which stages of life do you associate with...?

- nursery school / primary school / secondary school
- learning a language / learning to swim / learning to drive
- going to bed early / staying up late / sleeping late
- having your first boyfriend or girlfriend / your first job / your first grandchild
- going to work abroad / being self-employed / being retired

d Think of three people you know who are in different stages of life in **a**. Tell your partner about them.

My sister Ana is in her mid-thirties, but she looks younger. She's married and has a six-month old baby called Mario. She used to work as a nurse but now she's at home looking after Mario.

4 LISTENING

a Can you always tell how old someone is from their appearance? What other ways are there of telling a person's age, e.g. the kind of music they like?

b 2 10))) Listen to **Part 1** of a local radio news report on teenagers and answer the questions.

1. Who is able to hear the Mosquito Tone?
2. Were both the presenters able to hear it?
3. Were you able to hear it? How did it make you feel?

c 2 11))) Listen to **Part 2** of the news story. What is the Mosquito Tone being used for? Does everybody think it's a good idea?

d Listen to **Part 2** again. Complete the information in your own words.

1. Some shop owners think that teenage gangs can...
2. Shop owners think that the Mosquito Tone... for them.
3. They say that it doesn't...
4. Some groups of people are trying to... because they think it's harmful and unfair.
5. The Mosquito Tone has been released as...
6. This allows teenagers to...

e Do you think the shop owners and teenagers are using the Mosquito Tone in an appropriate way? Why (not)?

5 READING & SPEAKING

a Look at the headlines of three news stories. In groups of three, say what you think each one is about.

Under 16? This is no place for you!

Babies at the movies

Airline's new child rules cause controversy

b You are going to read one of the three articles and tell each other about it. Work in groups of three.
➤ **Communication** *News stories* **B** *p.105*, **C** *p.106*.

c **A** read the article below and find answers to the questions.

1 What new idea is being tried? Where?
2 What problem is this idea meant to solve?
3 Who will be affected by it?
4 What good points about this idea are mentioned?
5 What problems with the idea are mentioned?

Home | News | Sport | TV&Showbiz | Health | Science | Travel | Money

Under 16? This is no place for you!

As from today, teenagers under 16 will be banned from the centre of the Welsh town of Bangor at night. This is the first time a town in the UK has banned children from an entire city centre.

The aim of the new rule is to reduce crime and anti-social behaviour in the town centre. In the last year, the area has seen a large number of robberies committed by young people.

The new curfew, which applies between 9.00 p.m. and 6.00 a.m., means that any person under 16 who is caught in the centre of town without a parent or adult guardian could go to jail for three months or pay a £2,500 fine.

Both parents and some politicians have criticized the rule, which they say treats all young people like criminals. Sports groups, youth centres, and even churches could be affected, they say.

One mother said: 'My son is 16, and he wouldn't be allowed to walk home from the bus stop with these rules.'

Another resident said: 'The idea is simply crazy.'

Adapted from the Daily Mail

Glossary
1 __________ /ˈkɜːfjuː/ *noun* a time after which people are not allowed to go outside their homes
2 __________ /ˈænti ˈsəʊʃl bɪˈheɪvjə(r)/ *noun* a way of acting that is not considered acceptable by other people
3 __________ /bæn/ *verb* said officially that something is not allowed
4 __________ /faɪn/ *noun* a sum of money that you have to pay for breaking a law or rule

d Read the article again. Work out the meaning of the highlighted words and phrases, and then complete the glossary. Check the pronunciation of the words and phrases.

e Work in groups with **B** and **C**. Tell each other your stories. Try to use the words from the glossary and explain them to **B** and **C** if necessary.

f Discuss the questions with your group.

1 Do you think these are good ideas? Why (not)?
2 Are there any places in your town where babies, children, or teenagers aren't allowed?
3 Are there any places where you *don't* think babies / small children, teenagers, adults, or old people should be allowed? Why?

I don't think children should be allowed in spas. It's a place to relax, and children make a noise in the pool.

6 SPEAKING & WRITING

a What were you like as a child, or as a teenager? Tell a partner. Talk about three of the topics in either When I was a child… or When I was a teenager… . Say how you're different today.

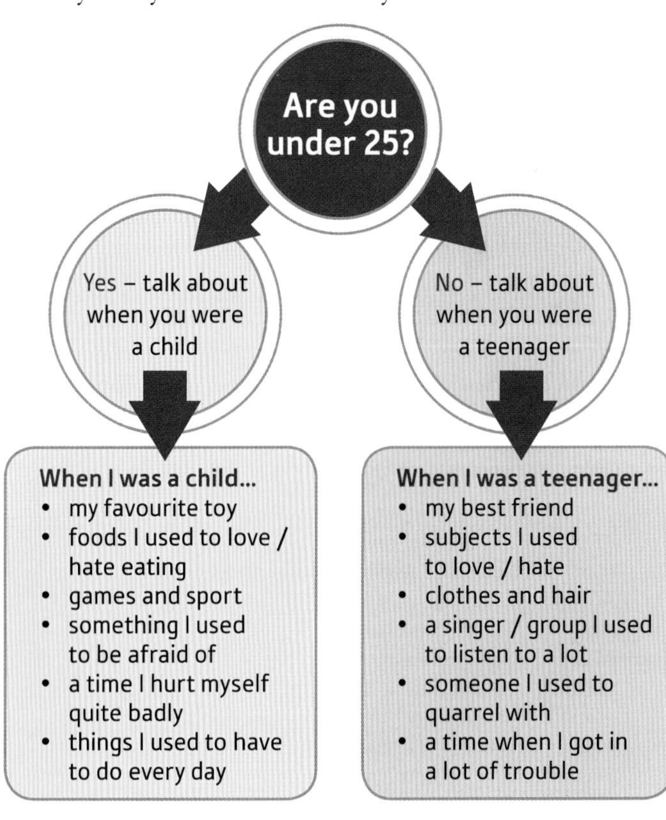

b Write a paragraph for the blog in **1** about what you used to be like as a child (or as a teenager) and if you have changed.

7 2 12)) SONG *Young folks* ♫

G prepositions
V photography
P word stress

Who's this picture of?

It's me when I was a child. It reminds me of all the wonderful family holidays we had.

3B In the picture

1 VOCABULARY photography

a Look at the photo. Where was it taken? Do you have any photos of yourself in front of a famous monument?

b Simon and Alice are tourists in Pisa. Complete the dialogue with the words below.

right background blurred take behind automatic

Alice	Excuse me, could you possibly [1]____ a photo of us?
Man	Yes, sure. Which button do I press?
Alice	This one here. It's [2]____. Just press it.
Man	Right. You want the tower in the [3]____, I suppose.
Alice	Yes, please.
Simon	Can you take it so it looks, you know, as if we're holding up the tower?
Man	All right, I'll try. Can you move back a little... a little to the [4]____... Just a minute. There's someone [5]____ you. OK, I think that's OK. Do you want to have a look?
Alice	Oh, that is so great. But I moved. It's a bit [6]____. Could you take just one more?
Man	Oh, all right...

c 2 13 Listen and check.

d ➤ **p.155 Vocabulary Bank** *Photography.*

2 PRONUNCIATION word stress

a 2 16 Underline the stress in the words beginning with *photo*. Listen and check. Practise saying the words.

1 pho|to|graph
2 pho|to|gra|pher
3 pho|to|gra|phy
4 pho|to|gra|phic
5 pho|to|ge|nic
6 pho|to|co|py

b Now underline the stressed syllable in the multi-syllable words in 1–7 below.

1 There's a tree in the **back|ground**.
2 In the **fore|ground** there's a girl.
3 You can see a house in the **dis|tance**.
4 There's a man **be|hind** her.
5 It's a **close-|up** of a watch.
6 It's out of **fo|cus**.
7 Is your **cam|era au|to|ma|tic**?

c 2 17 Listen and check. Practise saying the sentences.

d ➤ **Communication** *Spot the differences* **A** *p.107,* **B** *p.108.* Describe the picture to each other and find the differences.

3 LISTENING & SPEAKING

a How do you feel about having your photo taken? Do you think you're photogenic? Why (not)?

b 2 18 Listen to **Part 1** of an interview with Brian Voce, a professional portrait photographer. Make notes under the questions below.

1 How did he first become interested in photography?

2 What kind of people does he photograph and where?

3 Which famous person did he have an embarrassing experience with? What happened?

4 What's the favourite photo he mentions?

portrait by Brian Voce

portrait by Brian Voce

portrait by Annie Leibovitz

portrait by Brian Voce

c In **Part 2** of the interview, Brian explains how to look good in a portrait. Before you listen, read sentences 1–8. With a partner, decide whether you think they are **T** (true) or **F** (false).

1. Most people enjoy being photographed.
2. It's easier to relax if you are on your own with the photographer.
3. A professional photographer won't take long to get good photos.
4. What you wear is not really important.
5. Most people, including men, will look better with make-up on.
6. It's better to pose standing up than sitting down.
7. It's important to be in a comfortable position.
8. It's better not to look at the camera until just before the photographer shoots.

d **2 19**))) Listen and check your answers.

e Listen again and correct the false statements.

f Talk to a partner.

1. Are there any tips you've learned that you might put into practice next time someone takes a photo of you?
2. Do you think you're good at taking photos? Why (not)?
3. What do you normally take photos with?
4. Do you prefer taking photos of scenery or portraits of people? What else do you take photos of?

4 WRITING

➤ **p.115 Writing** *An article.* Write an article with tips on how to take good holiday photos.

5 GRAMMAR prepositions

a With a partner, complete the gaps with a preposition from the list.

at (x2) from in of (x2) over next to

I took this photo when we were flying [1]___ the Andes – I was going [2]___ Argentina to Chile. Luckily, I was sitting [3]___ the window, so I had a perfect view. I'm not usually very good [4]___ taking photos, but I think this one is beautiful, and I'm quite proud [5]___ it. Later on during the flight, we had a lot of turbulence, and by the time we finally arrived [6]___ Santiago I was feeling quite nervous. But when I look [7]___ this photo it reminds me [8]___ the feeling of calm that mountains always give me.

b Which preposition(s) in the text...?

1 show where a person or thing is
2 show where a person or thing is moving
3 are examples of prepositions used after certain verbs
4 are examples of prepositions used after certain adjectives

c ➤ **p.137 Grammar Bank 3B.** Learn more about prepositions and practise them.

d Complete 1–10 with a preposition. Then choose four topics to talk to a partner about.

1 A photo you took that you are very proud ___
2 Someone in your family that you really like talking ___
3 Something you're really looking forward ___ at the moment
4 Something your country is famous ___
5 Someone you often argue ___
6 A beautiful sight that you once flew ___
7 What you have ___ the walls of your bedroom
8 Someone you could rely ___ in a crisis
9 Something you usually ask ___ when you eat out
10 Somewhere you had to walk ___ a large number of steps

6 READING

a What do you do with the photos you've taken? Tell a partner. Which of these do you usually do?

- store them on your computer, phone, tablet, etc.
- back them up on a separate hard drive or CD-ROM
- email them to friends and family
- upload them to an online photo site
- print them out

b Read the article about storing digital photos and complete 1–5 with a heading from the list. There is one heading you don't need to use.

A Safe in the cloud?
B Hard drives don't hold enough photos
C Digital files can deteriorate
D Photo sites come and go
E Technology becomes obsolete
F How long will they last?

How safe are your digital photos?

In the past, your grandmother probably kept her photos in a box, or in an old album, and sadly, over time these memories faded or disappeared. But with today's technology, that shouldn't be a problem. A digital photo lasts forever, right?

Actually, think again. Though it is still a good idea to preserve all of your photos as digital computer files, there are plenty of things that can damage or even destroy those high-tech memories.

1 ___

Very few people realize this can happen, but if you store your photos as .jpgs (the most common file format), the file will actually deteriorate every time you copy or resave it. Experts disagree about how much damage this can do, but the damage is real.

2 ___

Your files may be safe on your hard drive, but how long will your hard drive last? The average is just five years. Before then, one big magnet could erase your drive in an instant. You could back up your photos on a CD-ROM, but they don't last much longer: about 10–20 years at most, experts say.

c Read the article again. Match the storage method with the problem it has.

1 ___ .jpg files	a only last for about five years
2 ___ hard drives	b only last for 10 to 20 years
3 ___ CD-ROMs	c are damaged when they're copied
4 ___ CD-ROM drives	d can go out of business
5 ___ 'the cloud'	e may not exist in the future
6 ___ photo sites	f can be damaged by storms

d Look at the highlighted words in the text related to digital photos and computers, and work out their meaning from the context.

e What do you think is the biggest threat to your own digital photos? After reading the article, will you do anything differently to protect your photos?

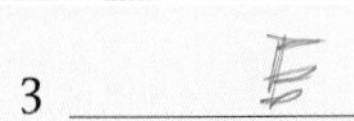

3 ___

Let's say all goes well and your CD-ROM full of photos lasts for 20 years. By then, will there still be any CD-ROM drives in the world that can read the disc? This is also true for flash drives, memory cards, and the rest. Today's high-tech storage solution is tomorrow's useless floppy disk.

4 ___

People talk about saving their files in a magical place on the internet, like Apple's iCloud or Dropbox. But this just means your files are in a company's data centre on – guess what? – a whole load of hard drives, which could die or go bad just as easily as your own. Just recently, a summer thunderstorm hit a cloud storage centre in the US, and major sites like Netflix, Pinterest, and Instagram were knocked offline for almost a whole day. Thousands of files were lost.

5 ___

Websites like Flickr and Instagram let you quickly upload photos and share them with others. But bear in mind that a photo site which is popular now could one day go out of business, taking your photos with it.

So what should you do? Experts say to make lots of copies of your photos and save them in many different ways – on your computer, on a backup drive, online, and even as traditional printed photos. It may be too late to save Grandma's photos, but you can still preserve yours.

7 LISTENING & SPEAKING

a 2 23 Listen to three people talk about their favourite childhood photos. Number the photos 1–3. There is one photo you don't need to use.

b Listen again. Which speaker…?

1 wanted to have the photo on his / her wall, but couldn't ☐
2 doesn't think he / she looks very good in the photo ☐
3 says the photo makes him / her feel better when he / she is a bit sad ☐
4 only saw the photo many years after it was taken ☐
5 likes the photo because of the emotion you can see in it ☐
6 used to keep the photo in his / her kitchen ☐

c Think of an interesting photo of yourself as a child. Tell a partner about it. Include the information below or your own ideas.

- How old are you in the photo?
- Who are you with?
- What's happening, or what has just happened?
- When and where was the photo taken?
- Why do you like it? Does it remind you of anything special?
- Where do you keep or display it?

d Show your partner some more photos on your phone and tell him or her about them.

Practical English All kinds of problems

EPISODE 2

1 HENRY'S CAR

VIDEO

a 2 24))) Watch or listen to Jenny and Henry. Where does Henry want to take her? Why can't he? How is Jenny going to get there?

b Listen again and (circle) the correct answer.

1 Jenny's suitcase *still hasn't been found* | *has been found.*
2 Henry thinks Jenny *will like Luke* | *won't understand Luke.*
3 Henry's car *has a flat tyre* | *has two flat tyres.*
4 He thinks the car was damaged by *neighbours* | *vandals.*
5 Jenny *doesn't know* | *knows* Luke's address.
6 Jenny had previously decided *to travel by public transport* | *to rent a car.*
7 She offers to *make dinner for Henry* | *take Henry out to dinner.*
8 Jenny *waits* | *doesn't wait* while Luke looks at her laptop.

Glossary
a spare (tyre) /speə 'taɪə/ = an extra tyre in a car
the AA = a breakdown service in the UK

British and American English
rent a car = American English
rent a car OR *hire a car* = British English

Who do you think vandalized Henry's car?
Who is the man who arrives as Jenny leaves?

2 RENTING A CAR

VIDEO

a 2 25))) Watch or listen to Jenny renting a car. Answer the questions.

1 How long does Jenny rent a car for?
2 What car does she rent?
3 Where does she want to leave the car?

What do you think is significant about the news on the TV? Do you think Jenny noticed it?

b Watch or listen again. Complete the **You Hear** phrases in the dialogue on p.33.

c 2 26))) Watch or listen and repeat some of the **You Say** phrases. Copy the rhythm.

d Practise the dialogue with a partner.

e In pairs, roleplay the dialogue.

A You're a visitor to the UK who wants to rent a car for a week. Talk to the assistant and choose the car you want. Use **Useful language** to help you.

B You're the assistant at a car rental company. Help **A** choose a car and get all of **A**'s details. Use **Useful language** to help you.

f Swap roles.

Useful language: describing cars
Kinds of drive: *automatic* or *manual*
Car types: *economy (small cars)*
compact (small, but larger than economy)
family (medium size)
luxury (large cars, 4x4s, sports cars)
convertibles (open-top cars)
people carriers (for more than five people)
Extras: *air conditioning, satnav*

You Hear	You Say
Hello. Can I help you?	Oh, hi. I'd like to rent a car, please.
Have you ________ from us before?	No.
OK, could I ________ your driving licence, please? Great. So what ________ of car are you looking for?	Oh, nothing too big. It's just for me.
OK, so a compact. ________-door?	Yeah, that'll be fine.
For how long?	Nine days.
Automatic or ________?	An automatic, please.
Any additional ________?	No, just me.
Great. Well, we have several ________ I can show you, but I'd recommend the Vauxhall Corsa. It's £________ per day and that includes insurance.	That sounds promising. Can I take a look?
Of course, but first I'd like to run through some of the basics. The ________ tank is full when you start, so if you return it with a full tank, there's no extra ________.	Great.
But if you get any ________ tickets or speeding fines you have to pay for them yourself.	Fair enough! Would it be possible to leave the car at the airport?
No problem, but that's a one-way rental so there's an additional charge of £________.	OK.
And one last thing – have you driven in ________ before?	Yes, I have. So driving on the left's not a problem.
That's good. OK, let's go out and take a look at the car. We can go through the paperwork afterwards.	Great.

3 VIDEO WHERE IS HENRY?

a 2 27 Watch or listen to Jenny's afternoon and evening. What has happened to a) her laptop? b) her suitcase? What does she hear on the news?

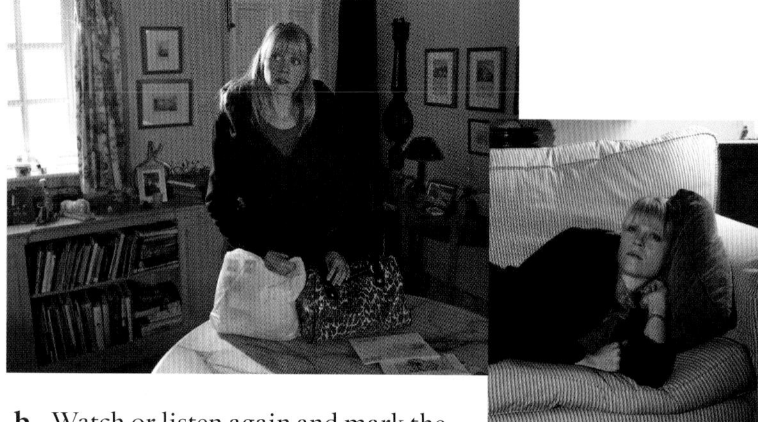

b Watch or listen again and mark the sentences **T** (true) or **F** (false). Correct the **F** sentences.

1 Henry is in his study when Jenny comes back.
2 Jenny reminds Henry about the dinner.
3 She isn't surprised by Luke's news about her computer.
4 Luke thinks that Henry has probably gone to the university to work.
5 Henry is always late for everything.
6 Jenny is feeling tired because of jet lag.
7 When she wakes up, Henry is back.
8 She phones Rob to say goodnight.

Who do you think was responsible for what happened on the news? What do you think Jenny is going to do next? What do you think has happened to Henry?

c Look at the **Social English phrases**. Can you remember any of the missing words?

Social English phrases

Henry I'm ________ I can't take your call at the moment.
Henry Please leave your message after the ________.
Luke Hi, Jenny. What's ________?
Jenny ________ on... my suitcase has arrived!
Jenny Well, at ________ it's back.
Jenny I'm ________ tired.
Jenny Thanks, Luke. See you ________.

d 2 28 Watch or listen and complete the phrases.

e Watch or listen again and repeat the phrases. How do you say them in your language?

Can you...?

- [ ] talk about transport options
- [ ] rent a car
- [ ] record a voicemail greeting and leave a message

G future forms: *will* / *shall* and *going to*
V rubbish and recycling
P /ɪ/, /aɪ/, and /eɪ/

When are they going to collect the rubbish?

They'll be here on Tuesday, I think.

4A That's rubbish!

1 LISTENING

a How often do you or your family throw away food? What kind of things? How do you feel about it?

b Look at the photo below. What do you think the woman is looking for? Why?

c You're going to listen to a journalist, Liz Scarff, talking about her experiences of living as a 'freegan'. Read the beginning of an article she wrote about freegans. Who are they? What do they do?

NEWS | VOICES | SPORT | TECH | LIFE | PROPERTY | TRAVEL | MONEY

My three days as a freegan

By Liz Scarff

They're not poor or homeless, but they look in rubbish bins for food to eat. They call themselves 'freegans' – a combination of the words 'free' and 'vegan' – and they are upset about how much food people waste. Around 17 million tonnes of food is thrown away in Britain every year, four million of which is perfectly good to eat. This is especially disturbing since four million people in Britain can't afford a healthy diet.

Their ideas are admirable, but taking and eating food from the rubbish sounds disgusting, embarrassing, and possibly unsafe. So, just how easy is it to live on food from bins? My challenge is to live as a freegan for three days. Too embarrassed to go on my own, I've brought my friend Dave. But first, we meet up with two London freegans, Ash and Ross, for a quick lesson in freeganism.

Adapted from The Independent

d 2 29 Listen to Liz Scarff talk about trying to live as a freegan. Mark the sentences **T** (true) or **F** (false).

Sunday

1 You should take gloves and a torch with you before going to look in bins. ☐
2 Large shops are better than small or medium size ones. ☐
3 In the first bin they found frozen chicken soup and *chilli con carne*. ☐
4 They also found some eggs, but they were past their sell-by date. ☐
5 Ross says you don't need to worry if the packaging is broken or if something is past its sell-by date. ☐
6 He says you should wash everything you find before eating it. ☐

Monday

7 Liz and Dave found the unlocked bin behind a large supermarket. ☐
8 They found fruit and vegetables in the bin behind the supermarket. ☐
9 They didn't feel embarrassed looking in the bins. ☐
10 They had soup and bread and baked apples for dinner. ☐

e 2 30 Listen to the second part of Liz's challenge. Answer the questions.

Tuesday

1 How did Liz feel on Tuesday morning?
2 What did they have for breakfast?
3 What did they find in the bins on Tuesday?
4 How does she feel about what people had thrown away?
5 What did they have for dinner on Tuesday evening?
6 Did all the ingredients come from the rubbish?

Wednesday

7 What was wrong with the bins in the market on Wednesday?
8 What did they find in them?
9 What did Liz learn from trying freeganism?

f What do you think are the advantages and disadvantages of being a freegan? Can you imagine ever trying it?

2 VOCABULARY rubbish and recycling

a Look at three sentences from the listening. Can you remember any of the missing words?

1 Ash and Ross walk confidently to the ____, lift the ____, and start looking for food.
2 At the bottom is a ____ of eggs.
3 If the ____ is open or it's past the ____ - ____ ____, don't take it.

b 2 31 Listen and complete the sentences.

c ➤ **p.156 Vocabulary Bank** *Rubbish and recycling.*

3 PRONUNCIATION /ɪ/, /aɪ/, and /eɪ/

a Look at the sound pictures. What are the words and sounds? Write the words from the list in the right column.

away bin date diet garbage lid lifestyle packaging reapply recycle tray waste

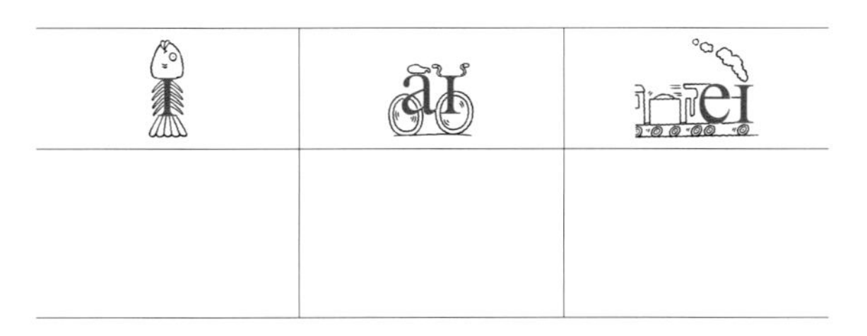

b 2 36 Listen and check. Practise saying the words.

c ➤ **p.166 Sound Bank.** Look at the typical spellings for the three sounds in **a**.

4 SPEAKING

a Read the questionnaire and think about your answers.

b Discuss the questions in groups of three or four.

What a waste!

What three things could you and your family do in order to throw away less food?

What kind of things do you recycle? Do you ever feel guilty about not recycling enough? Why (not)?

Have you ever eaten anything that was past its sell-by date? Why (not)? Did anything happen?

Have you ever taken something that someone else has thrown away? What was it? What did you do with it?

What do you do with clothes, books, or furniture that you don't want but could still be used?

Is there anything you are going to do differently now?

Other people

What could your local council do to make it easier to recycle where you live?

What do you think restaurants or supermarkets in your town should do with unused food? Do you know if any of them ever do it?

What kind of things do you think have too much packaging? When do you think packaging is really necessary?

Which of the things you've discussed do you think would make the most difference to your environment?

5 READING

a How long have you had your mobile phone? When do you think you'll get a new one? What will you probably do with your old phone?

b Read the article about mobile phone recycling. Find two reasons why recycling mobiles is better than throwing them away.

Home Reviews Videos **Phones** Tablets Cameras Components Computing Car Technology News Deals

Got a new mobile? Think twice before you throw the old one away!

Recycling our old mobile phones is something we often mean to do. But by the time we remember to do it, we decide that they're so old they're **worthless**, and we throw them away. But are they really?

[1] ______ 'Only about 3–4 per cent of the phones we receive can't be repaired,' says Simon Walsh, Sales and Marketing Director for a British phone recycler.

As a phone arrives at a recycling centre, it goes through a rigorous testing process, which starts with a check to ensure that it's not been lost or stolen. [2] ______ Many phones are then passed to specialized repair centres.

Even mobiles that can't be repaired are valuable. [3] ______ Batteries contain nickel, which can be used to make stainless steel for saucepans. The plastics in phones can be **melted down** to be made into traffic cones.

Of the phones that can be reused, about 20% stay in the UK. The rest of them are sent to places in Asia and Africa where they are specially needed because there are few landlines.

But there's more to it than that. It's good to recycle and reuse **second-hand** mobiles from the UK, but the countries which receive the mobiles also need to recycle them. [4] ______

This is a growing problem because some mobile phone parts contain **dangerous chemicals**. [5] ______. The phone's electrical circuits contain lead, which can cause brain damage.

It's estimated that there are more than 500 million used mobile phones around the world. If we send all of them to landfills, over 130,000 kilos of lead will be **released into the soil**. [6] ______.

The even greener alternative to recycling seems almost unthinkable. It's to keep your current phone for more than the usual 12 months!

Adapted from www.techradar.com

Glossary
nickel /'nɪkl/ a hard, silver-white metal
lead /led/ a soft, heavy, grey metal used in the past for water pipes or to cover roofs

c Read the article again and complete it with **A–F**.

A They contain small quantities of metals such as platinum, which are used to make jewellery.
B If they don't, the phones will still end up in landfill.
C As demand for mobiles and smartphones increases, the problem is going to get even worse.
D Some phone batteries have cadmium, a metal which can cause lung cancer.
E Then components such as the keypad are checked.
F In fact, most mobiles can be repaired and sold again.

d Look at the highlighted words and phrases connected with recycling and the environment. Work out their meaning from the context.

e What other electronic gadgets and appliances do you think people could recycle? Do they do it where you live?

6 **GRAMMAR** future forms: *will* / *shall* and *going to*

a Complete the dialogues with *will* | *shall* or *be going to* and the correct form of the verb.

1 **A** Could you take the rubbish out? It's beginning to smell.
B I ______ it as soon as this programme finishes, I promise. (do)

2 **A** ______ I ______ your plate now, madam? (take)
B Yes, thanks. It was delicious, but I couldn't finish it all.

3 **A** What ______ you ______ when you finish school? (do) I know you've made plans.
B I ______ a gap year, and work on a conservation project in Peru. (have)

4 **A** I'm a bit worried about the picnic. I think it ______ this afternoon. (rain)
B Well, on the internet it says it ______ sunny. (be) I wouldn't worry if I were you.

5 **A** Don't put bottles in the rubbish. We need to take them to the bottle bank.
B OK, OK. I ______ it again. (not do)

b **2 37** Listen and check. Practise the dialogues with a partner.

c ➤ **p.138 Grammar Bank 4A.** Learn more about future forms and practise them.

d Talk to a partner. Choose two topics from each group to talk about, or use your own ideas.

Talk about a plan you have...
- for this evening
- for the weekend
- for your next holiday
- to save money or spend less
- to improve your diet
- to learn something new

Make a prediction about...
- the environment
- your favourite sports club
- the economy and unemployment
- an actor, singer, or group you like
- your friends' or family members' careers
- the characters in a TV series you watch

Responding to plans and predictions

Plans
I'm going to...
Are you? So am I.
What a good idea! How nice!

Predictions
I don't think... will / is going to...
I think so too.
I don't think so either.
I hope so. I hope not.

G first and second conditionals
V study and work
P word stress

Why do you want to study business?

Because if I get a good degree, I'll be able to find an interesting job.

4B Degrees and careers

1 VOCABULARY study and work

a Read the job adverts. Would you like to do either of the jobs?

b Complete the adverts with a word from the list.

covering CV experience degree
references qualifications vacancy

c ➤ **p.157 Vocabulary Bank** *Study and work.*

2 PRONUNCIATION & SPEAKING word stress

a Underline the stressed syllable in these words.

a|ttend de|gree di|sser|ta|tion P|h|D
post|gra|du|ate pro|fe|ssor qua|li|fi|ca|tions
re|fe|ree re|si|dence scho|lar|ship se|mi|nar
tu|to|ri|al un|der|gra|du|ate va|can|cy

b 2 42 Listen and check.

c Work in pairs. What is the difference between...?

1. an undergraduate and a postgraduate
2. a master's degree and a PhD
3. a campus and a hall of residence
4. a professor and a tutor
5. a seminar and a webinar
6. a tutorial and a lecture
7. qualifications and skills
8. a covering letter and a CV

d Talk to a partner. Look at the points below. When you choose a subject to study, how important do you think these factors should be? How important were they for you?

- future career prospects
- how much you like the subject
- how learning the subject will allow you to help others
- your parents' wishes and dreams
- how hard you have to study
- the quality of the teaching
- other factors: ______________________

Bird Keeper

New

★ Add to shortlist

Bristol | £ Competitive

Bristol Zoo Gardens is hiring an Animal Keeper for our Bird Section. The successful applicant will be a bird keeper with at least two years' experience of working with a variety of bird species. Applicants should have [1] ______ such as an A-level in English or Biology. A [2] ______ in Zoo Management would also be an advantage.

To apply, please send a [3] ______ letter and [4] ______ to...

Art Handler

New

★ Add to shortlist

London | £27,000–£30,000

A fine-art mover is seeking to fill a [5] ______ for the position of Art Handler. The ideal candidate will have a minimum of two years' [6] ______ of moving and handling very expensive art and antiques for museums and galleries. Excellent [7] ______ from previous employers are also required, as well as a driving licence.

3 LISTENING

a Would you ever consider doing a job for no pay? Why (not)?

b You're going to listen to three people talking about their internships. First read the information below. What is an internship? What do you think the advantages and disadvantages are?

'It's slave labour,

Real interns speak out

For many young graduates, starting out in a new career means taking an unpaid internship, with no guarantee of a permanent job at the end. While internships can provide graduates with useful experience, referees, and skills for their CVs, they also require a lot of hard work. Many interns feel exploited by employers, who treat them as cheap labour. In fact, nearly 40% of internships are unpaid, especially in industries such as fashion, PR, the media, and politics. Legally, most interns in the UK are entitled to the minimum wage. However, few employers realize this. Many interns have to work in bars or restaurants at night to pay for their rent, food, and expenses, while others end up in debt.

We spoke to three recent interns about their experiences...

Adapted from the Daily Mail

c 2 43 Listen to Rosie, Joe, and Lauren talk about their experiences of internships. Who had a positive experience? Who had the most negative experiences?

d Listen again, and make notes in the chart.

	Rosie	Joe	Lauren
The kind of company			
The good side			
The bad side			

e Discuss the questions.

1 Have you ever done an internship? Do you know anyone who has worked as an intern? Did they have a good experience?

2 Do you think unpaid internships are fair? Why (not)?

4 GRAMMAR
first and second conditionals

a 2 44 Listen to the ends of two job interviews. Complete the conditionals. Which person do you think has a real possibility of getting the job?

1 If we __________ you the job, when you __________ to start?

2 If we __________ you the job, you __________ a lot of training.

b ➤ **p.139 Grammar Bank 4B.** Learn more about first and second conditionals and practise them.

c 2 47 Listen and write five first conditional sentences giving advice to people looking for work. Do you agree with the advice?

d Imagine you were in these situations. What would you do? Say why using a second conditional.

If I was offered a great job abroad, I'd probably take it, because...

1 You are offered a great job abroad.

2 Your partner is offered a job abroad in a country that you wouldn't like to live in.

3 You have to choose between a well-paid but boring job and a very interesting but badly paid job.

4 You are offered a job while you are still in the middle of your studies.

5 You have to choose between working at night or working at weekends.

5 READING

a In your country, do young people sometimes do part-time jobs in the evening or at weekends, or while they're at university? What sort of part-time jobs are common where you live?

b Read the newspaper article about Saturday jobs. Who is most positive about the job they did?

c Read the article again. Answer with A–E.

Which person...?

1 ___ felt that the job was badly paid
2 ___ liked the parts of the job where he / she could rest
3 ___ started very early and finished very late
4 ___ enjoyed spending time with the other workers
5 ___ was very unsuccessful in one of his / her jobs
6 ___ learned the importance of enjoying the work that you do
7 ___ learned the importance of punctuality
8 ___ got practice in something that later became his / her job
9 ___ and ___ aren't sure if they learned anything
10 ___ stopped getting any weekly money from his / her parents after starting his / her first part time job

The best Saturday job I ever had. . .

Shelf-stacker, dog-walker, and baby-sitter – most of us would have one of these classic Saturday jobs at the bottom of our CVs, if we were being strictly accurate. For the teenagers of today, however, it is far more difficult to find part-time work.

A Sir Ranulph Fiennes, explorer

When I was 16, I wanted to buy a canoe and needed £85. I washed the buses at Midhurst bus station between 3.00 a.m. and 7.00 a.m. during the week. Then I washed the dishes at the Angel Hotel from 6.00 p.m. to 10.00 p.m. I was paid £11 per week in all, and that's how I got the cash. It is too long ago to know if I actually learnt anything from the experience.

B Russell Kane, comedian

I did two humiliating Saturday jobs. The first was selling vacuum cleaners door to door. I didn't sell a single one. The other job was working with my granddad for a frozen-food delivery service. I doubt that a Saturday job really teaches you anything. Where I come from, it's automatic: at age 11 you get a job. It wasn't, 'Hey man, I'm really learning the value of work.' It was, 'If I want money, I must work for it.' My dad never gave me a penny of pocket money after the age of 11.

C Tony Ross, illustrator and author

In the fifties, when I was a boy, I used to work at the Post Office over Christmas. Many of us did it, and it was fantastic fun. I earned enough to buy an old motor scooter. My favourite part was going in the lorry to collect the mail bags from the station, because you didn't have to walk the streets all day. The other good thing was doing a round with your own house in it, because then you could stop for a cup of tea. I learnt the basics of working for money like arriving on time, and enjoying it no matter what. It was a good introduction because very few people work for fun. I think I'm probably the only one.

D Clive Stafford Smith, lawyer

I worked for a sand and gravel* company when I was 16. It was cold, damp, and so boring that I cried. I've learned various important things from that job. First, I know I'm very lucky to have a job now that I truly love. I also learned that it's crazy to pay bankers millions while paying minimum wage to people at gravel companies. It's terrible work and no one should have to do it. Anyone who says differently should be forced to work at that gravel company for a year.

E Adele Parks, author

When I was 16, I worked in our local supermarket, stacking shelves for two years. In a job like that you make the decision whether this is what you want to do for the rest of your life. I was doing my A-levels, and the other guys and girls were really quite pleased for me, as they were living through my experiences. I am good at talking and telling stories, and I think I learnt it there, because one of the things about stacking shelves or being at the checkout is that you get to pass the time with people. That's what I liked best.

* gravel = very small stones often used on paths or roads

Adapted from www.thetimes.co.uk

d Look at the highlighted words and phrases related to jobs, and work out their meaning from the context. Then match them with the definitions.

1 ________ *noun* a regular route that someone takes when collecting or delivering something
2 ________ knocking on people's doors to try to convince them to buy something
3 ________ *noun* taking things directly from e.g. a shop or business to people's homes
4 ________ *noun* a job which involves putting things on shelves, usually in a supermarket
5 ________ *noun* the place where you pay, e.g. in a supermarket
6 ________ *noun* the smallest amount of money a job can pay you according to the law

e Which of the jobs mentioned do you think sounds the best / the worst?

6 SPEAKING

In groups of three, discuss the questions about work and studies. Follow the arrows to ask the questions that are most relevant to you / your partners.

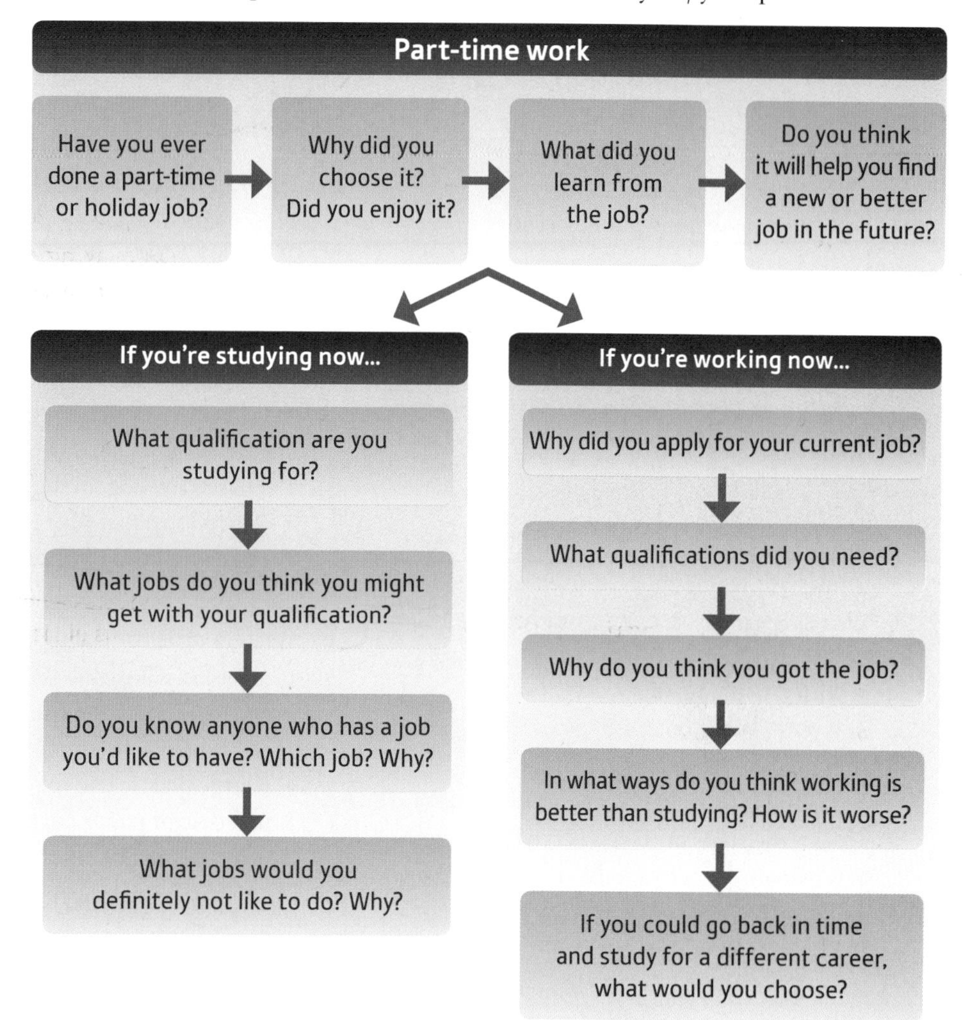

7 WRITING

➤ **p.116 Writing** *A LinkedIn profile*. Create your own profile for *LinkedIn* or a similar site.

8 2 48 SONG *5 o'clock world* ♫

3&4 Revise and Check

GRAMMAR

Circle a, b, or c.

1 I couldn't answer my phone because I ______.
a drove b used to drive c was driving

2 We ______ to a lot of different shops yesterday.
a went b used to go c were going

3 She ______ get up so late.
a didn't use b didn't use to
c didn't used to

4 When I was young I ______ playing football.
a love b was loving c used to love

5 We're very pleased ______ our holiday photos.
a with b to c of

6 **A** Are we going out?
B It ______ the weather.
a depends b depends on c depends of

7 ______ the steps until you get to the bottom.
a Go down b Go c Be down

8 **A** These bags are so heavy!
B ______ you with them.
a I help b I'm going to help c I'll help

9 **A** I've made an appointment to see my dentist.
B When ______?
a do you go b will you go c are you going

10 I'm really sorry. I promise ______ late again.
a I'm not b I won't be
c I'm not going to be

11 This job looks interesting. ______ I apply?
a Shall b Do c Will

12 I ______ to work abroad unless the pay was very good.
a don't want b won't want
c wouldn't want

13 I might get the job if I ______ more experience.
a will have b had c would have

14 If you ______ to earn some money, you shouldn't become an intern.
a will need b need c needed

15 You won't get into university ______ harder.
a unless you don't study b if you study
c unless you study

VOCABULARY

a Write a word or phrase connected with age.

1 15 years old ______
2 21 or 22 ______
3 18 months old ______
4 over 65 ______
5 58 ______

b Circle the right word or phrase.

1 My sister's a very good *photographer* | *photographic*.
2 It's very dark in here so you'll need to use *zoom* | *flash*.
3 I always *upload* | *download* my photos onto Facebook.
4 There's my dog, in the *bottom right-hand* | *right-hand bottom* corner.
5 What *document* | *file* format did you save the photo as?
6 Here's a photo of us on the beach – you can see our hotel in the *foreground* | *background*.

c Write words for the definitions.

1 a person whose job is to take the rubbish away ______
2 the material often used to make boxes ______
3 the top of a jar ______
4 a large plastic bag for putting rubbish in ______
5 a plastic or paper cover for a chocolate bar ______
6 a large area of land where waste is put ______

d Complete the words.

1 Don't forget to include a **c**______ letter with your CV.
2 I'm living in a hall of **r**______ in my first year at university.
3 He won't get the job. He doesn't have enough **q**______.
4 You need to **a**______ for a work permit to work in the US.
5 Most students attend **l**______ every day.
6 I'm trying to get a job, but there very few **v**______.
7 Her new job has a **t**______ period of six months.
8 The **m**______ wage in the UK is about £6.50 an hour.

PRONUNCIATION

a Circle the word with a different sound.

1	d	blurred	hoped	changed	saved
2	ɪ	behind	opposite	skills	lid
3	aɪ	recycle	apply	file	faculty
4	eɪ	reapply	waste	replay	data
5	əʊ	photo	front	overseas	focus

b Underline the stressed syllable.

1 pho|to|gra|pher
2 pho|to|co|py
3 re|cy|cle
4 un|der|gra|du|ate
5 qua|li|fi|ca|tions

CAN YOU UNDERSTAND THIS TEXT?

a Read the article once. Is it positive or negative about recycling in the UK?

Recycling facts and figures

UK households produced over 30 million tonnes of waste last year, of which 25% was collected for recycling. This figure is still quite low compared to some other EU countries, some of which recycle over 50% of their waste. There is still a great deal of waste which could be recycled that ends up in landfill sites.

Some interesting facts
- Up to 60% of the rubbish that ends up in the dustbin could be recycled.
- On average, 16% of the money you spend on a product pays for the packaging, which ultimately ends up as rubbish.
- Up to 80% of a vehicle can be recycled.
- Nine out of ten people would recycle more if it were made easier.

Aluminium
- 24 million tonnes of aluminium is produced annually, 51,000 tonnes of which ends up as packaging in the UK.
- £36,000,000 worth of aluminium is thrown away each year.
- Aluminium cans can be recycled and ready to use in just six weeks.

Glass
- Each UK family uses an average of 500 glass bottles and jars annually.
- Glass is 100% recyclable and can be used again and again.
- Glass that is thrown away and ends up in landfills will never decompose.

Paper
- It takes 70% less energy to recycle paper than to make it from raw materials.
- 12.5 million tonnes of paper and cardboard are used annually in the UK.
- The average person in the UK throws away 38 kg of newspapers per year.
- It takes 24 trees to make one ton of newspaper.

Plastic
- 275,000 tonnes of plastic are used each year in the UK – that's about 15 million bottles per day.
- Most families throw away about 40 kg of plastic per year, which could otherwise be recycled.
- The use of plastic in Western Europe is growing by about 4% each year.
- Plastic can take up to 500 years to decompose.

Adapted from recycling-guide.org.uk

b Read the article again. Mark the sentences **T** (true) or **F** (false).

1. The UK recycles more than most other EU countries.
2. Most of the rubbish that is thrown away could be recycled.
3. More than half of an old car can be recycled.
4. Most people think that recycling is easy.
5. Aluminium is an easy material to recycle.
6. Glass can only be recycled a few times.
7. Recycling paper uses less energy than making it.
8. The UK uses more plastic than paper and cardboard.
9. UK families recycle all their plastic.
10. Plastic doesn't last forever in landfill.

VIDEO CAN YOU UNDERSTAND THESE PEOPLE?

2 49 **In the street** Watch or listen to five people and answer the questions.

Jo

David

Paul

Marc

Kaley

1. Jo thinks children shouldn't be allowed in restaurants sometimes because ______.
   a they can be noisy b they don't appreciate the food
   c they shouldn't be out late
2. What kind of photos does David like taking?
   a photos of buildings b portraits of people
   c holiday photos
3. Paul ______.
   a buys a new phone every two years
   b is given a new phone every two years
   c changes his phone contract every two years
4. Which of these did Marc not study?
   a American history b British history
   c European history
5. In which of these places has Kaley worked?
   a a school and an office b an office and a restaurant
   c a laboratory and a shop

CAN YOU SAY THIS IN ENGLISH?

Do the tasks with a partner. Tick (✓) the box if you can do them.

Can you...?

1. ☐ talk about what you were like when you were a child or teenager
2. ☐ describe the different stages of a person's life
3. ☐ describe a favourite photograph of yours
4. ☐ say what you think about recycling
5. ☐ talk about your education, and about your work or your work plans

VIDEO **Short films** A New York sanitation worker
Watch and enjoy a film on iTutor.

G present perfect simple
V television
P /w/, /v/, and /b/

5A What's on?

How long has that quiz show been on TV?

It's been on for a long time, for at least three years.

1 VOCABULARY television

a How many hours of TV do you watch a day? Tell a partner about one TV programme you love and one you hate. Give reasons.

b 3 2 Listen to the excerpts from six TV programmes. Match each excerpt to a programme.

___ a chat show	___ d sitcom
___ b documentary	___ e sport
___ c drama series	___ f the news

c ➤ **p.158 Vocabulary Bank** *Television*.

2 PRONUNCIATION & SPEAKING /w/, /v/, and /b/

a 3 5 Listen and repeat the three sound pictures and words.

w	v	b
we switch weather	TV volume over	be button celebrity

b 3 6 Listen to the pairs of words. Can you hear the difference? Practise saying them.

1 a why	b buy
2 a ban	b van
3 a vet	b wet
4 a boat	b vote
5 a bake	b wake
6 a wine	b vine
7 a fiver	b fibre
8 a very	b berry

c 3 7 Listen and circle the word you hear.

d Practise saying the sentences.

Let's buy a wide-screen TV.
I never watch live sport.
Switch over to channel five.
It won't be over before eleven.

e Ask and answer with a partner.

1 Do you watch TV programmes...?
- on a TV (Where? What kind?)
- on your computer, tablet, or phone

2 Are there any TV programmes that...?
- you always switch off as soon as they start
- you watch although you know they are awful
- you only watch because the rest of your family like them

3 Which channel do you usually watch...?
- when there is a big news story
- for live sport

4 Do you ever...
- turn the volume right down (or off) during a programme? What kind of programme?
- get bored halfway through a programme but still carry on watching? Why do you carry on watching?

3 LISTENING

a Do you watch any cartoon series on TV? Which one(s)? What do you think of them?

b 3 8 Listen to **Part 1** of a chat show where the guests are two sisters who write for a new US animated series called *Bob's Burgers*. Tick (✓) the topics they discuss.

1 ___ who the series is for
2 ___ what the series is about
3 ___ how they got the job
4 ___ how much money TV writers earn
5 ___ their daily routine
6 ___ how many episodes they write in a year
7 ___ how long it takes to create an episode
8 ___ the process of creating an episode
9 ___ the actors in the series
10 ___ their favourite episodes in the series

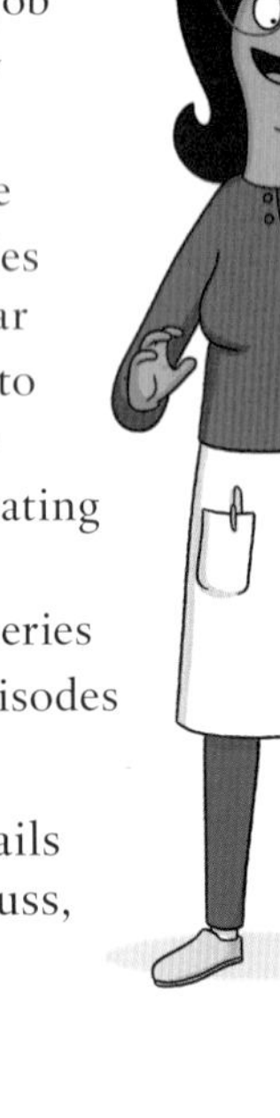

c Listen again for more details about the topics they discuss, and make notes.

d 3 9))) Listen to **Part 2** of the programme. Why do they mention the following?

1 Loren Bouchard
2 baked potatoes
3 Jon Hamm
4 their other sisters
5 *Game of Thrones* and *Homeland*
6 *The Real Housewives of Beverly Hills*

e How important is a good script in a TV series? Think of examples of programmes that you think are well written or badly written.

4 GRAMMAR present perfect simple

a Complete the questions with a word from the list.

already ever for just since yet

1 Have you _ever_ watched a UK or US period drama series? What was it? Did you like it?
2 Are there any programmes that have been on TV in your country ________ five years or more? Do you ever watch them?
3 Do you sometimes re-watch an episode of a series that you've ________ seen?
4 What TV actors or presenters did you like when you were a child? Have they made any good programmes ________ then?
5 Is there anything that has ________ happened in the news today?
6 Is there a new TV series that everyone is watching? Have you seen it ________?

b Ask and answer the questions with a partner.

c ➤ **p.140 Grammar Bank 5A.** Learn more about the present perfect simple and practise it.

d Tell your partner about...

- a series you've just finished watching
- a film you've seen more than three times
- a DVD or film download that you've had for over a month but not watched yet
- a film or TV programme that everyone you know has seen but you haven't

5 READING

a Read the Wikipedia entry about Netflix. Does anything similar exist in your country? Would you like it to?

b Now read the article below. Is the journalist positive about…?

1 the series *House of Cards*
2 Netflix
3 both

Article Talk Read Edit View history

Netflix

From *Wikipedia, the free encyclopedia*

Netflix Inc. is an American provider of on-demand internet streaming media, available in North and South America, the UK, and several other European countries. In its simplest form, video is streamed to the user's computer. TV series and films can be paused or restarted at will. According to a 2011 report, Netflix is the biggest source of North American web traffic.

ALL IN ONE SITTING

We have all been there: you settle in to watch one episode of a TV show, and eight hours later you've watched the whole season…

On the day when Netflix released the entire 13-episode first season of its political drama series *House of Cards* in one go, it reminded viewers on Twitter to #watchresponsibly: 'Don't forget to shower, eat something, get up and walk around!' All through that day, people were tweeting: 'What episode are you on?' Netflix's strategy was to encourage subscribers to 'binge-watch' the show – the TV equivalent of binge-eating.

House of Cards of course is not rubbish; it is a highly praised political drama. Originally a novel by Michael Dobbs, it follows the congressman Francis 'Frank' Underwood (Kevin Spacey), his scary wife, Claire, and young reporter, Zoe Barnes, as they struggle for power and influence in Washington. At 2.00 a.m., two episodes into the series, I simply couldn't stop. It was going to be a long night.

The show is clearly and cleverly structured for binge-consumption. Each episode is called a 'chapter'. There are no introductory flashbacks, common in traditional series. And at the end of nearly every episode, the cliffhanger makes the temptation to find out what is going to happen unbearable. By 10.00 a.m. the next day, and minutes away from the end of the final episode, I was searching for a release date for season two.

Initial reviews of Netflix's strategy and the show were mixed. Liz Shannon, a fellow binge-watcher, was sceptical. 'I'm not convinced that substituting the buzz that traditional shows acquire during a whole season for the buzz of binge-watching will be a success.' Laura Hudson was slightly more critical. 'It's not a great show; it's debatably a good one, but more importantly, it was just good enough to make me press "next" every time the episode finished.' That's precisely the point.

What's clear is that with DVDs and on-demand video, consumers have never had more choice in their own media consumption habits. Why pay the very expensive monthly cost for cable service when you're only watching three or four shows on as many channels? And why wait each week or months at a time for your favourite show? And with Netflix another advantage is that there are no commercials.

Netflix knows that it's already succeeded, at least in the US. *Breaking Bad*, for example, another good show for binge-watching, has been a hit. According to the *Wall Street Journal*, '73% of members who started streaming season one of *Breaking Bad* finished all seven episodes. Seasons two and three were longer – thirteen episodes each – but the number of viewers jumped to 81% and 85% respectively.'

As for me, I've heard great things about *Friday Night Lights*. Netflix, here I come.

Whether it's *Downton Abbey* or *The Big Bang Theory* – tell us about your TV binge experiences…

Adapted from The Guardian

c Read the article again. Choose a, b, or c.

> **Tip: Multiple-choice reading**
> - Read the text first to get an idea of what it's about and how it's organized.
> - Read the questions and try to eliminate any options that you know are wrong.
> - Finally, re-read the parts of the text that go with the other options and try to choose the correct one.

1 *Binge* + a verb means ____.
   - a to share your experience of doing something with other people
   - b to do something too much in a short period of time
   - c to do something late at night

2 *House of Cards* is ____.
   - a an addictive sitcom
   - b a soap opera about politics
   - c a drama series based on a book

3 One of the features of *House of Cards* is that each episode ____.
   - a ends making you want to watch the next one
   - b begins with some scenes from previous episodes
   - c is based on one chapter of the book

4 The first reviewers ____.
   - a made both positive and negative comments about the show and Netflix's strategy
   - b thought the series was good but Netflix's strategy was irresponsible
   - c thought that people would return to watching shows weekly

5 According to the article, nowadays ____ than before.
   - a more TV series are being made
   - b people have more choice as to how to watch TV series
   - c people watch more channels

6 In the series *Breaking Bad* ____.
   - a the first season was longer than the second one
   - b the second season was nearly twice as long as the first one
   - c fewer people finished watching the third series

d Look at the highlighted words related to TV. With a partner work out their meaning from the context.

e Talk to a partner.

1 Do you think you would enjoy *House of Cards*? Why (not)? Have you seen any of the other series mentioned in the article?

2 What was the last TV series you got 'addicted' to?
   - Did you watch it in weekly episodes, on DVD, or online?
   - How many seasons did you watch?
   - How many episodes did you usually watch in one sitting?

3 Have you ever 'binge-watched' any other series? Why (not)? Do you know anyone who has?

6 SPEAKING

a Look at the statements and decide if you agree or disagree with them. Think of reasons why.

1. You enjoy a series more if you watch it weekly and don't binge-watch.
2. Children under the age of five shouldn't watch any television at all.
3. TVs should be banned from bars and restaurants.
4. Violent programmes shouldn't be shown before 10.00 p.m.
5. There aren't enough good programmes to fill all of the channels available today.
6. Families shouldn't have the TV on while they are having meals.
7. The news on TV is not objective, as most channels are controlled by the government.

b Work in small groups. Choose statements from **a** where you don't all agree. See if you can persuade the other students to agree with you.

I agree with ***1****. There's more suspense when you have to wait a week for the next episode...*

G present perfect continuous
V the country
P vowel sounds; sentence stress

How long have your parents been living in the country?

For two years. They moved back to their village when they retired.

5B The country in other countries

1 VOCABULARY the country

a Look at photos from three different places in Europe. With a partner, answer the questions.

1 Which country do you think they were taken in?
2 What do you think it would be like to live in each of these places? Which would you prefer?
3 Can you name at least three things in each photo?

b ➤ **p.159 Vocabulary Bank** *The country.*

2 PRONUNCIATION vowel sounds

a Look at the pairs of words below. Are the vowel sounds the same or different? Write **S** or **D**.

1	leaf	wheat	☐
2	bush	mud	☐
3	plant	grass	☐
4	grow	cow	☐
5	pick	chicken	☐
6	pond	stone	☐
7	lamb	farm	☐
8	sheep	field	☐

b 3 14))) Listen and check. Practise saying the words.

3 LISTENING & SPEAKING

a 3 15))) Listen to Melisa, who used to live in the country in Turkey, and Eric, who lives in the country in the USA now. Answer the questions.

	Melisa	Eric
1 What's the countryside like where they live / used to live?		
2 How do / did they entertain themselves?		
3 What disadvantages do they mention?		

b Talk to a partner.

1 Do either of the two places described attract you? Why?
2 Does the countryside they describe sound like the countryside near you? Why (not)?
3 Do you ever go to the country? Why do you go? Do you enjoy yourself there? Why (not)?
4 Answer the questions below.

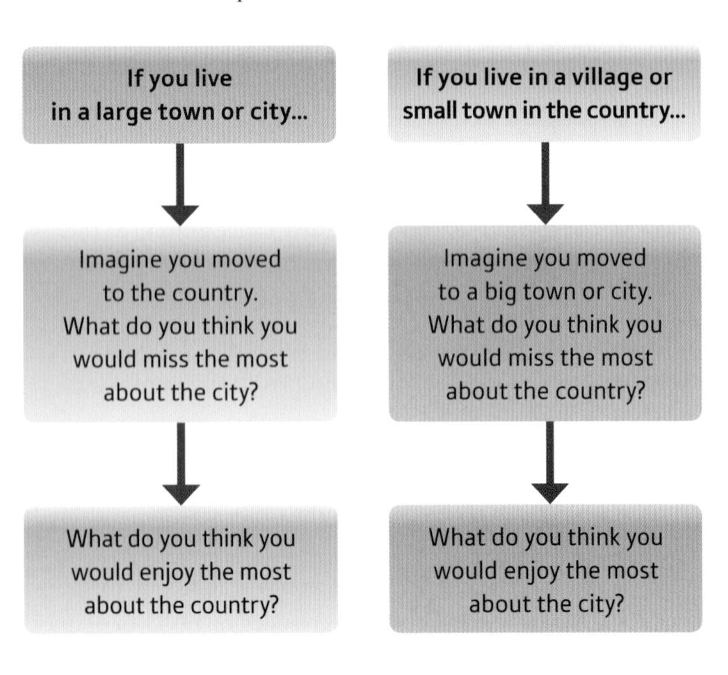

4 READING & SPEAKING

a Read the introduction to the article. Why do you think people move from the city to the country? Why do some people move back?

From the city to the country

(and sometimes back again)

Not everyone who moves to the country ends up staying there. In fact, for the first time in years, as many people are moving back to cities as are moving out to the country.

b Work in pairs **A** and **B**. **A** read about Liz Jones, **B** read about Rob Penn. Answer questions 1–5.

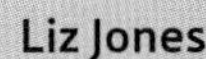

Liz Jones

'I was just divorced, and bored with my easy, if super-busy, London life. I wanted to live somewhere quieter, simpler, more beautiful, so I sold my house and bought a big farmhouse with 50 acres of land. I'll look after horses, I thought, I'll get a dog. I'll grow all my own food. It will be idyllic and friends will come to stay and tell me how lucky I am to live here.

But even from the first week, it was a nightmare. When I moved in, the house was cold and absolutely filthy, and the cooker didn't work. I discovered everything in the countryside is more expensive: you have to drive miles to find a shop where everything costs twice as much as in my local supermarket in London. I never fitted in. I think that in the country, if you are a woman, you will never be accepted unless you are a full-time mum. Another thing I hated was the shooting! I just couldn't pass a group of men with guns, shooting rabbits and deer, without getting out of my car and saying: "Do you really have nothing better to do on a Saturday morning?" That didn't make me very popular. I became so lonely, I often used to sit in my car and listen to the kind voice of the satnav lady.'

After five years Liz decided to go back to London. 'On my last night in the country, I sat outside underneath millions of stars and I thought to myself: "I've come to the end of a five-year prison sentence."'

1 Why did Liz move to the country?
2 What was she dreaming of doing there?
3 What problems did she have at the beginning?
4 Why does she think people didn't accept her?
5 How long did she stay? What did she compare living in the country to?

Glossary
1 __________ *phrasal verb* leaving a car
2 __________ *phrasal verb* started to live in a new home
3 __________ *phrasal verb* was able to live and work well with other people
4 __________ unit of land, equivalent to 4,050 square metres

Rob Penn

Rob Penn, a writer, left London for some peace and quiet in the Black Mountains in Wales. 'I've been living here in a small farmhouse for eight years now,' says Penn. 'It wasn't easy at first. The fact that I ride a bicycle every day caused suspicion. In the countryside you only use a bike if something is wrong. A local farmer said to me, "I see you on the bike. How long have you lost your driving licence for, then?"'

Over time, however, Penn has managed to fit in with his new neighbours. 'I'm lucky. I live in a place with a strong sense of community. My local pub is an active part of that. We have two village halls as well. Between them, they put on activities or meetings every night of the week – singing workshops, the garden club, zumba, as well as monthly films and occasional quiz nights.

'In the city, you choose your community. It may be through work, your football team, or your kids' school or your colleagues,' says Penn. 'In the country, your neighbours are your only community.'

Penn has no plans to move back to London. 'I stood in a field this week, listening to the first sounds of spring. I love to hear the birds singing in the sunshine. I wouldn't live anywhere else. The rural sights, sounds and, above all, communities beat the city any day.'

1 Who is Rob Penn? Where did he move to?
2 Why did he move?
3 How long has he been living there?
4 What problems did he have at first? Did he solve them?
5 Why did he decide to stay?

Glossary
1 __________ *phrasal verb* organize an event, e.g. a play, a workshop
2 __________ *phrasal verb* integrate, be able to live and work well with other people
3 __________ *phrasal verb* go to live in a place where you lived before

c Read your article again. Work out the meaning of the highlighted words, and then complete the glossary.

d Cover the articles and use your answers to questions 1–5 to tell each other about Liz and Rob in your own words. Try to use the phrasal verbs from the glossary, and explain them to your partner if necessary.

e Answer the questions in small groups.

1 What was one problem that both Liz and Rob had? Do you think this would be the main problem for people moving from the city to the country in the area where you live? Why (not)?
2 Why do you think one of them succeeded and the other failed?
3 Do you know anyone who's moved from the city to the country? Did they stay? Why (not)?
4 Do you know anyone who's moved from the country to the city? Did they stay? Why (not)?

5 GRAMMAR present perfect continuous

a Look at the photos and speech bubbles. Circle the correct verb form.

b Compare answers with a partner. Explain why you chose each answer.

c ➤ **p.141 Grammar Bank 5B.** Learn more about the present perfect continuous and practise it.

6 PRONUNCIATION & SPEAKING sentence stress

a Complete sentences 1–10 with the present perfect continuous of the verbs.

1 I __________ really hard this week. (work)
2 I __________ well lately. (not sleep)
3 My neighbours __________ a lot of noise recently. (make)
4 I __________ about getting a new phone for a while. (think)
5 I __________ with my family a lot recently. (argue)
6 I __________ TV at all lately. (not watch)
7 I __________ very stressed for the last few weeks. (feel)
8 I __________ a lot of exercise this month. (do)
9 I __________ a lot recently. (go out)
10 I __________ a lot of time on Facebook this week. (spend)

b 3 17 Listen and check. Then listen and repeat, copying the rhythm.

c Work with a partner. For each sentence in **a** say if it is true for you or not, and give reasons.

1 is true for me. I've been working really hard this week because I have exams soon.

d Now think of two things you have or haven't been doing this week or recently. Work in pairs **A** and **B**. **A** tell **B** what you've been doing. **B** show interest by asking for more details. Then swap roles.

I've been eating out a lot recently.

Oh really? Why?

Because some friends of mine are visiting, so we've been going out together.

7 READING & LISTENING

a Are there any radio or TV programmes you know that have been running for a long time in your country? Do you watch them? What do you think of them? Why do you think they've been so successful?

b 3 18 Read and listen to an article about *The Archers*, a BBC programme that is the world's longest-running radio soap opera. Answer the questions.

1 What is the programme about?
2 What was its original aim?
3 Who were the original main characters?

1954

1994

A British Institution

Just before 7 o'clock every evening, people all over Britain, from Camilla, Duchess of Cornwall (a major fan, who actually appeared on the show) to students, housewives, and farmers, tune in to BBC Radio 4, and listen to an introductory tune that has been playing every night for more than 60 years. It is the theme tune to *The Archers*, the longest running radio soap opera in the world, and a British institution. *The Archers*, which is about life in the fictional village of Ambridge, was conceived by the Ministry of Agriculture as a way of providing information about new farming methods to British farmers and smallholders in order to increase productivity after the Second World War, during the years of food shortages and rationing. It was originally about the lives of three farmers: Dan Archer, who farmed efficiently with little cash, Walter Gabriel, who farmed inefficiently with little cash, and George Fairbrother, a wealthy businessman who farmed for a hobby. The programme was hugely successful – at the height of its popularity it was estimated that 60% of adult Britons were regular listeners, and today its listeners number over a million. The involvement of the Ministry of Agriculture ended in the 1970s, but *The Archers* still contains many storylines and discussions about farming, and has a separate 'agricultural story editor'.

Glossary
smallholder /'smɔːlhəʊldə/ a person who owns or rents a small piece of land for farming
rationing /'ræʃənɪŋ/ the policy of limiting the food, fuel, etc. that people are allowed to have, when there is not enough for everyone to have as much as they want; it started in the UK in the Second World War in 1940 and ended in 1954.

c 3 19 You are going to hear an interview with an actor who plays one of the main characters in *The Archers*. Do these statements describe (**A**) the actor, (**C**) his character, or (**B**) both?

1 His name is David Archer. ____
2 He's very honest and dependable. ____
3 He was born on a sheep station in Tasmania. ____
4 His father worked as a farmer. ____
5 He lives in Ambridge. ____
6 He has a cottage in Norfolk. ____

d Listen again and make notes. What does he say about these things?

1 how long he's been working on the programme
2 his character's grandfather
3 why his father went to Devon
4 what the other actors know about the country
5 what city and country people like about *The Archers*
6 where he lives now and why

e Are there any radio or TV programmes in your country about farming or the countryside? Have you ever watched them? How popular are they?

8 WRITING

➤ p.117 **Writing** *An informal email.* Write an email about things you've been doing recently.

9 3 20 SONG *Country boy* ♫

Practical English Time to tell the police EPISODE 3

1 VIDEO A WORRIED PHONE CALL

a 3 21 Watch or listen to Jenny talking to Rob on the phone. In the end, what does Rob say she should do?

b Watch or listen again. Answer the questions.

1. Is Jenny sure the man in the news is the man she met on the plane? Why (not)?
2. What time were Jenny and Henry planning to have dinner?
3. What time is it now? Why is Rob worried about this?
4. How does Jenny describe the house?
5. What doesn't she think she'll be able to do?

If you were Jenny, would you stay in Henry's house alone?

2 VIDEO MAKING A POLICE REPORT

a 3 22 Watch or listen to Jenny and Luke at the police station. What information does the police officer ask for about Henry? How do Luke and Jenny describe him?

b Watch or listen again. Complete the **You Hear** phrases in the dialogue on p.53.

c 3 23 Watch or listen and repeat some of Jenny's **You Say** phrases. Copy the rhythm and intonation.

d In groups of three practise the dialogue.

e ➤ **Communication** *Reporting a missing person* **A** *p.107*, **B** *p.108*.

You Hear	You Say
... You also said that your father-in-law – Henry Walker – hasn't returned home yet. How long has he been ________?	He was supposed to be home three hours ago.
OK. It's a bit early to report him missing but I'll ________ a statement. So, your name's Jenny Zielinski.	That's right.
And you're staying at The Grange, Marsh Lane, Long Crendon.	Yes.
OK. Can you ________ Mr Walker?	He's 62, I think. He's average height and build. He has grey hair and glasses. I don't know what colour his eyes are. *They're brown. Here is a photo of him.*
When did you ________ see him?	This morning. Around ten.
Where were you?	At his house in Long Crendon.
And do you remember what he was ________?	Oh, just a brown jacket, a dark green shirt, and jeans.
Do you remember anything ________ about the last time you saw him?	Yes, actually. We were going to go to Oxford but Henry's two front tyres had been punctured.
Really? So you left for Oxford and he stayed to fix the car?	Yes.
Do you know what his ________ were for the rest of the day?	No.
Can you give me some idea of his normal ________?	Not really... *Well, he's an academic. He teaches at the university a few days a week but he often works from home. He takes a lot of long walks, but never this late.*
And Jenny, do you ________ seeing anything unusual when you got back to the house this afternoon?	Well, there was my suitcase. The airport had returned my lost luggage and the lock was broken.
Is there anything ________?	There were some books on the floor. *Really? That's weird. Henry's normally really tidy.*
OK. Try not to ________, we'll look into this. In the meantime, perhaps you should stay with Luke, and if you think of anything else, or he turns up, give me a call.	

3 VIDEO A THREATENING MESSAGE

a 3 24 Watch or listen to Jenny and Luke talking the next morning. What's the good news? What's the bad news?

b Watch or listen again. Circle the correct phrase.

1. Jenny feels *safer* | *less safe* in Luke's house.
2. The username on the laptop *is* | *isn't* Jenny's.
3. When Luke opens a file he finds *a photo* | *a formula*.
4. Jenny receives *a text message* | *a video message* from Henry.
5. Henry says the people who are holding him want her *laptop* | *suitcase*.
6. Henry shows them *today's* | *yesterday's* newspaper.
7. He asks Jenny and Luke *to go* | *not to go* to the police again.
8. He asks them *to give Rob a message* | *not to say anything to Rob*.

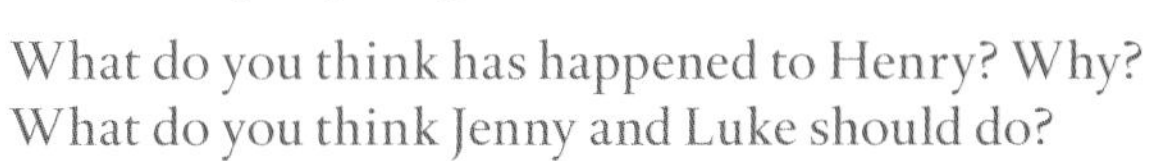

What do you think has happened to Henry? Why? What do you think Jenny and Luke should do?

c Look at the **Social English phrases**. Can you remember any of the missing words?

Social English phrases

Jenny	Thanks for ________ me stay.
Jenny	What does it ________?
Luke	I have ________ idea.
Jenny	It's a ________ from Henry!
Henry	As you can see, I'm ________.
Henry	Listen ________.

d 3 25 Watch or listen and complete the phrases.

e Watch or listen again and repeat the phrases. How do you say them in your language?

Can you...?

- [ ] describe someone's appearance and routine
- [ ] report a problem to the police
- [ ] thank someone for helping you

G obligation, necessity, prohibition, advice
V DIY and repairs; paraphrasing
P consonant clusters

This lamp doesn't work. Can you fix it?

I think we just need to change the bulb.

6A Do it yourself

1 VOCABULARY DIY and repairs; paraphrasing

a Look at the photo of the shop. What kind of things does it sell? Do you ever go to shops like this?

b 3 26 Listen to a person asking about things in a DIY store. Which of the four objects above does he want to buy?

c Listen again and complete the dialogue. Then practise the dialogue with a partner.

A Excuse me.
B Yes, can I help you?
A Yes, thanks. I'm [1]_______ for some... Sorry, I don't know the [2]_______. They're the [3]_______ that you put in the wall. I want to put some pictures on the wall.
B You mean nails?
A Ah, yes, that's it. And I need one more thing. My [4]_______ doesn't [5]_______. I need a new er...
B Bulb?
A Yes, thank you.
B You'll find them over there, behind the gardening things.

d ➤ **Communication** *What's it called?* **A** *p.109*, **B** *p.110.*

e ➤ **p.160 Vocabulary Bank** *DIY and repairs.*

2 PRONUNCIATION consonant clusters

Consonant clusters
Some words have three (or even four) consonant sounds together, and these can be difficult to pronounce. These are common in:
1 words beginning with *scr*, *spr*, or *str*, e.g. ***scr**ipt*, ***spr**ing*, ***str**uggle*
2 in the middle of a word, e.g. *su**ngl**asses*, *de**scr**ibe*
3 when you add an *s* to a word ending in two consonant sounds, e.g. *pou**nds***

a 3 30 Listen and repeat the groups of words.

1 screw screwdriver scream screen
string stress stream straight
2 paintbrush toothbrush electrician handle
3 needles shelves lamps bulbs

b Practise saying the sentences.

1 I need some screws and a screwdriver.
2 Go straight down the next street.
3 Two electric toothbrushes, please.
4 That's strange – the string's not very strong.
5 Put some new bulbs in the lamps.

3 LISTENING & SPEAKING

a Have you ever been to IKEA or similar stores that sell self-assembly (or flat-pack) furniture? Did you buy anything there? What?

b Read the information about IKEA. What information does the author give…?

1 to show that IKEA is very popular outside Sweden
2 to show that there are also problems with IKEA

It looks so easy at first...

Started in 1943, the Swedish furniture store IKEA has transformed homes around the globe with its cheap, modern Scandinavian style. It has also changed the way we live: one in ten Europeans now sleeps in an IKEA bed, and its catalogue is in more homes than any other publication, including the Bible, the Yellow Pages, and the complete works of Shakespeare.

But along with the pleasure of inexpensive furniture is the pain. The frustrating one-way system used to navigate the stores, for example, or some of the strange names given to the products (Snille chair, Odda chest of drawers, etc.). Most of all, there's the problem of getting the furniture home and trying to put it together. We asked three IKEA shoppers to share their experiences...

c 3 31 Listen to three people describe an experience with IKEA furniture. What did they buy? Who was the least successful at assembling it?

d Listen again. Which speaker…?

A ☐ didn't have all the parts he / she needed
B ☐ doesn't blame IKEA for the experience
C ☐ had problems understanding what to do
D ☐ had to assemble the furniture twice
E ☐ hadn't expected to have a problem
F ☐ learned a lesson from the experience

e 3 32 Listen to some extracts from the listening, and write the missing words. What do you think they mean?

1 After hours and hours, and a lot of _______, I finally managed to put it together.
2 So I had to _______ it to _______, move all the bits into the bedroom…
3 I'm quite _______, quite practical, so I thought, 'No problem'…
4 I realized I'd put the door handle on the _______ _______ round.
5 It's _______, but at least it has four legs!

f Talk to a partner. Choose two things that you (or someone you know) have done and tell your partner about it. Use the questions in the box to help you.

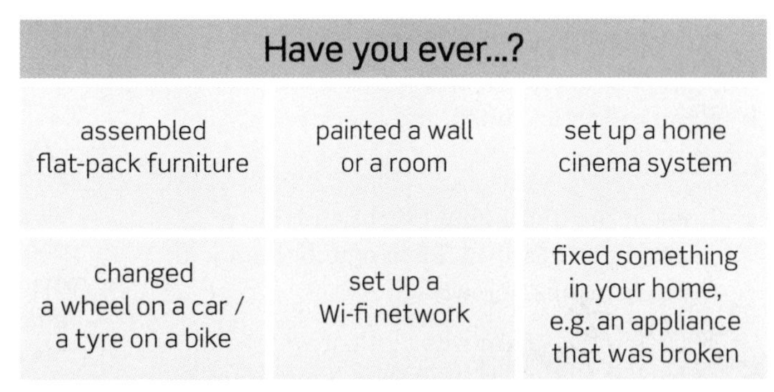

Have you ever...?		
assembled flat-pack furniture	painted a wall or a room	set up a home cinema system
changed a wheel on a car / a tyre on a bike	set up a Wi-fi network	fixed something in your home, e.g. an appliance that was broken

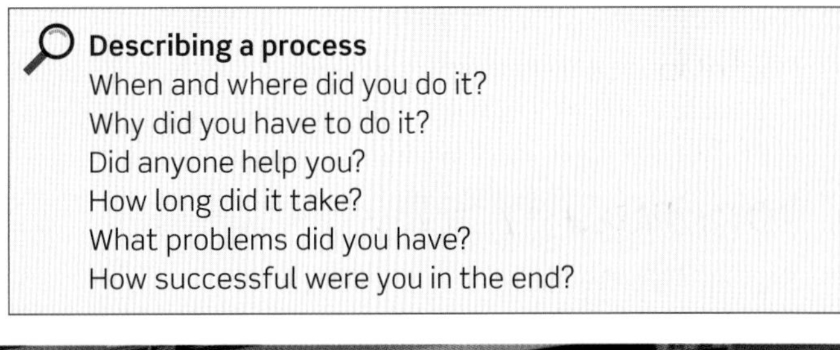

Describing a process
When and where did you do it?
Why did you have to do it?
Did anyone help you?
How long did it take?
What problems did you have?
How successful were you in the end?

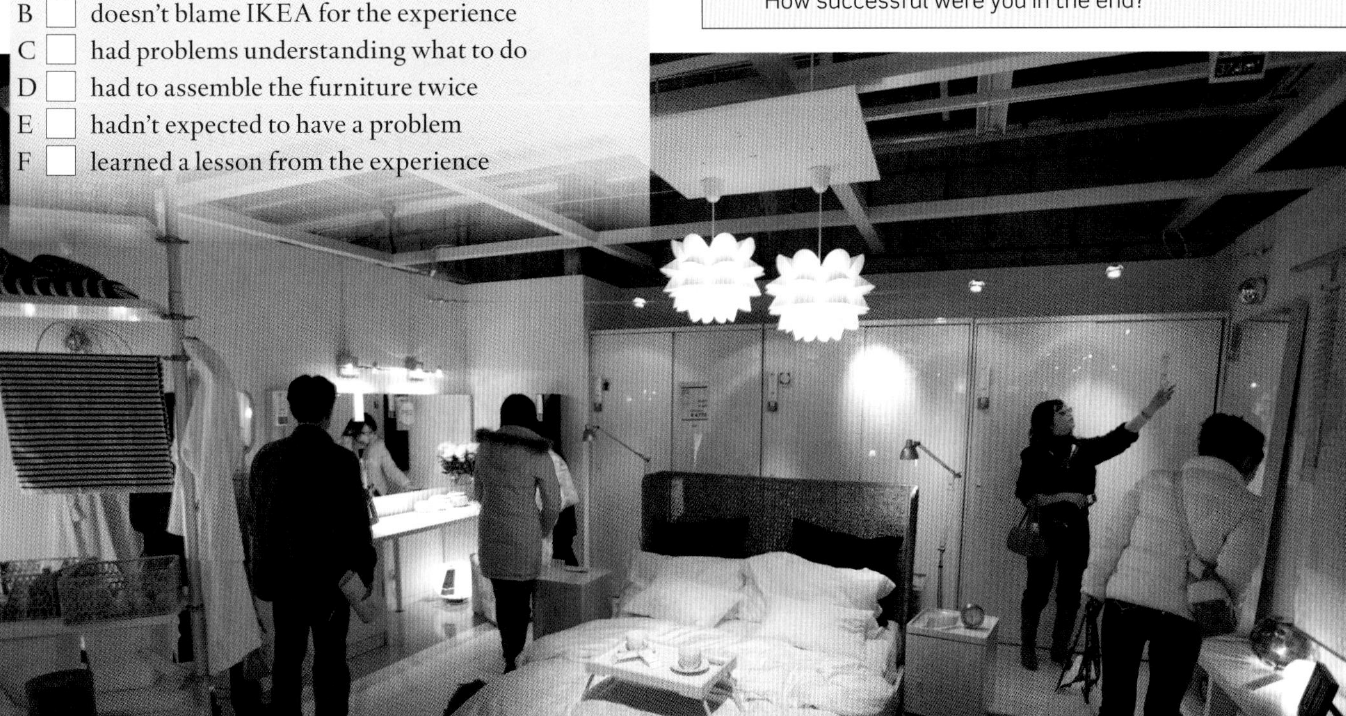

4 READING & SPEAKING

a You're going to read about some unusual uses for everyday things. Before you read, with a partner, try to complete sentences 1–5.

rice   a bowl   a potato   a banana   mayonnaise

1 You can use ________ to take out a broken light bulb.
2 You can use ________ to make a speaker for your mobile.
3 You can use ________ to remove water marks from wood.
4 You can use ________ to repair a phone that has got wet.
5 You can use ________ to fix a scratched DVD.

b Read the article once, and check your answers.

c Look at the **highlighted** verbs and try to guess their meaning. Then match them with the definitions below.

1 ________ to move a cloth or your hand backwards and forwards on something while pressing hard
2 ________ to clean or dry something with a cloth or towel, e.g. you ~ the windows of your car after you have washed them
3 ________ to connect an electronic device to another device, or to the electricity supply
4 ________ to let something fall
5 ________ marked on the surface by something sharp
6 ________ to make something shine, e.g. your shoes, a mirror
7 ________ to take out something
8 ________ to turn something in a particular direction, e.g. the lid of a jar
9 ________ to make something louder

d Read the article again. Then with a partner, try to remember exactly what to do for each of the problems in **a**.

e Are there any tips you think you might try?

Brilliant uses for everyday things

It's been a bad day. First you dropped your mobile in the pool and now the DVD you wanted to watch is scratched. But don't worry, you needn't buy new ones. You can fix them with everyday things you already have at home! Read on for some good DIY tips from the internet.

Mobile phones make our lives easier, but it's so easy to lose them, or drop them, worst of all, into water. If that happens to you, you may think the phone is ruined. In fact, you don't have to throw it away. *Reader's Digest* says all you have to do is to take the battery out and put the phone in a bowl of rice overnight. You must use uncooked rice, and it will absorb all of the water. Next morning put the battery back, and the phone will work again.

Another problem with mobile phones is that you probably have a lot of great music on yours, but if you're with a group of friends and you all want to listen, you need to plug it into a speaker, and you may not have one at hand. Or do you? Next time, try this easy trick from *Real Simple* magazine. Put the phone into a bowl and press 'play'. The bowl will amplify the sound from your mobile's speakers. Now everyone can hear the music! A jar or glass will also work if you don't have a bowl.

In addition to rice, a potato can also make a great DIY tool. Here's an example. The other day I was trying to kill a fly that was buzzing around a ceiling light and the worst happened: I missed the fly but broke the light bulb. Now, it can be very difficult to remove a broken bulb, and of course, you mustn't ever do it with bare hands. Luckily, there's another way. According to the *Martha Stewart* website, simply cut a potato in half, press the potato into the remains of the bulb, then twist and remove it. Remember you must switch off the light first.

Another useful DIY tool is a banana. Check out this idea from *Apartment Therapy*. If you have a scratched DVD that won't play, rub the inside of a banana skin over the scratch. Then polish the DVD with a soft cloth and – *voila!* – problem solved. This trick works because the waxy substance in the banana skin fills in the scratch. For deep scratches, you should rub some toothpaste in first.

Even mayonnaise has surprising uses. Everyone knows that you shouldn't put a wet glass on a wooden table, because it will probably leave an ugly mark on the wood. But sometimes you forget. Don't worry, again according to *Apartment Therapy*, just rub some mayonnaise into the mark and leave it for 15 minutes or longer. Wipe clean, and the mark will be gone. For best results, you should do this as soon as possible after the mark is made.

5 GRAMMAR obligation, necessity, prohibition, advice

a Look at some extracts from the article in **4**. Complete the chart with the **bold** phrases.

You needn't buy new ones.

In fact, **you don't have to** throw it away.

Reader's Digest says all **you have to** do is to take the battery out.

... but if you're with a group of friends and you all want to listen, **you need to** plug it into a speaker.

...and of course, **you mustn't** ever do it with bare hands.

Remember **you must** switch off the light first.

For deep scratches, **you should** rub some toothpaste in first.

Everyone knows that **you shouldn't** put a wet glass on a wooden table, because it will probably leave an ugly mark on the wood.

1 It's an obligation / necessity.	________ ________ ________
2 It isn't an obligation / necessity.	________ ________
3 Don't do it! It's prohibited / dangerous.	________
4 It's a good idea.	________
5 It isn't a good idea.	________

b ➤ **p.142 Grammar Bank 6A.** Learn more about expressing obligation, necessity, prohibition, and advice.

c Look at the problems and possible solutions below. Make three sentences using the expressions in **bold**.

1 Your microwave has a bad smell.
  a) buy a new one
  b) put half a lemon in a glass of water and cook it on high
  c) clean it with strong detergent

mustn't / don't have to / should

You don't have to buy a new one.

2 Your leather sofa has a scratch.
  a) paint the scratch with a permanent pen
  b) pay a professional to repair it
  c) rub some olive oil on it

needn't / shouldn't / should

3 Your cups have tea and coffee stains.
  a) only use dark coloured cups for tea and coffee
  b) wash them with water and bleach*
  c) clean them with a mixture of salt and lemon juice

should / mustn't / don't have to

* a chemical that makes something become white

6 SPEAKING & WRITING

a What would you suggest in these situations? Compare your ideas with a partner.

What shall I do?

you spill red wine on your white trousers

you think your computer might have a virus

one of the screws in your glasses keeps coming out

you have a biro mark on your jeans

the heel breaks on one of your shoes

there's a power cut, and you have a freezer full of food

you can't get good reception on your phone

the zip on your suitcase breaks at the airport

your car is nearly out of petrol and the nearest petrol station is 20 km away

one of your shoelaces breaks while you're out

Responding to other people's suggestions
That's a brilliant idea!
Yes, that really works.
Are you sure that would work?
I suppose that might work.
That sounds dangerous to me.
I wouldn't want to try that.

b Choose the best solution you discussed in **a** and write a short paragraph about it for a competition on the internet. Describe the problem and give instructions for solving it.

G *can, could,* and *be able to*
V at a restaurant
P word pairs with *and*

6B At your service

Excuse me, can you help me?

I'll be able to help you when I finish with this customer.

1 READING

a What really annoys you about customer service when you go shopping? With a partner, write down three things you consider to be bad customer service.

b Read an article about bad customer service. Write the correct headings in the article. There is one you don't need to use.

A Too few shop assistants
B Inappropriate offers
C It's a shop, not a social club
D Too much pressure to buy
E Too much stock
F Keeping too few checkouts open
G Silent cashiers
H Terrible changing rooms

The 7 worst customer service crimes

Mary Portas – broadcaster, writer, and shopping expert – names some of the most irritating aspects of shopping...

1 *Keeping too few [1] checkouts open*
So many stores are guilty of this. The worst are the supermarkets. Then they ring the bell to get a new [2] **cashier** from out the back, and leave their finger on the bell, making a really irritating noise.

2 ______
Cashiers at supermarket checkouts now don't even say the final price – you're supposed to see it on the [3] **till**. They've lost basic communication skills. Even worse is when they dump the [4] **receipt** and the change into your hand in one lump. Horrible.

3 ______
At the newsagent's, you go to the [5] **counter** to buy a newspaper and they offer to sell you a huge chocolate bar for £1, as well. A massive bar of chocolate at 7.30 in the morning? How about just smiling and saying good morning?

4 ______
There's a long queue to try things on, but they say, 'You can only take in four items'. You should be able to take a big armful in. And there's nowhere to hang your clothes, so you have to put them on the floor. Except the floors are filthy.

5 ______
Again, many fashion stores are guilty of this. The [6] **rails** are so full of clothes that you can't even see the sizes. You have to pull the [7] **hangers** apart to look in, then they fall onto the floor.

6 ______
I hate it when assistants stand next to the till gossiping to each other. It's all too common in department stores, hairdressers, and coffee shops. All you want to do is pay, but it's as if you're invisible.

7 ______
This is why I hate beauty counters. You walk through the ground floor of many department stores and a woman runs after you and sprays you with perfume, asking, 'Could I just interest you in...?' Her face is usually orange, with eyebrows drawn on with a pencil. It says, 'You too could look like me'. You can't be serious! Why would I want to look like you? No, thanks!

Adapted from The Daily Telegraph

c Look at the highlighted words in the text, and match them with A–G in the photos.

d Read the article again. Tick (✓) the opinions that Mary Portas agrees with.

1. Supermarkets should make sure people don't have to queue for too long to pay.
2. Cashiers should be more friendly.
3. Cashiers shouldn't chat to customers.
4. Shop assistants shouldn't encourage you to buy things you haven't asked for.
5. Instead of chocolate, the newsagent's should offer people fruit to buy.
6. It's important to limit the number of items customers take into changing rooms so that they don't spend too long in there.
7. Changing rooms are generally uncomfortable and dirty.
8. It should be easy to see what size clothes are.
9. It's unreasonable to expect shop assistants not to chat to each other while they are working.
10. People on beauty counters usually look great because they use the products they are selling.

e Which of the customer service 'crimes' she mentions are a problem in your country? Which of the opinions in **d** do you agree with?

2 SPEAKING

a Look at the list of places below. Think about the ones you go to, how good or bad the service usually is there, and experiences that you have had.

- supermarkets
- clothes shops
- banks
- chemists
- mobile phone / computer shops
- gyms
- department stores

b Work in groups of three or four. For each place talk about:

- how often you go there
- how convenient the opening and closing times are
- what the facilities are like (queuing, changing rooms, background music, seating areas, etc.)
- what the staff are like (enough of them, helpful, etc.)
- what the customer service is like if you have a problem
- any especially good or bad experiences you have had

c In your groups, decide on three things that would really improve customer service in these places.

3 GRAMMAR *can, could,* and *be able to*

a Right (✓) or wrong (✗)? With a partner, correct the mistakes in the highlighted phrases.

1. If you wait till the sales, you'll can get it more cheaply.
2. People are still in the shop, so it can't be closed.
3. I wanted to buy some jeans, but I didn't can find any that I liked.
4. I think you could to try a smaller size.
5. I'd love to can sing well.
6. You can park over there but you can't leave your car there for more than two hours.

b ➤ **p.143 Grammar Bank 6B.** Learn more about *can, could*, and *be able to* and practise them.

c Complete the statements with your own ideas, then compare answers with a partner.

1. Everybody **should be able to**...
2. I hate **not being able to**...
3. I've never **been able to**...
4. I'd love **to be able to**...
5. Even though it was very difficult, I **was able to**...
6. If I work / study hard, I hope **I'll be able to**... in a few years' time.

4 3 39)) SONG *Hit 'em up style (Oops!)* ♫

5 VOCABULARY at a restaurant

a Do you know a restaurant, café, or bar where the service is bad? What's bad about it?

b ➤ **p.161 Vocabulary Bank** *At a restaurant*.

6 PRONUNCIATION word pairs with *and*

a Look at the photo. What do you think the '*n*' stands for? Why do you think it's written like that?

b 3 42 Listen and repeat the phrases.

fish and chips
oil and vinegar
salt and pepper
cup and saucer
bread and butter
knife and fork

c Ask and answer with a partner.

What's the difference between...?

1 a cup and a glass
2 a spoon and a teaspoon
3 a plate and a saucer
4 a jug and a mug
5 a tablecloth and a napkin
6 a plate and a dish
7 a meal and a course
8 'clear the table' and 'lay the table'
9 'take orders' and 'order food'
10 'pour the wine' and 'try the wine'

7 READING & LISTENING

a Have you ever worked as a waiter / waitress in a bar or restaurant? Do you know anyone who has or does? What are the main advantages and disadvantages?

b Read the article about the TV reality show *Service*. Answer the questions.

1 How is *Service* different from other restaurant reality shows?
2 What are the prizes at the end of the show?
3 Who is Michel Roux and where does he work?
4 What examples does he give to show that service is as important as food?
5 What is surprising about Danielle's and Ashley's previous experience of restaurants?

Le Gavroche

Michel Roux with restaurant manager Fred Sirieix and the eight trainees

Michel at work

MICHEL ROUX'S SERVICE

FROM SCHOOL DROPOUTS TO TOP WAITERS

We've seen plenty of cookery competitions where amateur chefs compete, hoping to become professionals, but BBC2's *Service*, a programme from chef Michel Roux, one of the judges on BBC's *Masterchef*, focuses on another side of restaurants. Over eight episodes, eight young people with no restaurant experience at all are taught the skills to become top waiters and waitresses. Rather than having competitors voted off each week, after the eight weeks two winners are chosen to receive six-month scholarships with the Academy of Food & Wine Service.

'Great service is as important as great food,' says Roux, who owns several well-known restaurants, including Le Gavroche, a two-Michelin star restaurant in London. 'If the food at one of my restaurants was OK, but the service was brilliant, the customers would still come back. But I'd never see them again if the service was rubbish, even though the food was brilliant.'

'There is a great career to be had in restaurant service,' says Roux. 'Head waiters can earn as much as a top chef. And, like chefs, their skills can take them all over the world.'

Roux's trainees include Brooke Arnold, 18, who has previously worked for McDonald's, Nikkita Palphreyman, 19, a single mother, and Niki Bedson, 22, an unemployed history graduate. 24-year-old James Marvin used to work in sales, and Danielle Menagh, 19, was a hairdresser. 'Before the show I'd never drunk wine,' she says.

The most unlikely trainee is 21-year-old Ashley Flay. 'I left school at 14,' he says. 'Before the show, I'd never eaten in a place which had table service.'

c 3 43 Listen to a breakfast radio show where a critic talks about the series. Mark the sentences **T** (true) or **F** (false).

1. Ryan only watched the final episode.
2. In the first episode the trainees weren't very successful working at a pizza restaurant.
3. Ashley and Nikkita had a fight.
4. Michel Roux and his colleagues made the trainees feel more confident.
5. Brooke had a disaster when she cooked *crêpes Suzette*.
6. In the final episode the trainees served at a restaurant in Paris.
7. Michel Roux was very nervous for them beforehand.
8. Only Danielle and Ashley won scholarships.
9. The show was a success both for the trainees themselves and as a programme.

d Listen again and correct the **F** sentences.

e Discuss the questions with a partner.

1. When you go to a restaurant, which do you think is more important, the service or the food? Why?
2. Think of some places where you like to eat out. Are there waiters or are they self-service places? How do the staff treat you? How do you treat the staff?

8 WRITING

➤ **p.118 Writing** *A restaurant review.*
Write a review of a restaurant you've been to recently for a website.

5&6 Revise and Check

GRAMMAR

Circle a, b, or c.

1 **A** What's this programme?
B I don't know. I've ______ turned it on.
a already b just c yet

2 We've never been to Madrid, but ______ to Barcelona last year.
a we went b we've been c we've gone

3 **A** Shall I make some photocopies?
B No, it's OK – ______ them.
a I already did b I already have done
c I've already done

4 They've lived here ______.
a for two months b two months ago
c since two months

5 Where have you been? ______ since 9.00!
a I'm waiting b I've been waiting
c I've waited

6 How long ______ to your family?
a is this farm belonging
b has this farm been belonging
c has this farm belonged

7 The fields are really wet. ______ a lot recently.
a It's raining b It rains c It's been raining

8 You ______ pay if you don't have any money.
a mustn't b don't have to c needn't to

9 I didn't have any screws so I ______ use nails instead.
a had to b must to c must

10 You ______ pay me back till next week.
a needn't b don't need c don't have

11 She thinks I ______ sell my car.
a need b ought c should

12 When we're on holiday ______ go swimming every day.
a we'll can b we'll be able to
c we'll be able

13 She ______ to come to the party.
a might not can b might not be able
c might not

14 The exam was really hard, but I ______ pass.
a was able to b could c could to

15 He ______ be from Paris – he doesn't speak French.
a could b can c can't

VOCABULARY

a Circle the word that is different.

1 sheep	cow	barn	hen
2 remote control	stand	speakers	sitcom
3 rope	drill	hammer	screwdriver
4 knife	fork	tray	spoon
5 mug	bowl	cup	glass

b Complete the words.

1 Can you **t**______ the TV up? I can't hear it.
2 I find some **s**______ operas really addictive.
3 Have you seen the weather **f**______ for tomorrow?
4 I'm not very interested in **c**______ affairs.
5 We need a TV with a bigger **s**______.

c Write words for the definitions.

1 trees grow these in spring and lose them in autumn ______
2 a small, narrow river ______
3 an area of low land between hills or mountains ______
4 to take fruit from the plant where they are growing ______
5 a young sheep ______

d Circle the right word.

1 I'm not tall enough – do you have a *hammer* | *ladder*?
2 This torch needs new *batteries* | *matches*.
3 Do you have a needle and *string* | *thread*?
4 I've lost one of the *nails* | *screws* from my glasses.
5 We need to *set up* | *put up* our new computer.

e Complete the phrases with a verb.

1 ______ for the bill
2 ______ a tip
3 ______ our order
4 ______ a button back on
5 ______ a table for 9 o'clock

PRONUNCIATION

a Circle the word with a different sound.

1	path	plant	grass	tap
2	bush	bucket	mug	country
3	cookery	should	wood	cartoon
4	ought	work	forecast	torch
5	bowl	cow	stone	grow

b Underline the stressed syllable.

1 com|mer|cial
2 har|vest
3 screw|dri|ver
4 ba|tte|ry
5 tea|spoon

CAN YOU UNDERSTAND THIS TEXT?

a Read the article once. Is tipping in the UK similar to tipping in your country?

Tipping in the UK

Tipping is not expected in the UK in the way it is in the United States or Canada. All staff in the UK must be paid at least the national minimum wage, whether they receive tips or not. Therefore, unlike in much of North America, the need for tipping is much less.

Cafés and coffee shops

In a café, you may receive waiter / waitress service to bring your tea, coffee, sandwiches, or whatever you have ordered to the table. In these establishments tipping is not usual. If you feel the service has been especially pleasant you can leave a pound (or the change) in appreciation.

In coffee shops such as Starbucks, there may be a tip jar on the counter, but very few customers leave tips, and you certainly don't have to. In self-service cafés where you collect your food and put it on a tray (as found in tourist attractions, for example) you don't tip either.

Restaurants and pubs

In pubs, where you usually choose and pay for your order at the bar, but the food is brought to your table, tipping is uncommon. You can leave a pound or two if you wish.

In restaurants where you place your order with a waiter / waitress and receive your food and your bill at your table, you should tip around 10% of the bill. This varies from place to place – in more expensive restaurants where you receive personal service, a tip would always be expected (it would be considered rude not to leave one unless there was a problem with the service), whereas in the most casual of restaurants tipping is not universal. If you have been very unhappy with the service, you could consider not leaving a tip.

In some restaurants, a service charge may automatically be added to the bill, typically 10% or 12.5%, sometimes only for larger groups. This should be noted on the menu. But if you're not happy with the service, you can ask for it to be removed, and explain why you're unhappy.

If a service charge is added, or the menu says 'service included', you needn't add any further tip. In some cases if you pay by credit card the machine may ask if you want to add a tip. Check your bill carefully to see if a service charge has been added before paying, and if it has, be sure not to add any more. In some cases a restaurant may print 'service not included' on the menu or the bill. This is a request for a tip!

Adapted from tripadvisor.co.uk

b Read the article again and answer the questions.

1 Is tipping more common in the UK or in the US?
2 When might you leave a tip in a café?
3 Do you need to leave a tip in all types of restaurant in the UK?
4 When might you decide not to leave a tip in an expensive restaurant?
5 Do all restaurants add a service charge? Do you have to pay it?
6 Why should you be careful if you pay by credit card in a restaurant?

c Choose five new words or phrases from the text. Check their meaning and pronunciation and try to learn them.

VIDEO CAN YOU UNDERSTAND THESE PEOPLE?

3 44 **In the street** Watch or listen to five people and answer the questions.

Andrew

Diarmuid

Mairi

Chris

Christopher

1 Andrew doesn't watch ______ very often.
 a comedies b chat shows c the news
2 Diarmuid thinks the countryside is ______.
 a somewhere he wouldn't like to live at the moment
 b a good place for families to live
 c not as safe as it used to be
3 Mairi is ______ the bed that she put up.
 a worried about b a bit disappointed with
 c quite pleased with
4 Chris had problems with his IKEA bed because ______.
 a he assembled it badly
 b he didn't have all the right pieces
 c the instructions were badly written
5 Christopher says that when he needs a shop assistant ______.
 a he can never find one b they are always chatting
 c he goes to look for one

CAN YOU SAY THIS IN ENGLISH?

Do the tasks with a partner. Tick (✓) the box if you can do them.

Can you...?

1 ☐ describe your TV-watching habits
2 ☐ compare living in a city with living in the country, and describe your own experience
3 ☐ describe two of your favourite shops and say why you like them
4 ☐ describe a DIY job that someone has done in your home
5 ☐ agree or disagree with these statements, and say why:
- Most TV programmes aren't worth watching.
- To be successful, a shop must have good customer service.

VIDEO **Short films** The history of flat-pack furniture
Watch and enjoy a film on iTutor.

iTutor

G phrasal verbs
V cash machines; phrasal verbs
P linking

What shall I do with this old T-shirt?

Either give it away or throw it away.

7A Giving it away

1 VOCABULARY & LISTENING
cash machines

a Look at the words and expressions. Do they refer to the same thing or four different things? Which is the most common in the UK and in the US?

cash machine   ATM   hole in the wall   cashpoint

b Do the quiz with a partner.

What do you press on a cash machine...?

1 if you want to take out money
2 if you want to know how much money you have
3 if you want a paper record of what you did
4 if you want to put money into your account
5 if you make a mistake and need to start again

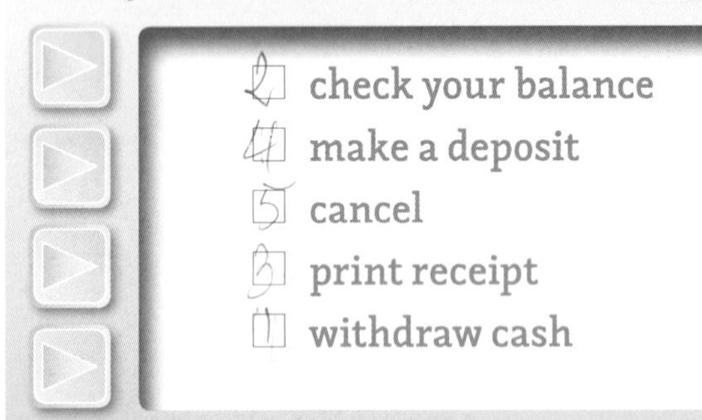

What do you have to do if you see the following?

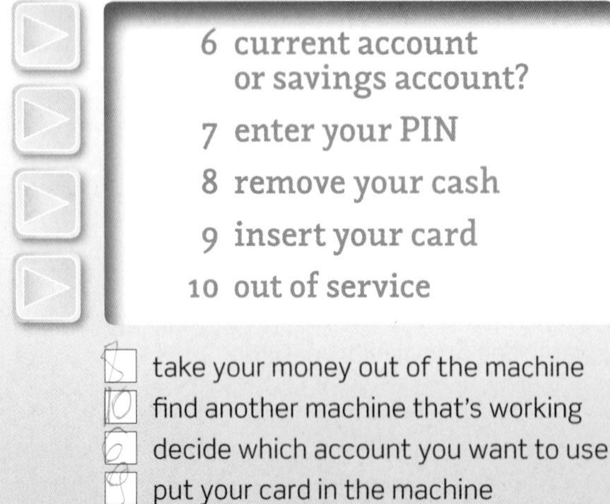

c 4 2))) Listen and check.

d 4 3 Listen to two true news stories and answer the questions.

	Story 1	Story 2
1 What was strange about each machine?		
2 Who was responsible?		
3 What happened in the end?		

e Listen again and answer with a number.

Story 1

How much money…

1 did you get if you tried to take out £20? £______
2 was given out by cash machines in Coventry? £______
3 did three family members collect? £______

Story 2

4 How much money were the ATMs missing? $______

f Talk to a partner.

1 How often do you go to a cash machine? Do you do anything apart from withdraw cash?
2 Have you ever had a problem with a cash machine? What happened? What did you do about it?
3 If a cash machine gave *you* more money than you asked for, what would you do?

2 GRAMMAR phrasal verbs

a Look at some sentences from the news stories in **1d**. With a partner, circle the correct form. Tick (✓) if both forms are possible.

1 Over a hundred people were queuing, *looking for free money* / *looking free money for.*
2 Eventually, police arrived and stood guard over the machine until the bank was able to *switch off it* / *switch it off* remotely.
3 If you've *taken money out* / *taken out money* recently at an ATM in New York City, you might want to check your wallet for fake notes.
4 Police have warned customers and shops to *look out for the fakes* / *look out the fakes for* after they were found in two ATMs on Monday.
5 The man went on holiday to the Dominican Republic to enjoy the stolen cash, but he was immediately arrested when he *came ten days later back* / *came back ten days later.*

b ➤ **p.144 Grammar Bank 7A.** Learn more about phrasal verbs and practise them.

3 PRONUNCIATION linking

a Match **1–6** with **a–f.**

1 ☐ He keeps arguing with the referee.
2 ☐ He's still asleep.
3 ☐ I can't finish this steak.
4 ☐ This chicken's past its sell-by date.
5 ☐ The rubbish is beginning to smell.
6 ☐ It's probably in Wikipedia.

a Take‿it‿out.
b Throw‿it‿away.
c Send him‿off.
d Take‿it‿away.
e Look‿it‿up.
f Wake him‿up.

b 4 7 Listen and check.

c 4 8 Listen and repeat **a–f**, linking the words.

d Work with a partner. **A** cover **a–f**. **B** say a sentence from **1–6**. **A** say a response from **a–f** from memory. Then swap roles.

e 4 9 Listen to the sentences. Make another sentence to follow each one with a phrasal verb from the box and a pronoun (*it*, *me*, or *them*).

fill in pick up switch off pay back take off ~~try on~~ turn down turn up

1 *It'll look great on you!*

Try it on.

4 READING & SPEAKING

a You're going to read an article about a man who calls himself Mr Lucky. Why do you think he has given himself this name?

b Read an article about him, and answer the questions.

1 Who is Mr Lucky? What do we find out about him?
2 What is *Wearelucky*?
3 What kind of things have people done with the money?

c Read the article again. Complete the gaps with a sentence or phrase below.

A At first he didn't know what to do with all the money
B Each lucky person's story is recorded on the *Wearelucky* website
C Giving away money is an incredible feeling
D He was moved by her openness, and her dedication to her shop
E Some people are especially generous
F They are people he meets, in cafés or on the Tube

d Look at the highlighted words related to money, and with a partner work out their meaning.

e If Mr Lucky gave you £1,000, what would you do with it? If you were Mr Lucky, who would you give the money to?

Login | Subscribe | Contact us   Search

When luck comes to town

What good deed would you do with a gift of £1,000? Sonia Zhuravlyova meets the mystery man making strangers' dreams come true.

You Are Lucky.

You have been personally selected to participate in our exciting new project.

ω

£1000 is yours, to spend on something good.

{Once that's sunk in, please turn over.}

We all know the old saying 'money can't buy happiness', but one man disagrees. He thinks he has come up with a way to make his money give him pleasure – by giving it to strangers. '1__________,' says Mr Lucky, the mystery millionaire behind *Wearelucky*, a project that has seen nearly 100 people receive £1,000 each in cash. But there is a catch. You must promise to do something 'good' with it.

Mr Lucky wishes to remain anonymous but I can reveal that he is a Londoner, and is in his forties. The name *Wearelucky* came to him when he was thinking about his own good fortune – he took a job abroad with an insurance company and earned so much that he could afford to retire in 2011 aged 37. 2__________, whether to give it to a charity in a developing country, or to an individual in the UK. So he decided to get other people to decide for him. *Wearelucky* was born.

So far, the lucky people have included web designers, nurses, taxi drivers, bar owners, and photographers – anyone qualifies. 3__________, who have responded positively to his idea for the project. If he likes you and your idea for the money, then you get an invitation. He also sometimes gives an invitation to someone he trusts, and asks them to choose someone to give it to. Since 2011, 92 people have qualified. 'I am constantly looking out for "lucky" people,' he explains. The invitation comes in a square black envelope and asks the person to get in touch within 48 hours, explaining in detail the good deed they will do with the money. 4__________, and Mr Lucky, who is an amateur photographer, takes their photo.

The project's definition of the 'good' deed is quite open. During a recent walk in London, Mr Lucky met Lucy, who runs a small bookshop on Charing Cross Road. 5__________. She decided to pass on the money by giving a bonus to a colleague, which the bookshop couldn't previously afford to do, and by investing the rest in microfinancing. Jane, a bar owner from St-Fort-sur-Gironde in France, is spending the money on promoting cultural events at her bar for the benefit of her community, and buying late Christmas presents, which she couldn't afford at the time, for her four granddaughters. 6__________. Rufus, an 81-year-old football coach in Kerala, India, spent the £1,000 on training – and often feeding – local children. Mr Lucky says, 'I'm enjoying giving the money to someone and they're enjoying the process of giving the money to someone else, so there is this chain reaction of positive feeling.'

Recently Mr Lucky gave an invitation to Paul 'Chilli' Churchill, a London taxi driver, and asked him to give it to someone he likes. Just think, the next time you get into a cab, it could be your lucky day!

Glossary
microfinancing /maɪkrəʊˈfaɪnænsɪŋ/ a system of providing services such as lending money to people who are too poor to use banks

Adapted from The Times

5 VOCABULARY phrasal verbs

a Look at three sentences from the article. Can you remember what the missing words are in the phrasal verbs? What do you think they mean?

1 He thinks he has **come** ____ **with** a way to make his money give him pleasure.

2 '**Giving** ____ money is an incredible feeling.'

3 She decided to **pass** ____ the money by giving a bonus to a colleague.

b ➤ **p.162 Vocabulary Bank** *Phrasal verbs.*

6 SPEAKING

Ask and answer the questions with a partner. Give background information, and details or examples where you can.

I tried to learn Polish. I got to about pre-intermediate level and then I gave up. The thing that made me give up was the grammar – it was unbelievably difficult...

Think of something you have tried to do and failed. How long was it before you **gave up**? What made you finally **give up**?

Has your car ever **broken down** on the motorway? What did you do?

If someone offered to **take** you **out** for a meal to a restaurant of your choice, where would you go?

When you started school (or university) did you find it difficult to **fit in**?

If you invited people to your house for a meal, how would you feel if they **turned up** half an hour late?

Have you ever left something on a bus or train, or in a taxi? Did you ever **get** it **back**?

Have you ever lent money to someone who never **paid** you **back**?

What would you do if a friend borrowed your laptop but it didn't work when he or she **gave** it **back**?

G verb patterns
V live entertainment
P /ɔː/, /ɜː/, and /ə/; words with two pronunciations

Do you enjoy going to clubs?

Not much. I prefer spending time with my friends at home.

7B Going out and staying in

1 VOCABULARY
live entertainment

a What are the advantages and disadvantages of seeing a concert or a sporting event live instead of on TV?

b 4 12))) Listen to three conversations. Match them with the events below. Are the people talking before, during, or after the event?

- ☐ a concert
- ☐ a play
- ☐ a sporting event

c 4 13))) Listen and repeat some words related to live entertainment.

arena audience box office crowd curtain extra time fans final whistle half time interval matinee opponent performance plot programme row scene score spectators stage stalls / circle theatre tickets

d With a partner, put the words in **c** in the right column. Some words can go in more than one place.

Play, musical, or concert	Sporting event

2 PRONUNCIATION
/ɔː/, /ɜː/, and /ə/; words with two pronunciations

a 4 14))) Listen and repeat the three sounds. Which sound is short, and always on an unstressed syllable?

b Look at the groups of words. Circle the word where the pink letter is pronounced /ə/. What sound do the other two words have?

1 audience stalls arena
2 interval circle curtain
3 score spectator performance

c 4 15))) Listen and check. Practise saying the words.

d 4 16))) Read the information box. Then listen and repeat the sentences. What do the words mean in each sentence?

> **Words with the same spelling but different pronunciations**
> A few words in English are spelled exactly the same but pronounced differently, and have different meanings, e.g. *bow* /baʊ/ = to put your head down, e.g. at the end of a concert or play when people are clapping, but *bow* /bəʊ/ = a weapon that you use to shoot an arrow.

1 We went to a live concert last weekend.
2 We live next to the concert hall.
3 We sat in the front row.
4 After the concert we had a row.

e Practise saying the sentences.

3 SPEAKING

a You're going to tell a partner about a live event you went to (a concert, play, sporting event, or other). Read the prompts on the right and think about what you're going to say.

b Work in pairs. Tell each other about the event you went to. Would you like to have gone to your partner's event?

what the event was
who you went with
how you got the tickets
the queues
the seats
the food and drink
how long it lasted
what you thought of it
if it was worth the money
what you did afterwards

4 LISTENING

a Read the description of a play called *Sleep No More*. How is it different from an ordinary play?

b 4 17 Listen to a radio programme where Jill, a theatre critic, is reviewing *Sleep No More*. Number the photos in the order she mentions them.

c Listen again. Mark the statements **T** (true) or **F** (false).

1. There are no tickets available now for *Sleep No More*.
2. *Sleep No More* is frightening, but enjoyable.
3. The performance takes place in a well-known hotel.
4. There are more than 100 different rooms.
5. You're allowed to touch anything in the rooms.
6. In the hospital room, there were drawers containing human hair.
7. All the actors wear identical white masks.
8. Jill was very nervous when she had to interact with the actors.
9. At the end of the play, all of the audience end up in the same place.
10. The critic thought that the plot was very clear.

d Would you like to attend a performance like *Sleep No More*? Why (not)? Have you ever seen anything similar?

SLEEP NO MORE

The thrilling new show *Sleep No More* is loosely based on Shakespeare's *Macbeth* – but it's unlike any *Macbeth* you've ever seen. Or any play you've ever seen.

In this performance, produced by London's Punchdrunk company, you don't just sit and watch the show. You stand up and walk through it, and the cast interacts with you.

Adapted from www.nypost.com

5 GRAMMAR verb patterns

a Complete the sentences with the correct form of the verb in brackets (infinitive, *to* + infinitive, or verb + *ing*).

1 If a friend asked me _______ to a classical music concert, I think I'd _______ no. (go, say)
2 I love _______ films in 3D – they're much better than ordinary ones. (watch)
3 My parents didn't use to let me _______ out late during the week when I was a teenager. They wanted me _______ my evening _______. (stay, spend, study)
4 I hate _______ to clubs. I don't like _______ in places where there are lots of people and noise. (go, be)
5 I never feel like _______ out on New Year's Eve. I prefer _______ in. (go, stay)

b With a partner, say if the sentences are true for you or not, and why.

c ➤ **p.145 Grammar Bank 7B.** Learn more about verb patterns and practise them.

d Complete the sentences with a verb phrase so that they are true.

1 I've often tried...but I've never been able to do it.
2 My parents used to try to make me...
3 When I'm on holiday I really enjoy...
4 How do I feel about housework? Well, I can't stand...but I don't mind...
5 I can't imagine not...
6 When I'm away from home I really miss...
7 I would like it if people in my country stopped...
8 At the moment I'm planning...
9 When I leave the house in the morning I often forget...

e Compare your sentences with a partner.

6 SPEAKING

a If you stay in at the weekend and friends come round, what do you like doing? Tick (✓) or cross (✗) the activities in the list, and add one more option.

WHAT DO YOU LIKE DOING?

- playing board games or role-playing games
- watching films or DVDs together
- cooking and having a meal together
- getting a takeaway
- watching sport on TV
- listening to music and chatting
- playing video games or online games
- _______________

b Compare your list with a partner. Say why you like / don't like doing each of these.

c ➤ **Communication** *Going out or staying in?* **A** *p.107,* **B** *p.108.*

d Think about the last time you spent an evening with friends at your house or theirs. What did you do?

7 READING

a What games do you play on your phone, tablet, or laptop? Do you play any online games?

b Do you know anyone who plays *World of Warcraft*? Read a short summary of the game. What do the **highlighted** words mean?

Article | Talk | Read | Edit | View history

World of Warcraft

From *Wikipedia, the free encyclopedia*

World of Warcraft (or WoW) is a multiplayer online **role-playing game** set in the **virtual reality** fantasy Warcraft universe, where players control their **avatar** to fight monsters or other players. Gold coins are used to repair armour or buy items (**weapons**, food, **potions**, etc.), but to get these coins you have to complete **quests** which often take a very long time. Some items like **mounts** are very expensive, so players who want one for their avatar need a lot of gold.

c Read the article once. Which of these does the article mention?

1 what a 'gold farmer' is
2 the pros and cons of being a gold farmer
3 other jobs in the gold-farming industry
4 how to play *World of Warcraft*
5 how much 'gold' costs
6 why people pay for virtual gold
7 why people play *World of Warcraft*
8 other online games

WELCOME TO THE NEW GOLD MINES

Being paid to play games all day long sounds like a dream job – but for thousands of 'gold farmers', the virtual reality is hard work.

Li Hua makes a living playing computer games. Working from a cramped office, he kills dragons and robs them of virtual gold in ten-hour shifts. Next to him, rows of other young workers do the same. 'It is just like working in a factory, the only difference is that this is the virtual world,' says Li. 'The working conditions are hard. We don't get weekends off and I only have one day free a month. But compared to other jobs it is good. I have no other skills and I enjoy playing sometimes.'

Li is just one of more than 100 workers employed by WoW7gold, an internet-based company that makes more than £1m a year selling in-game advantages to *World of Warcraft* players. Apart from gold, customers may ask for their avatar's skill level to be increased, or for a virtual magic sword.

For thousands of workers such as Li, 'gold farming' is a way of life. They can expect to earn between £80–£120 a month which, given the long hours and night shifts, can amount to as little as 30p an hour. After completing his shift, Li is given a basic meal of rice, meat, and vegetables, and falls into a bed in a room that he shares with eight other gold farmers. His wages may be low, but food and accommodation are included.

The gold farming industry may be about playing games, but these companies take their work seriously. At WoW7gold, there are different departments, including production, sales, advertising, and research. While young, largely unskilled workers such as Li spend their days in the virtual field, highly skilled graduates, mainly female, receive better salaries working as customer service operators.

Eva Yuan is one such operator. A 26-year-old graduate who speaks three languages, she has been working for WoW7gold for more than a year. 'Most of our customers are from America, but they are people of all ages and careers,' she says. 'The biggest transaction I have seen was one person who bought 100,000 gold pieces, which costs £2,000 to £3,000.' Yuan thinks her job is worthwhile. 'Everything that appeals to some people in the world needs some people to produce it. We are allowing people to buy what they want, and we care about that.'

Thousands of miles away, I ask Jamie, a 24-year-old gamer from the UK, what makes him spend his money on these sites. 'The reason people buy gold is the same reason they pay people to wash their car – they would rather spend money on it than do it themselves,' he says. 'You could spend time getting gold, say 20 real-life hours. Or you could go to work for two hours and pay someone else for the gold. If I'm playing, I want to play, not do boring tasks.'

Most multiplayer game operators do not allow players to buy gold from gold farmers. WoW7gold is no longer active, though similar services can be found online.

d Read the article again and choose a, b or c.

1 For Li Hua, the advantage of his job is that ______.
   a he enjoys doing it, and it's quite well paid
   b it's sometimes fun, and it's better than other jobs
   c he gets his meals free and his own room

2 WoW7gold is a company that ______.
   a pays its employees in virtual money
   b charges its customers virtual money for their services
   c sells its customers virtual money and services

3 Eva Yuan thinks that ______.
   a she is overqualified for the job that she is doing
   b if people want to buy virtual gold there is no reason why companies shouldn't sell it
   c people spend a ridiculous amount of real money on virtual gold

4 Jamie prefers to buy his virtual gold because ______.
   a he doesn't enjoy the process of getting the virtual gold
   b he think the gold farming industry needs to be encouraged
   c his job doesn't give him enough free time to be able to get virtual gold

e From what the article says, do you think people like Jamie are cheating at the game? Why (not)? Would you pay real money for a virtual object?

8 4 21 **SONG** *We don't need money to have a good time* ♫

Practical English Is it a clue?

EPISODE 4

1 ROB GETS INVOLVED

VIDEO

a 4 22 Watch or listen to Jenny, Luke, and Rob talking about Henry's disappearance. What are two possible clues they notice in the video?

b Watch or listen again. Mark the sentences **T** (true) or **F** (false). Correct the **F** sentences.

1 Rob thinks they should ask the police for help.
2 Rob and Luke agree that they shouldn't give the laptop to the criminals.
3 Rob noticed something strange about how his father looked.
4 The phrase that really surprises Rob is *his old dad*.
5 He doesn't know how to interpret the clue.
6 Rob has booked a flight to the UK.
7 Jenny is going to go back to Henry's house.

What do you think the clues might mean? Who do you think Simon is?

2 TALKING ABOUT HOUSE RULES

VIDEO

a 4 23 Watch or listen to Luke telling Jenny about the rules in his house. Complete Rules for guests. Why does he ask her to move her car?

Rules for guests

1 This is a no-__________ house.
2 Don't cook __________ or leave __________ products in the fridge.
3 If you need to use the internet, the __________ for the Wi-fi is *lukeandsimonrule.*
4 If you use the washing machine, please use the __________-__________ detergents in the cupboard.
5 Please help us save energy – don't use a __________ water programme.
6 There isn't a __________. Hang your clothes on the __________ __________ instead.

b Read the dialogue between Luke and Jenny. Can you remember any of the missing words? Watch or listen again and check.

Luke It's a great location, and the rent is cheap, but Simon can be a bit difficult.
Jenny Oh, right.
Luke He's got a few rules. After all, it is his house.
Jenny That's fine.
Luke To start with, it's a no-smoking house.
Jenny Great.
Luke And he's a strict vegetarian so ________ ________ cook meat or leave meat products in the fridge.
Jenny Uh huh.
Luke He just feels really strongly about not eating ________.
Jenny That's not a ________.
Luke What about you? Is there ________ you need?
Jenny There is one thing – could I ________ my phone to your Wi-fi?
Luke ________. The ________ is *lukeandsimonrule*, all lower case, all one word.
Jenny Got it.
Luke Anything ________?
Jenny Yeah. I have some clothes I need to wash. Is it ________ if I use your washing machine?
Luke Of ________ you can. But Simon prefers us to use the eco-friendly detergents. There's some in the cupboard.
Jenny Cool.
Luke Oh, and you ________ use a hot water programme. He's very keen on saving energy.
Jenny OK, and ________ you ________ if I use your dryer too?
Luke ________, we don't have one, but you can hang it out on the washing line.
Jenny Great. Is there ________ else I ________ know?
Luke No, I don't think ________ – oh! You should probably move your car.
Jenny I guess Simon doesn't like cars either.
Luke Well no, but it's not that. We know the kidnappers have been watching us, right? They might see it and recognize us.
Jenny You're right. I'll move it right away.
Luke Look, I'll come with you and we can get a coffee. There's a nice café round the corner.
Jenny Thanks, Luke.

c 4 24 Watch or listen and repeat the highlighted phrases. Copy the rhythm.

d In pairs, practise the dialogue with a partner.

e ➤ **Communication** *Renting a room* **A** *p.109*, **B** *p.110*.

3 TAKING A RISK
VIDEO

a 4 25 Watch or listen to Jenny and Luke discussing the situation with Rob. Where are they going to go tonight? Why?

b Watch or listen again and answer the questions.

1 Who is more optimistic at the beginning, Jenny or Luke?
2 Has Rob managed to get a flight to London? Why (not)?
3 What does Rob think the words *old man* might refer to?
4 What does he think Luke and Jenny need to do?
5 How are they going to get to the house?
6 Why does Luke know the back way well?

What do you think will happen when they go to the house?

British and American English
flashlight = American English
torch = British English

c Look at the **Social English phrases**. Can you remember any of the missing words?

Social English phrases
Jenny It's all ________ a mess.
Jenny I hope ________. I just don't know.
Jenny Any ________?
Rob I know, but I'll ________ trying.
Rob I've been thinking about Dad's message. That 'old man' ________.
Jenny Did you ________ that?

d 4 26 Watch or listen and complete the phrases.

e Watch or listen again and repeat the phrases. How do you say them in your language?

Can you...?
- ☐ ask about the rules in a house
- ☐ explain the rules in a house
- ☐ suggest and agree on a plan of action

G *have something done*
V looking after yourself
P sentence stress

I love your hair! Where did you have it done?

At a new place near my office.

8A Looking after yourself

1 VOCABULARY looking after yourself

a Look at the website for a spa and gym. Would you like to go there? What would you do if you went there? Do you have any similar places near where you live?

Our 1200 m² Wellbeing Centre offers you everything you need to recharge your mind and body.

- The spa area has a large pool, a hammam, and massage rooms offering a variety of treatments. The whole area is beautifully illuminated, with relaxing music, aromas, and gentle lighting.
- The gym has the most advanced fitness equipment, and a spacious aerobics studio. Yoga, t'ai chi, and Pilates classes are also offered either individually or in groups.
- The lounge and bar area offers a healthy assortment of all-organic snacks and juices.

b ➤ **p.163 Vocabulary Bank** *Looking after yourself.* Do parts 1 and 2.

2 SPEAKING

a Look at the topics below. Work with a partner. How important are these things if you want to look after yourself?

LOOKING AFTER YOURSELF

KEEPING FIT
- doing exercise (where? who with? how often?)
- walking, e.g. to work
- doing sport

BEAUTY
- looking after your skin / face
- using sunscreen
- looking after your hands and feet

WELLBEING
- having a healthy diet
- cutting down on some food / drink (e.g. red meat, etc.)
- cutting out some food / drink (e.g. alcohol, etc.)
- having regular check-ups at the doctor's / dentist's

BOOSTING YOUR BRAIN POWER
- reading (books / newspapers, etc.)
- doing puzzles (crosswords, Sudoku, etc.)
- playing computer games
- learning new things

ANYTHING ELSE?

Giving opinions

I think the most important thing if you want to keep fit is *doing regular exercise.*
I think *going to a gym* is better than *doing exercise at home* because...
I don't think you need to *have medical check-ups* unless...
I also think it's important to...

b Imagine the government in your country was planning to introduce **three** new campaigns to encourage people to look after themselves better. What do you think the best ideas would be?

c Report your ideas to the class and have a class vote on the three best ideas.

We think first they should make it obligatory to do more sport at school. Nowadays people only do two hours a week. Secondly, we think they should ban fizzy drinks...

3 READING & SPEAKING

a Look at the photos of two spa treatments. What do you think they are?

b Work in pairs **A** and **B** and read about the treatments. **B** go to **Communication** *Hot or Cold? p.110.*

c **A** read the article on the right and find answers to the questions below.

1. Where did the journalist have the treatment? Where does it come from?
2. In what sort of room do you have the treatment?
3. What shows how hot the room gets?
4. What are the health benefits?
5. How do you protect yourself during the treatment?
6. How hot was it inside? How does this compare to a normal sauna?
7. How long did the journalist stay for?
8. How did the journalist feel afterwards?

d Read the article again. Work out the meaning of the highlighted words and phrases, and then complete the glossary. Check the pronunciation of the words and phrases.

e Imagine you had the treatment in the article. Think about how you felt before, during, and afterwards. Describe the experience to **B** in your own words. Use your answers in **c** to help you. Explain the words in the glossary if necessary.

I was on holiday in New Jersey and I went to a really amazing sauna...

f Now listen to **B**'s story and ask about any new words.

g Talk to your partner.

1. Which of the two treatments would you prefer? Why?
2. Do you ever have saunas? How long do you stay in the sauna? Do you enjoy it?
3. Have you ever had a treatment that involves very cold water or temperature? What was it like?
4. What are the hottest / coldest places you've ever been in? What were you doing there? How did you feel?
5. Do you find it easier to put up with extreme heat or extreme cold?

Sauna or oven? Sweating next to cooking eggs

In New York City, there are some very hot saunas. But none of them come close to the heat you can find inside the Bul Hanzung Mok room at King Spa Korean Sauna in nearby New Jersey.

A Korean tradition for over 500 years, this brick room gets its heat from wood burned in a fire each morning. The brick holds so much heat that spa workers put cartons of eggs inside the room to cook (they're later sold in the spa restaurant). The spa says the heat helps remove impurities from the body and is also good for aches and pains.

Inside the sauna, I sit on a mat to stop my legs from burning. What can I say? Nothing. It's too hot to talk. Opposite me one Korean woman (or is it a man?) is wrapped in a heavy blanket and has a handkerchief around her face for protection.

Sitting on the floor, slowly breathing the hot and humid air, I see a thermometer near where the eggs are cooked. As I stand up to look at it, I feel the heat on my scalp and nose. I look to see how hot it is but I can hardly see because so much sweat is dripping into my eyes. Finally, I can see the temperature: 220 degrees – an ordinary sauna is only 70–100 degrees! Like most people, I manage to stay inside for only a few minutes, but others last longer. But I definitely feel lighter, as if I've lost a few kilos, and more relaxed. Maybe I'll have to go back.

Adapted from nymag.com

Glossary

1. __________ /ˈhæŋkətʃɪf/ *noun* a small square piece of cloth used to blow your nose
2. __________ /ræpt ɪn/ *verb* covered in
3. __________ /skælp/ *noun* the skin on the top of your head
4. __________ /ˈblæŋkɪt/ *noun* a cover made of wool that people have on beds to keep them warm
5. __________ /drɪpɪŋ/ *verb* falling in small drops
6. __________ /eɪks ən peɪnz/ continuous bad feelings in your body, e.g. because you are ill

4 GRAMMAR *have something done*

a Look at the photos. Who...?

1 is **having** his / her hair **cut**.
2 is **cutting** his / her hair.
3 is **painting** his / her flat.
4 is **having** his / her flat **painted**.

b ➤ **p.146 Grammar Bank 8A.** Learn more about *have something done* and practise it.

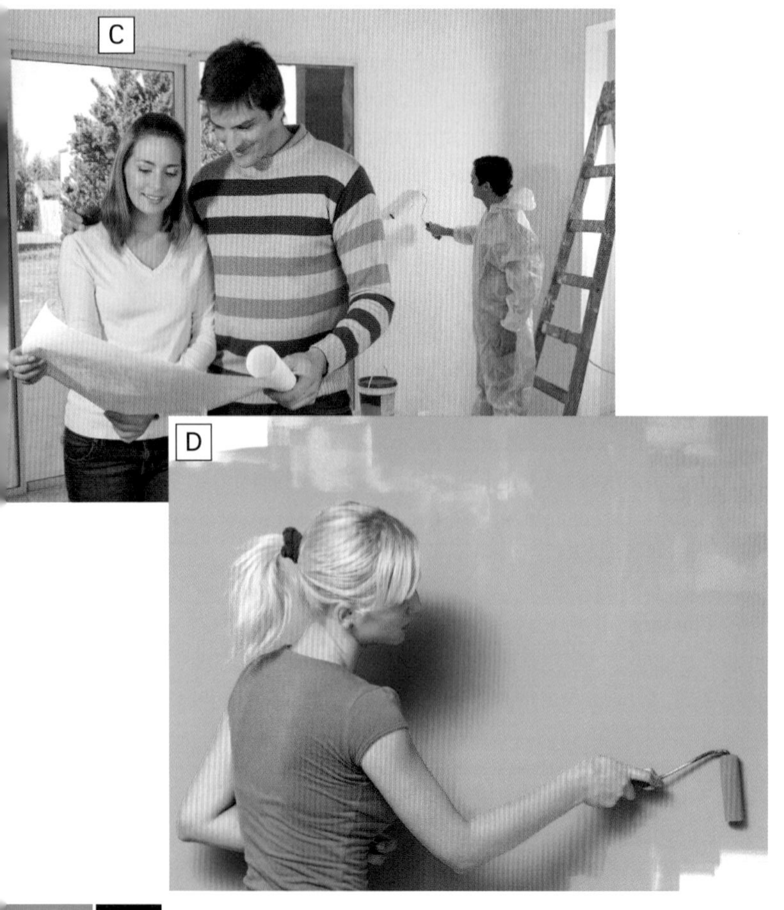

5 PRONUNCIATION sentence stress

a 4 30))) Listen and repeat the sentences. Copy the rhythm.

1 I **had** my **hair cut yesterday**.
2 Do you **usually have** your **shopping delivered**?
3 I **think** you **ought** to **have** your **eyes tested**.
4 We're **going** to **have** our **flat repainted soon**.
5 Have you **ever had** your **fortune told**?
6 I **hate having** my **photo taken**.

b Talk to a partner. Give more information for each question and ask follow-up questions.

How often do you (or your family)...?

- have your teeth cleaned at the dentist's
- have your eyes checked
- have prints made of your digital photos
- have things delivered when you go shopping
- have your clothes dry-cleaned
- have your car washed

Have you ever...?

- had your fortune told
- had clothes made for you
- had the locks changed at your flat or house
- had your photo taken by a professional

6 VOCABULARY at the hairdresser's

a Have you ever had any of these hairstyles? Would you like to have any of them?

b ➤ **p.163 Vocabulary Bank** *Looking after yourself.* Do part 3.

c Talk to a partner.

1 How often do you go to the hairdresser's or barber's? What do you usually have done?
2 Are there any hairstyles that are very popular in your country at the moment?

7 LISTENING & SPEAKING

a You are going to listen to an interview with Dino Karveli, a hairdresser at his salon in London. Read the information about Dino. With a partner, think of two questions you might ask him if you were interviewing him.

b 4 32)) Listen once. Did he answer your questions?

c Listen again. Mark the sentences **T** (true) or **F** (false).

1 Dino's father was a barber in Greece. ____
2 When he came to the UK he worked for Vidal Sassoon for two years. ____
3 He does a wide variety of hair treatments. ____
4 He thinks it's important for hairdressers to be sociable. ____
5 He thinks men get just as stressed about their hair as women. ____
6 It's easy to fix a mistake in hair colour. ____
7 A woman once got very upset with him because he cut her hair very short. ____
8 Dino would never say no to a client's request. ____
9 He thinks to have good hair you need to go to a good hairdresser. ____

d Discuss the questions with a partner.

1 What's the best or worst haircut you've ever had?
2 How long have you had your current hair style? What was your hair like before?
3 Do you know anyone (friends, celebrities, family) who has great hair? What do they do to maintain it? Where do they have it cut?

Dino Karveli

Introduction
Home
Hairdressing
Gallery
Contact
Offers
Opportunities
Biography

Dino Karveli is a hairdresser in London. His parents are Greek, and he came to live in London in 1990. He has been working as a hairdresser since 1993.

Where was Queen Elizabeth II crowned?

In Westminster Abbey. Nearly every British monarch has been crowned there.

8B The rest is history

1 VOCABULARY history

a Look at the quiz **Know your history**. With a partner, work out the meaning of the highlighted words. Then choose the right answer.

KNOW YOUR HISTORY!

1 Which country was Mustafa Kemal Atatürk the leader of?
a Morocco b Poland c Turkey

2 What year were the 9 / 11 attacks on New York and Washington, D.C.?
a 2000 b 2001 c 2003

3 Which of these countries is *not* a monarchy today?
a Denmark b Ireland c Japan

4 Which of these countries has *not* fought a civil war in its history?
a England b Spain c Germany

5 When did the Russian Revolution take place?
a the early 18th century
b the early 19th century
c the early 20th century

6 Which army fought with 300 men at Thermopylae?
a the Spartan army
b the Persian army
c the Roman army

7 During which war was the battle of Gettysburg fought?
a the Vietnam war
b the American War of Independence
c the American Civil War

b 4 33))) Listen and check your answers.

c Look at some stills from classic historical films. Which events from the quiz are the films connected to?

d What historical films or TV series have been on recently? Did you see any of them? Did you learn anything from them?

2 PRONUNCIATION the letters *ar*

a Look at three words with the letters *ar*. How are they pronounced? Put them in the correct row.

war monarchy army

ɑː	
ɔː	
ə	

b 4 34))) Listen and check.

c Now add these words to the correct rows.

dark warm farmer warning afterwards reward avatar start bargain quarter wardrobe standard towards

d 4 35))) Listen and check. After which letters is *ar* usually pronounced /ɔː/?

3 READING & SPEAKING

a Bill Bryson is an American travel writer. Read an extract from his book *The Lost Continent* where he describes revisiting the site of the battle of Gettysburg. Answer the questions.

1 Why did he decide to go there?
2 What historical things did he see?
3 How did he feel about the visit as a whole?

b Read the extract again. How did the writer feel about these things? Write + (positive) or – (negative). Underline the phrases in the extract that tell you how he felt.

1 the places he went to on holiday as a child ____
2 the museum at the site ____
3 the display about the Gettysburg Address ____
4 the truth about when Lincoln gave the speech ____
5 the appearance of the battlefield ____
6 the shops and restaurants near the battlefield ____
7 being at the site when he was a child ____

c Look at the highlighted words connected to war and history and try to work out their meanings. Then match them to the definitions below.

1 ________ *noun* the place where a battle is fought
2 ________ *verb* destroying something by exploding it
3 ________ *noun* large guns on wheels used in battles
4 ________ *noun* small metal objects that are fired from a gun
5 ________ *noun* members of an army
6 ________ *noun* a long gun you hold against your shoulder to shoot with

d 4 36))) Listen and check. Then listen again and repeat the words.

e Tell a partner about one of the following places.

- a historical site you've visited
- a place that you enjoyed as a child, but you found disappointing when you returned as an adult
- a place you know that has been spoiled by tourism

On another continent, 4,000 miles away, I became quietly seized with that nostalgia that overcomes you when you have reached the middle of your life. I wanted to go back to the magic places of my youth – to Mackinac Island, the Rocky mountains, Gettysburg – and see if they were as good as I remembered them...

I drove to Gettysburg, where the decisive battle of the American Civil War was fought over three days in July 1863. There were over 50,000 casualties. I parked at the visitors' centre and went inside. It contained a small museum with glass cases containing bullets, brass buttons, belt buckles, and that sort of thing. [...] There was little to give you any sense of the battle itself.

One interesting thing was a case devoted to the Gettysburg Address, where I learned that Lincoln was invited to speak only as an afterthought and that everyone was taken aback when he accepted. It was only ten sentences long and took just two minutes to deliver. I was further informed that he gave the address many months after the battle. I had always imagined him making it more or less immediately afterwards, while there were still bodies lying around. [...] The truth, as so often in this life, was disappointing.

I went outside and had a look at the battlefield, which sprawls over 3,500 acres of mostly flat countryside, fringed by the town of Gettysburg with its gas stations and its motels. The battlefield had the great deficiency common to all historic battlefields. There was nothing much to distinguish this stretch of empty fields from that one. You had to take their word for it that a great battle was fought there. There were a lot of cannons scattered about, I'll give them that. [...] Through my dad's old binoculars I could clearly see

how troops had advanced from the direction of the town, a mile or so to the north, sweeping across the Burger King parking lot, skirting the [...] Tastee Delite Drive-in and re-grouping just outside the Wax Museum and Gift Shop. It's all very sad. Ten thousand soldiers fell there in an hour, two out of every three Confederate soldiers didn't make it back to base. It's a pity, that so much of the town of Gettysburg has been spoiled with tourist tat and that it is so visible from the battlefield.

When I was little, my dad bought me a Union cap and a toy rifle and let me loose on the battlefield. I was in heaven. I dashed about the whole day crouching behind trees, blowing up parties of overweight tourists with cameras around their necks. [...] Now, however, I found it difficult to summon any real excitement for the place.

Glossary
The Gettysburg Address = a famous speech made by President Lincoln after the battle
The Confederate army = the army of the southern US states
The Union army = the army of the northern US states

4 LISTENING

a Look at the pictures of Westminster Abbey in London. What famous events have taken place here? Do you know anything else about it?

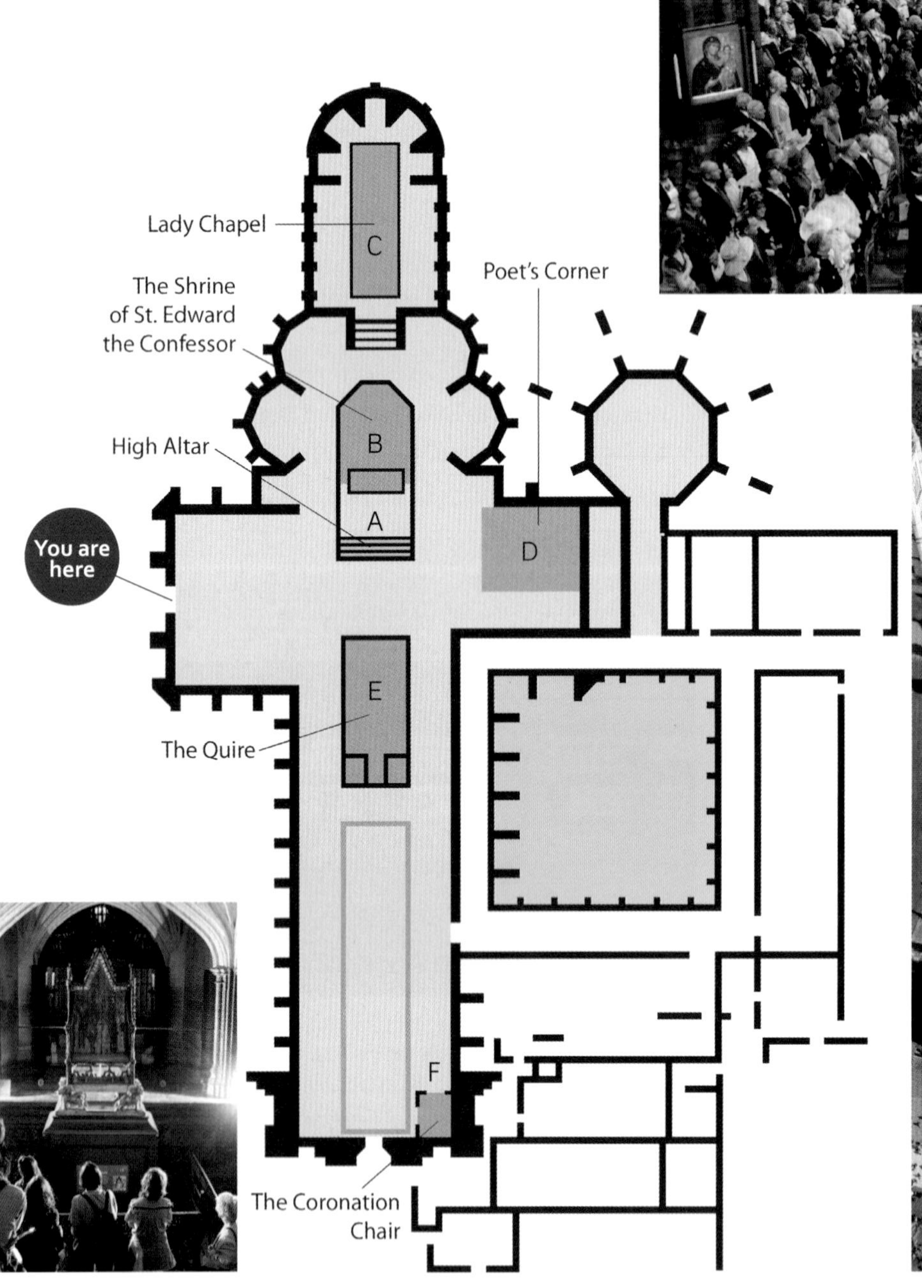

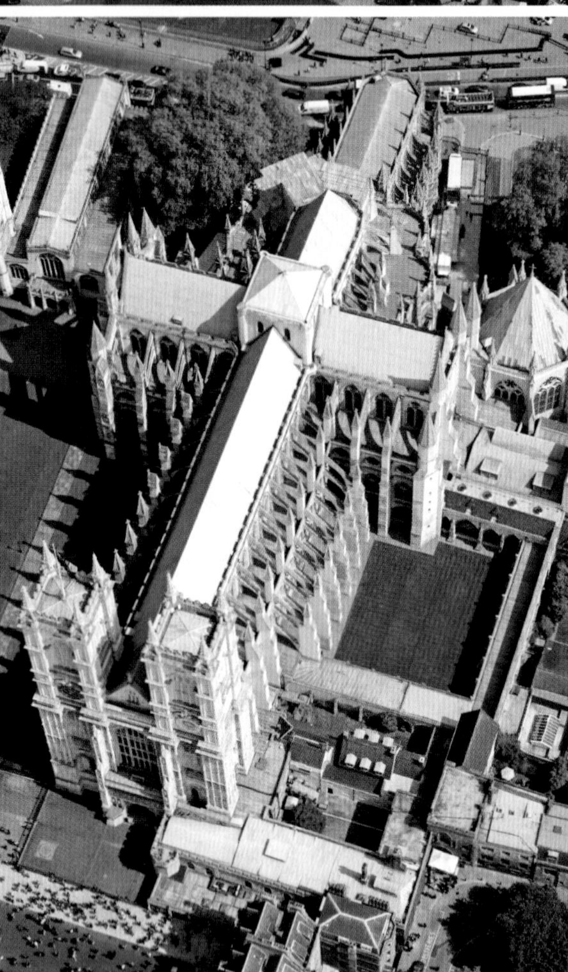

b 4 37 Listen to a guided tour of Westminster Abbey. Follow the route, and match places A–F with the correct information.

1 Nearly every king and queen has been crowned here. ____
2 Some well-known scientists are buried near here. ____
3 Prince William and Kate Middleton stood here at their wedding. ____
4 Here you can see the tomb of the first king of England to be buried in the Abbey. ____
5 Geoffrey Chaucer and Charles Dickens are buried here. ____
6 Queen Elizabeth I is buried here. ____

c Listen again, pausing after each area and taking notes. What does the guide say about these people and things?

1 Princess Diana
2 Edward I and Eleanor of Castile
3 Queen Mary
4 Shakespeare and Jane Austen
5 what the Quire is used for
6 the writing on the Coronation Chair

5 GRAMMAR the passive; impersonal *you*

a Complete the information about Westminster Abbey with the verbs in the right form of the passive. What does the word *you* refer to in the last sentence of the text?

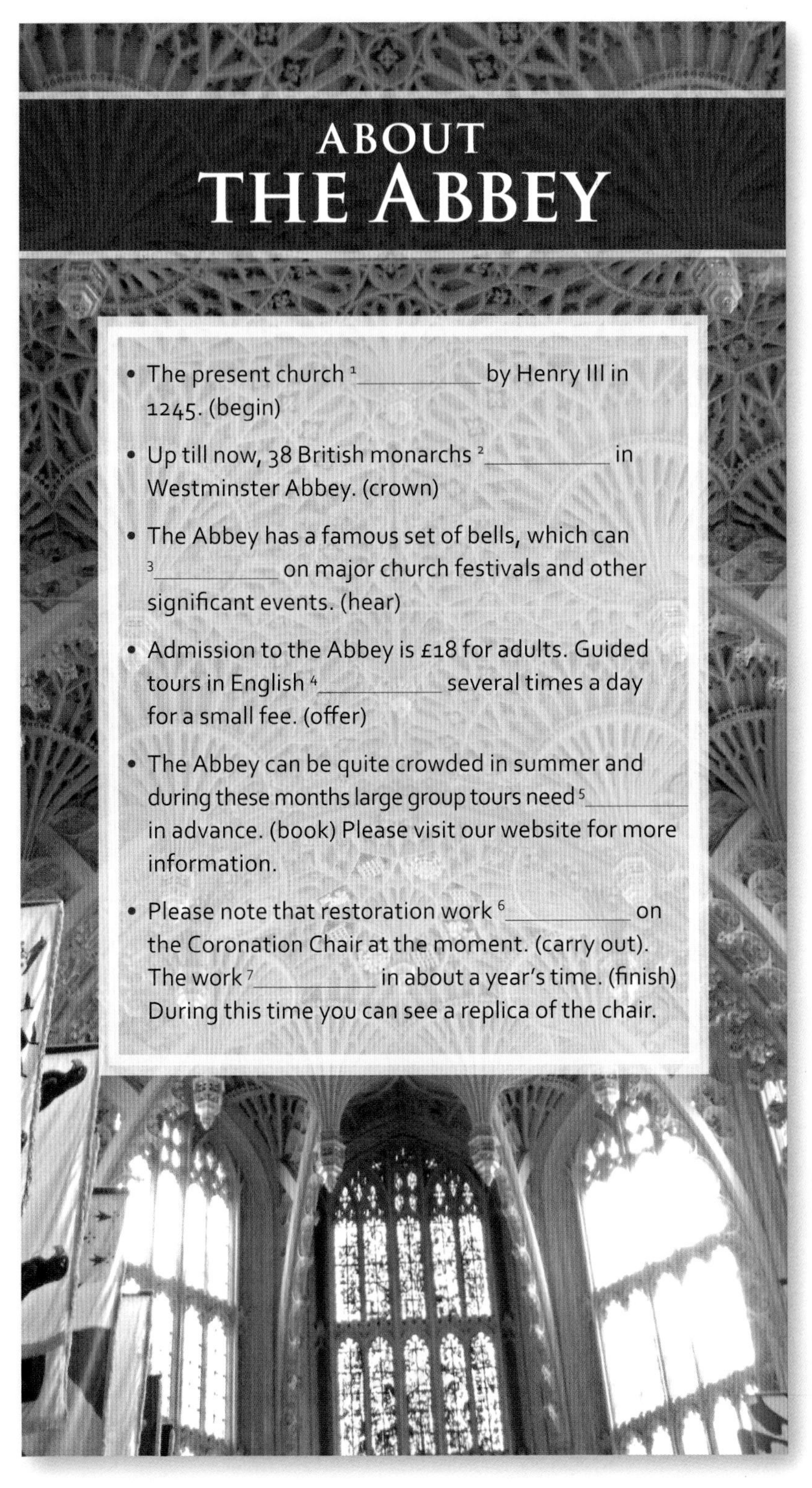

ABOUT
THE ABBEY

- The present church [1]__________ by Henry III in 1245. (begin)
- Up till now, 38 British monarchs [2]__________ in Westminster Abbey. (crown)
- The Abbey has a famous set of bells, which can [3]__________ on major church festivals and other significant events. (hear)
- Admission to the Abbey is £18 for adults. Guided tours in English [4]__________ several times a day for a small fee. (offer)
- The Abbey can be quite crowded in summer and during these months large group tours need [5]__________ in advance. (book) Please visit our website for more information.
- Please note that restoration work [6]__________ on the Coronation Chair at the moment. (carry out). The work [7]__________ in about a year's time. (finish) During this time you can see a replica of the chair.

b ➤ **p.147 Grammar Bank 8B.** Learn more about the passive and impersonal *you* and practise them.

c ➤ **Communication** *Local history* **A** *p.111*, **B** *p.112*. Roleplay being a tourist and ask your partner about the history of your town.

6 SPEAKING & WRITING

a Tell a partner about a famous building you've visited (not in your town). Use the questions to help you and add your own ideas. Include any interesting details or anecdotes that you can remember.

The Shard

FAMOUS BUILDINGS

- Where is it?
- When was it built?
- What was it used for originally?
- What is it used for now?
- What did you learn about it while you were there?
- How long did you spend there?
- How much did you have to pay to visit it?
- Would you recommend visiting it?

b ➤ **p.119 Writing** *Describing a building.* Write a description of an interesting building in your town or country for a tourism website.

7 4 40 SONG *Believe in humanity* ♫

7&8 Revise and Check

GRAMMAR

a Circle a, b, or c.

1 That story's not true. He ______.
a made up it b made it up c made up
2 Why don't you ______?
a come later round b later come round
c come round later
3 He really doesn't get ______.
a on with his parents b on his parents
c on his parents with
4 Those shoes don't fit – why don't you ______ to the shop?
a take back b take back them
c take them back
5 They decided ______ to a concert.
a to go b go c going
6 You should ______ more careful.
a to be b be c being
7 Are you going to keep on ______ that noise all night?
a to make b make c making
8 He wanted ______ him.
a me help b me to help c that I help
9 My mother never used to let me ______ late.
a to stay out b stay out c staying out

b Complete the second sentence so that it means the same as the first.

1 I'm going to pay someone to take my photo.
I'm going to have ______ ______ ______.
2 The hairdresser cut my hair last week.
I had ______ ______ ______ last week.
3 I'd like someone to paint my flat.
I'd like to have ______ ______ ______.
4 They built the cathedral in the 15th century.
The cathedral ______ ______ in the 15th century.
5 Most people think that the government should pay nurses more.
Most people think that nurses ______ ______ ______ more.
6 I don't like it when people tell me what to do.
I don't like ______ ______ what to do.

VOCABULARY

a Complete the phrasal verbs.

1 They're going to be late – their car's ______ down.
2 That's a fantastic idea! Who ______ up with it?
3 I lent him some money but he never ______ me back.
4 Do you want to ______ round for dinner at the weekend?
5 Don't ______ on doing that. It's very annoying.
6 He finally turned ______ two hours late.
7 I'm 35 – I can't move ______ to my parents' house!
8 That expensive deli has closed ______.
9 She's given all her old clothes ______.
10 I can't do this – it's too hard. I give ______.

b Write words for the definitions.

1 the place where theatre tickets are sold ______ ______
2 a short period of time separating parts of a play or concert ______
3 the events that form the story of a novel, play, or film ______
4 an afternoon performance of a play ______
5 the person that you are playing against in a game ______

c Complete the words.

1 She's had her hair **d**______ orange.
2 My nails look terrible – I need a **m**______.
3 You need to do more exercise if you want to lose **w**______.
4 A **m**______ is a very good way to relax.
5 It's important to **s**______ after you've been running.
6 A **m**______ has a king or a queen.
7 The **a**______ on the army base killed and injured dozens.
8 The historical battlefield was full of old bullets and **c**______.
9 The **w**______ between Iran and Iraq lasted for eight years.
10 50,000 **s**______ were killed in the battle.

PRONUNCIATION

a Circle the word with a different sound.

1	start	dark	quarter	parting
2	war	reward	warning	army
3	audience	circle	curled	turn
4	cash	cancel	fake	tan
5	theatre	arena	receipt	leader

b Underline the stressed syllable.

1 de|po|sit
2 ma|ni|cure
3 per|for|mance
4 spec|ta|tors
5 ae|ro|bics

CAN YOU UNDERSTAND THIS TEXT?

a Read the article once. What is 'event cinema'? Why is it popular?

Event cinema: opera in cinemas takes off

Cinemas are proving to be a goldmine for some of the UK's finest opera and ballet companies. Hollywood films are facing competition from live performances being shown in cinemas around the country, in a development called 'event cinema'.

In recent weeks tens of thousands of Britons have gone to the cinema to watch live screenings of ballet or opera. *La Bohème* has beaten *Gangster Squad* at the box office, and *The Nutcracker* came ahead of the latest Bond film when it was shown last month.

Over the past three years the number of cinemas showing ballet and opera performances has risen from fewer than 100 to around 250. More than 120 different events were shown at cinemas last year, a 400% increase from five years ago. And it is not just opera and ballet. Plays are also enjoying big audiences, with 20,000 tickets already sold for a cinema screening of a performance of Alan Bennett's *People* at the National Theatre next month.

Advances in digital technology have allowed opera and ballet companies to broadcast their events live, and cinemas have realised that the growing demand for an alternative to blockbuster films can help increase their own profits, especially when they can charge more – at around £15 on average – than for a movie.

For one company, Picturehouse Cinemas, event cinema already represents more than ten per cent of its ticket sales. And experts predict that very soon more than two million Britons a year will go to the cinema to see live performances or events – double the number that do so already. By the end of this decade at least one in 20 cinema tickets will be for something other than a movie, according to David Hancock, head of film and cinema at *IHS Screen Digest*. 'There is great demand – especially for cultural products,' he said, though sport and pop concerts have also made an appearance.

Melissa Keeping, who chairs the recently established Event Cinema Association, said: 'Opera and ballet are expensive and are generally located in large cities, so even if tickets are affordable the journey makes it difficult for a lot of people to go. But bring the performance live to your local cinema, in real time, at a fraction of the cost – what's not to like?'

Adapted from independent.co.uk

b Read the article again. Mark the sentences **T** (true) or **F** (false).

1 Cinemas don't make much money from showing opera and ballet performances.
2 Operas and ballets shown in cinemas are never as popular as films.
3 'Event cinema' was more popular five years ago.
4 'Event cinema' wouldn't be possible without digital technology.
5 Opera tickets are more expensive than cinema tickets.
6 Picturehouse Cinemas show more operas and ballets than most cinemas.
7 Some people go to the cinema to watch live sport.
8 Only cinemas in big cities show opera and ballet.

VIDEO CAN YOU UNDERSTAND THESE PEOPLE?

4 41))) **In the street** Watch or listen to four people and answer the questions.

Mairi

Lindsay

Dexter

Charlie

1 In the past Mairi ______.
  a used to go to the hairdresser's more often
  b used to have a lot of bad haircuts
  c used to have more things done at the hairdresser's
2 Lindsay prefers to go to the bank rather than use online banking because ______.
  a she doesn't trust online banking
  b she likes talking to people face to face
  c it's really near where she lives
3 One of the reasons why Dexter likes video games is because ______.
  a you use your body as well as your mind
  b you can read books about the characters after you've played the games
  c you interact a lot with other people
4 When Charlie visited the ruins of Pompeii, she also ______.
  a had a problem with a dog b walked up the volcano
  c saw a documentary about Roman civilisation
5 It was an appropriate place for her to visit because ______.
  a she had always been fascinated by Roman society
  b she had just read a book about Pompeii
  c it was connected to something she was studying at school

CAN YOU SAY THIS IN ENGLISH?

Do the tasks with a partner. Tick (✓) the box if you can do them.

Can you...?

1 ☐ describe a concert or sporting event that you've been to
2 ☐ talk about the entertainment options where you live
3 ☐ talk about different ways that people can look after themselves, and describe what you do
4 ☐ describe a famous building you know, including its history

VIDEO **Short films** The Globe Theatre
Watch and enjoy a film on iTutor.

G reported speech
V word families
P word stress

I told you not to forget to phone her.

Sorry, I thought you said you'd do it.

9A Can't remember, can't forget

1 SPEAKING

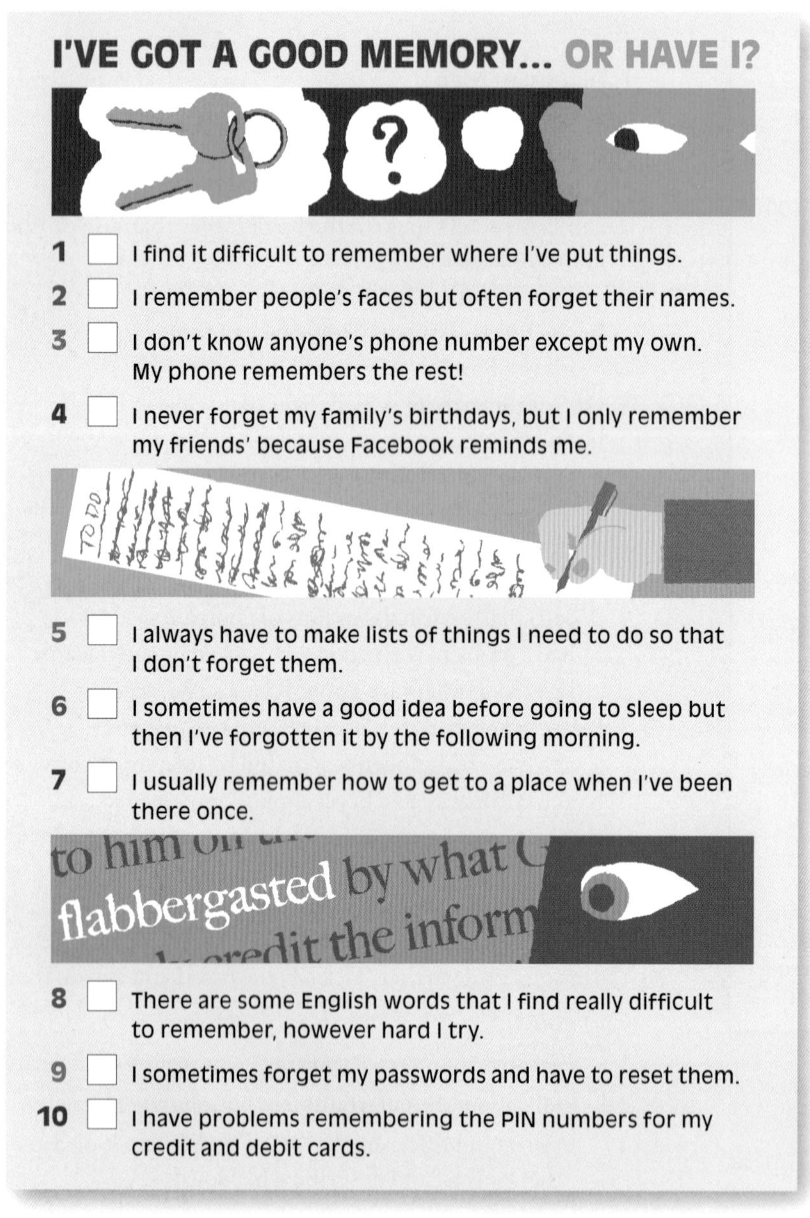

I'VE GOT A GOOD MEMORY... OR HAVE I?

1 ☐ I find it difficult to remember where I've put things.

2 ☐ I remember people's faces but often forget their names.

3 ☐ I don't know anyone's phone number except my own. My phone remembers the rest!

4 ☐ I never forget my family's birthdays, but I only remember my friends' because Facebook reminds me.

5 ☐ I always have to make lists of things I need to do so that I don't forget them.

6 ☐ I sometimes have a good idea before going to sleep but then I've forgotten it by the following morning.

7 ☐ I usually remember how to get to a place when I've been there once.

8 ☐ There are some English words that I find really difficult to remember, however hard I try.

9 ☐ I sometimes forget my passwords and have to reset them.

10 ☐ I have problems remembering the PIN numbers for my credit and debit cards.

a Tick (✓) the sentences above which apply to you. Compare with a partner. Give examples.

> **Giving examples**
> *I often forget where I've put things* **like / such as** *my phone and my car keys.*
> *I make lots of lists,* **for example / for instance** *when I go shopping.*

b What kind of things would you like to be able to remember better? Do you know any tricks for remembering things like PIN numbers and passwords?

2 LISTENING

a Read the website about the *StoryCorps* project. What does it aim to do and why? Why do you think Gweneviere Mann decided to use it?

b 5 2))) Listen to the news report about Gweneviere and check. Tick (✓) the things she has had problems remembering.

1 the date
2 her name
3 her phone number
4 whether she has had a meal or not
5 what city she lives in
6 how to get home from work
7 who her boyfriend is
8 who her colleagues are
9 how much time has passed

c Listen again and answer the questions.

1 What kind of people does Brian mention who have recorded stories on *StoryCorps*?
2 What does she do to remember the date?
3 What might happen if she doesn't write down when she eats?
4 When did Gweneviere's memory problem start?
5 What was Gweneviere afraid of?
6 Do Gweneviere and Yasir have a positive attitude?
7 Where did she use to say that she lived?
8 Who did she think was her mother? How were the two women different?
9 What did she ask Yasir not to let her do when she ran the marathon?

d Is there anyone you know who you think should record a story for *StoryCorps*? Why?

StoryCorps

Recording and preserving America's stories.

GREAT QUESTIONS | BLOG | NEWSLETTER | CONTACT US

Search

ABOUT STORYCORPS

StoryCorps is an oral history project which provides people of all backgrounds with the opportunity to record, share, and preserve the stories of their lives. Since 2003, we have collected more than 45,000 interviews with nearly 90,000 participants.

RECORD YOUR STORY

Think of a person whose stories you would like to hear, like a grandparent, parent, or friend. Then bring your friend or loved one to the StoryCorps facility and record your story together. At the end, you'll receive a free CD of your story, and a second copy will be kept at the Library of Congress in Washington, D.C.

STORIES

Gweneviere Mann talks to her boyfriend, Yasir Salem, about losing her short-term memory after suffering a stroke. They visited *StoryCorps* in New York City.

MORE STORIES

3 GRAMMAR reported speech

a Look at some extracts from the radio programme. With a partner say what you think the missing words are.

1 The doctors told her that her condition ________ improve in a couple of years.
2 She lives in New York, but after her stroke she always used to say that she ________ in San Francisco.
3 And she often used to ask him ________ one of her colleagues ________ her mother.
4 She told Yasir ________ ________ let her look at any of the distance signs along the way.

b 5 3 Listen and complete the gaps.

c Complete the sentences in direct speech.

1 The doctors said: '________ condition ________ ________ in a couple of years.'
2 After her stroke Gweneviere always used to say: '________ ________ in San Francisco.'
3 She often used to ask Yasir: '________ that woman ________ mother?'
4 She told Yasir : '________ ________ ________ look at any of the distance signs along the way!'

d ➤ **p.148 Grammar Bank 9A.** Learn more about reported speech and practise it.

e Work in pairs **A** and **B**. Write down **three** questions to ask your partner. Then ask your questions and try to remember your partner's answers. Don't write them down!

f Now test your memory. Tell a new partner what you asked your previous partner and what he or she said.

4 READING & SPEAKING

a With a partner, look at the list of days and dates. Can you remember where you were and what you did on these days? Try to remember as many details as you can, e.g. who you were with, what you were wearing, what you had to eat, and so on.

last Saturday night
the first day of this course
your last birthday
31 December last year
25 December 2012

b Read the article about Jill Price. What is unusual about her memory? Why is it a problem for her?

c Read the article again. Find out why the following are mentioned. Don't write your answers.

1	24 January 1968	6	California
2	24 January 1986	7	1980
3	a restaurant in Beverly Hills	8	crying
4	Prince Andrew and Fergie	9	2000
5	New Jersey	10	Michael

d With a partner, compare what you remember.

e Look at the highlighted verbs from the text. With a partner try to work out their meaning from the context.

f Can you think of any advantages of having superior autobiographical memory like Jill? If you had to choose, would you rather not be able to remember things (like Gweneviere Mann), or not be able to forget things (like Jill Price)?

NEWS | SPORT | BUSINESS | COMMENT | TRAVEL | DRIVING | CULTURE | STYLE

Search

The woman who remembers everything

Can you remember exactly what you did, who you saw, and what you said, on any day, at any time 10, 20, or even 30 years ago? Jill Price can. But is it a gift or a curse?

Jill Price asks me my date of birth and I tell her: January 24, 1968. 'Okay – 1986 you were 18. I could tell you on January 24, 1986, I was working in an ice cream shop, it was a Friday. I had turned 20. We were four days away from the Challenger explosion. I hated my job and Saturday night I went out with Tim and Candace.' She could probably tell me what she ate, what they ordered, and what time she got home.

We have met for dinner at a restaurant in Beverly Hills. 'As I sit here with you, it's 6.30 on Wednesday night,' she says. 'Today would have been the 22nd wedding anniversary of Prince Andrew and Fergie. That was also on a Wednesday. It was a friend's birthday and he got some balloons that he didn't want so he gave them to me. And then I went to see a friend of mine who worked at the Hard Rock Cafe.'

Jill Price doesn't try to remember these things; she simply isn't able to forget them. She was born in New Jersey on December 30, 1965. When she was eight, she thinks her brain 'snapped' due to the move the family made from New Jersey to California, and she began to remember in great detail. By the time she was 12, she realized she could remember every single day of the previous year. Since 1980, her memory has been near perfect. Any date she is given from that year onward she can instantly recall.

There is a downside to this: painful and unpleasant memories are as vivid as if they had just occurred. Awkward moments from school, battles with her weight, or hurtful comments from her childhood never fade in her memory. 'I can't forget,' she says. Crying helps her to cope with the unhappiness that her memory can cause. 'I cry all the time. Up to 10 times a day. I cry in the shower every morning.'

Doctors have been studying Jill since 2000. At first, they didn't know how to classify her, and have only recently given a name to her condition – superior autobiographical memory. They have only found three other people in the world who share the condition.

No one else in Jill's family has a memory like hers. Her brother, Michael, is happy not to remember everything. Jill has recently published her memoirs, *The Woman Who Can't Forget*, but Michael hasn't read it yet because there might be things in it he doesn't want to know. When I asked him what he would do if he was the one who had this memory, he answered, 'I would be making a fortune counting cards in Vegas.'

Glossary
the Challenger explosion a US space shuttle exploded in 1986 shortly after taking off, killing all seven astronauts on board
Beverly Hills a famous district of Los Angeles where many celebrities live
Prince Andrew and Fergie Queen Elizabeth II's second son and his ex-wife, Sarah Ferguson
New Jersey the state south of New York
Vegas Las Vegas, the famous US casino city in Nevada

5 VOCABULARY & PRONUNCIATION
word families and word stress

a 5 7))) Listen to these word families and underline the stressed syllable. In which word family a) is the stress always on the same syllable b) does the stress change on one of the words?

remember: me|mo|ry me|mo|ra|ble me|mo|rize me|mo|ri|al me|moirs
forget: for|get|ful un|for|get|ta|ble

b Match the words from the word families with their definitions.

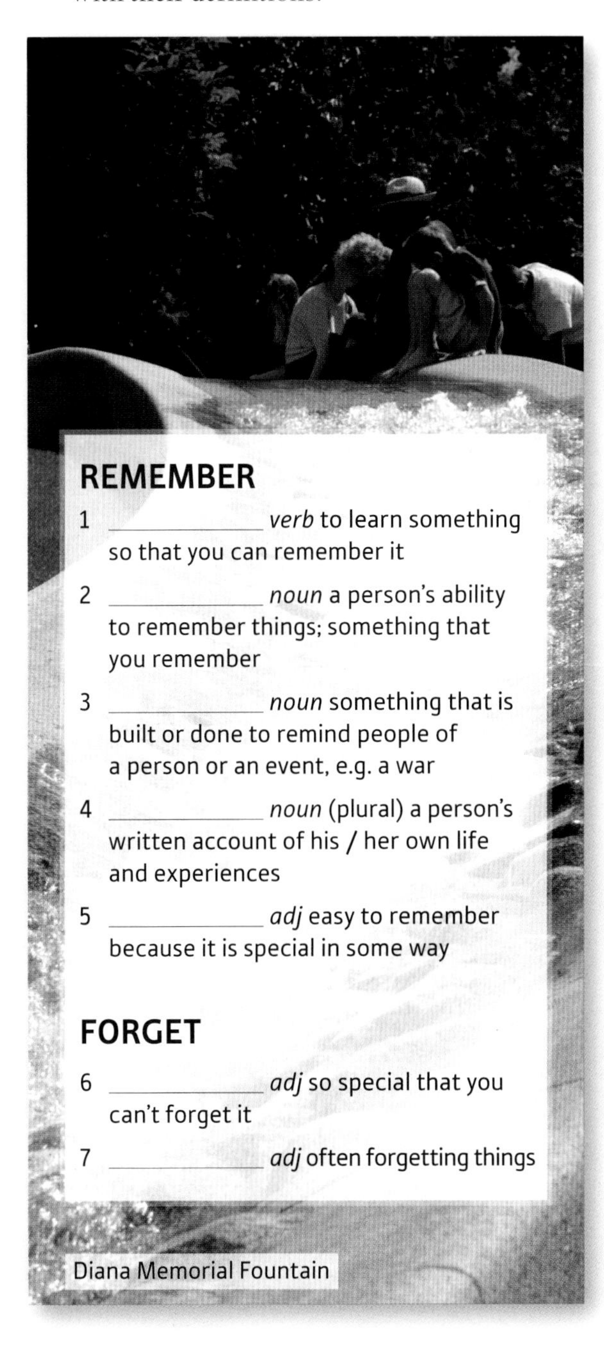

REMEMBER

1 ____________ *verb* to learn something so that you can remember it
2 ____________ *noun* a person's ability to remember things; something that you remember
3 ____________ *noun* something that is built or done to remind people of a person or an event, e.g. a war
4 ____________ *noun* (plural) a person's written account of his / her own life and experiences
5 ____________ *adj* easy to remember because it is special in some way

FORGET

6 ____________ *adj* so special that you can't forget it
7 ____________ *adj* often forgetting things

Diana Memorial Fountain

6 SPEAKING

a Choose two of the topics below, and think about what you are going to say, e.g. examples or details.

- a **memorable** moment from your school days
- an **unforgettable** birthday or Christmas
- something you were made to **memorize** as a child and found difficult
- a person you know who's very **forgetful**
- a **memorial** that you think is very beautiful
- someone's **memoirs** that you've read and really enjoyed
- someone you know who has an incredibly good **memory**
- something from your past that you wish you could **remember** better
- a time when you **forgot** an important date or appointment

b Work in groups of three or four. Talk about your topics, and listen and respond to the other people in the group.

Starting an anecdote or story
I'll never forget the time when...
This happened to me when...
When I was at school, we had a history teacher who...
I'm going to tell you about a friend of my mother's, who's incredibly forgetful...

c From memory, tell the rest of the class about something someone in your group told you.

7 5 8))) SONG *Memories* ♫

G uses of the past perfect
V weddings
P sentence stress

Why didn't he tell her he'd changed his mind?

It wouldn't have made any difference if he'd told her.

9B Wedding dramas

1 READING & LISTENING

a You're going to read a short story by William Somerset Maugham. Read the information about him below. Do you think it was acceptable for Maugham to write about people he met? Why (not)?

Article Talk Read Edit

William Somerset Maugham (1874–1965)

From *Wikipedia, the free encyclopedia*

William Somerset Maugham (ˈsʌməset ˈmɔːm) was a well-known English novelist and short story writer whose stories often took place in China, Singapore, Burma (now Myanmar), Malaysia, and other East Asian countries. Maugham wrote at a time when many of these places were colonies of Great Britain. He was famous for writing stories about real people who he met when he was travelling, and many of these people were very upset to recognize themselves in his books.

b 5 9))) Read and listen to **Part 1** of *Mabel*. Answer the questions with a partner.

1. Who were George and Mabel?
2. Why couldn't they get married for seven years?
3. What do you think *his nerve failed him* in line 8 means? Why did it happen?
4. What was George's dilemma?
5. What did he decide to do?

What do you think of his behaviour? What do you think will happen next?

c 5 10))) Listen to **Part 2.** Mark George's route on the map.

Mabel

Part 1

George was working in Burma for the British colonial government. He and Mabel became engaged when he was back in England. When he returned to Burma, it was arranged that she would join him there in six months. But one difficulty came up after another. Mabel's father died, the war came, then George was sent to a district which was unsuitable for a white woman. In the end it was seven years before she was able to start. He made all the arrangements for the marriage, which was going to take place on the day of her arrival, and went down to Rangoon to meet her. Then, suddenly, without warning, his nerve failed him. He had not seen Mabel for seven years. He had forgotten what she was like. She was a total stranger. He felt a terrible feeling in his stomach. He couldn't go through with it. He must tell Mabel that he was very sorry, but he couldn't, he really couldn't marry her. But how could a man tell a girl a thing like that when she had been engaged to him for seven years and had come 6,000 miles to marry him? He didn't have the nerve for that either. There was a boat just about to sail for Singapore; he wrote a letter to Mabel, and without any luggage, just in the clothes he was wearing, he boarded the boat. The letter Mabel received said:

Dearest Mabel,
I have been suddenly called away on business and do not know when I will be back. I think it would be much wiser if you returned to England. My plans are very uncertain.
Your loving George.

Glossary
Burma is now called Myanmar.
Rangoon is now called Yangon, and is the country's largest port.
The **'war'** is the First World War, which started in 1914.

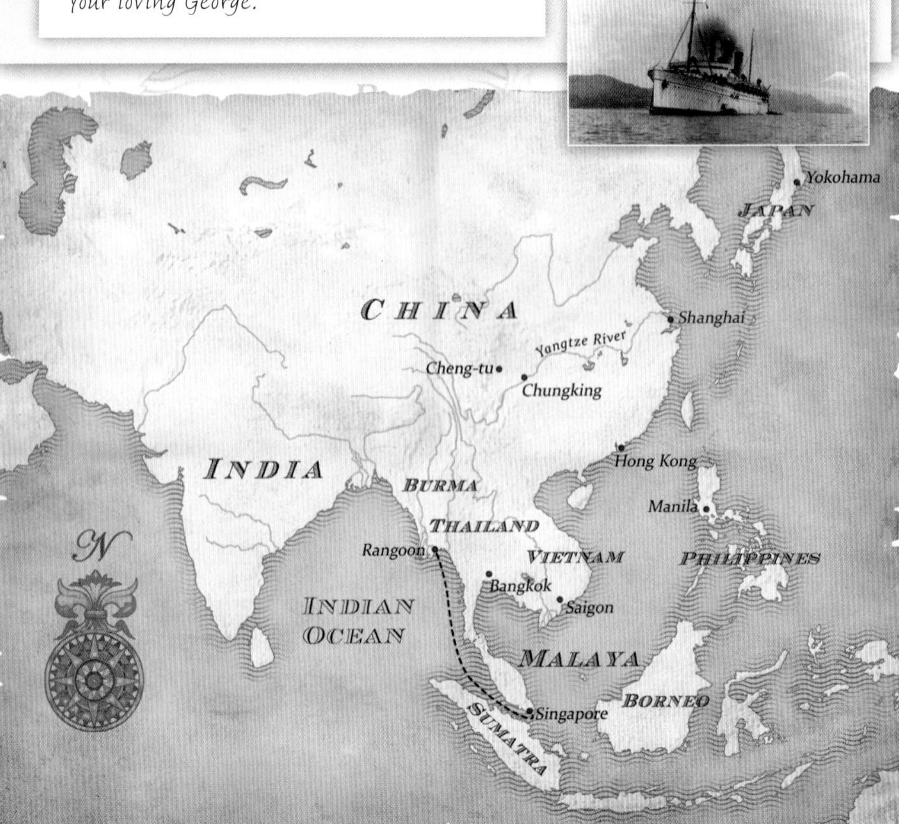

d Listen again, and complete Mabel's four telegrams.

1 URGENT: DELIVER WITHOUT DELAY
TELEGRAM
MESSAGE GOES HERE. BE BRIEF.
Quite ________.
________ ________.
Love Mabel

3 URGENT: DELIVER WITHOUT DELAY
TELEGRAM
MESSAGE GOES HERE. BE BRIEF.
So ________ I ________
you at ________.
Love Mabel

4 URGENT: DELIVER WITHOUT DELAY
TELEGRAM
MESSAGE GOES HERE. BE BRIEF.
________ ________.
Love Mabel

What do you think George will do now?

e Read **Part 3** (Don't listen yet). Continue drawing George's journey on the map. Then complete the gaps with an adverb or adverbial phrase from the list.

after that ~~already~~ lazily never now one morning only

Part 3

1 No, no, she wasn't going to catch him so easily. He had [1] *already* made his plans. He could catch the last ship along the Yangtze river to Chungking. [2]________, no one could get there until the following spring. He arrived at
5 Chungking, but he was desperate [3]________. He was not going to take any risks. There was a place called Cheng-tu, the capital of Szechuan, and it was 400 miles away. It could [4]________ be reached by road, and the area was full of thieves. A man would be safe there.
10 George set out. He sighed with relief when he saw the walls of the lonely Chinese city. He could rest at last. Mabel would [5]________ find him there. The British consul was a friend of his and he stayed with him in his luxurious house. The weeks passed [6]________ one after the other.
15 [7]________ George and the consul were in the courtyard when there was a loud knock at the door.

f 5 11 Listen and check. What do you think *he sighed with relief* means in line 10?

g 5 12 How do you think the story ends? Listen to **Part 4** and check.

h Discuss the questions with a partner.

1 Do you think Mabel and George had a happy marriage? Why (not)?
2 How do you feel about what Mabel did in the story?
3 Do you know anyone whose 'nerve failed them' before their wedding? What did they do about it?

2 GRAMMAR uses of the past perfect

a Look at three extracts from *Mabel*. Which highlighted phrase…?

a describes an event that happened before another event in the past
b says how the past could have been different
c reports what someone said or asked in the past

1 He went straight to the club and asked if he had received any telegrams.
2 Then, suddenly, without warning, his nerve failed him. He had not seen Mabel for seven years.
3 It would have been terrible if I hadn't been able to marry you after all.

b p.149 Grammar Bank 9B. Learn more about uses of the past perfect and practise them.

3 PRONUNCIATION sentence stress

a 5 16 Listen to five sentences. Try to write down the stressed words in the pink rectangles.

1 *When* *read* *email* *understood* *left.*

2

3

4

5

b Look at the stressed words and try to remember what the unstressed words are. Write in the unstressed words.

c Listen again and repeat the sentences.

4 VOCABULARY weddings

a Look at the wedding photo. Who is...?

the bride ____
the (bride)groom ____
the best man ____
a bridesmaid ____
a pageboy ____

b Read the blog post about a wedding. What nearly went wrong at the wedding?

c Complete the text with the words and phrases in the box.

bride guests reception speech
ceremony wedding dress

Search More ▾ Next Blog» Create Blog Sign In

I nearly caused a wedding disaster!

Last weekend was my wife's sister's wedding in a little town in southern Egypt, and I nearly ruined it. I flew in from the UK two days before, and my one job was to bring the [1] __________, which the [2] __________ had had specially made by a well-known designer in London.

Well, my flight to Cairo was delayed so when I landed, I was in a hurry. I quickly picked up my suitcase and caught the overnight train heading south. As soon as I got there I went to my hotel, opened my suitcase, and to my horror realized that it wasn't mine. My suitcase – with the dress inside – was presumably still at the airport in Cairo, or even worse, in the hands of a stranger. The [3] __________ was at 11 o'clock the following morning!

I immediately went to the station and took the first train back to Cairo and amazingly found the suitcase still at the airport. After another overnight train, I was back just in time for the wedding. I hadn't slept much at all, but I had the dress. The bride looked great and the [4] __________, which was at a hotel, was beautifully organized. All the [5] __________ had a great time, but I was so exhausted that by the time the best man was giving his [6] __________ I had already fallen asleep at the table.

d 5 17 Listen and check.

e Talk to a partner.

- What are weddings like where you live?
- Who are the main people?
- Where are wedding ceremonies usually held, e.g. a church, a registry office, the town hall, etc.?
- Where do people usually hold receptions? What kind of food and drink is typical? Do the bride and groom cut a cake?
- Do people make speeches at the reception? What are the speeches like?
- Do people have stag parties (the groom and his male friends) and hen parties (the bride and her female friends) before the wedding? What usually happens?

5 LISTENING

a In an English wedding ceremony, the priest or registrar asks the bride, 'Do you take this man to be your husband?' What words does the bride answer?

1 'I do.'
2 'Yes, please.'
3 'Yes, I do.'

b Look at the headlines of three news stories about weddings that went wrong. What do you think happened in each wedding?

1 **Bride ruins wedding with joke**

2 **Groom sets fire to wedding**

3 **Better late than never?**

c 5.18 Now listen to the news stories. Did you guess right?

d Listen again and complete the chart.

	1	2	3
Where was it?			
Who were the people?			
What went wrong?			
Did the wedding take place?			

e Have *you* heard any stories about wedding disasters? What went wrong?

6 SPEAKING & WRITING

a Tell a partner about the last wedding you went to. Talk about:

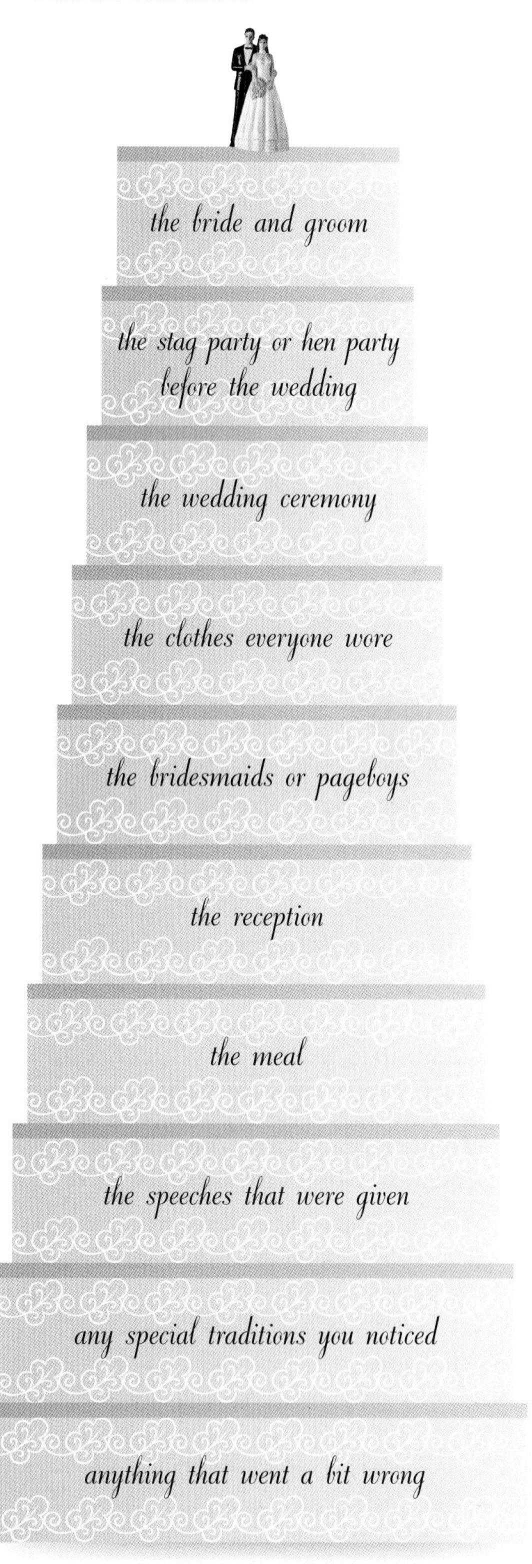

b ➤ p.120 **Writing** *A story.* Write a story describing a significant event.

Practical English Finding Henry

EPISODE 5

1 VIDEO WHAT THE CLUE MEANS

a 5 19))) Watch or listen to Jenny and Luke looking in Henry's study. What does *old man* refer to? Where do they think Henry is?

b Watch or listen again. Complete the sentences with **Jenny**, **Luke**, or **Rob**.

1 ________ has checked all the paintings.
2 ________ thinks maybe the *old man* thing wasn't a message.
3 ________ suggests looking on top of the bookcase.
4 ________ finds the two paperweights.
5 ________ discovers that Proteus is a company in Oxford.
6 ________ phones the Police Inspector.
7 ________ downloads the plans of the Proteus building.
8 ________ is going to guide the police officers.

What do you think they are going to find in the building?

2 VIDEO GIVING DIRECTIONS IN A BUILDING

a 5 20))) Look at the plan of the building. Watch or listen. Mark the rest of the police officers' route. Where do they end up, A, B, or C?

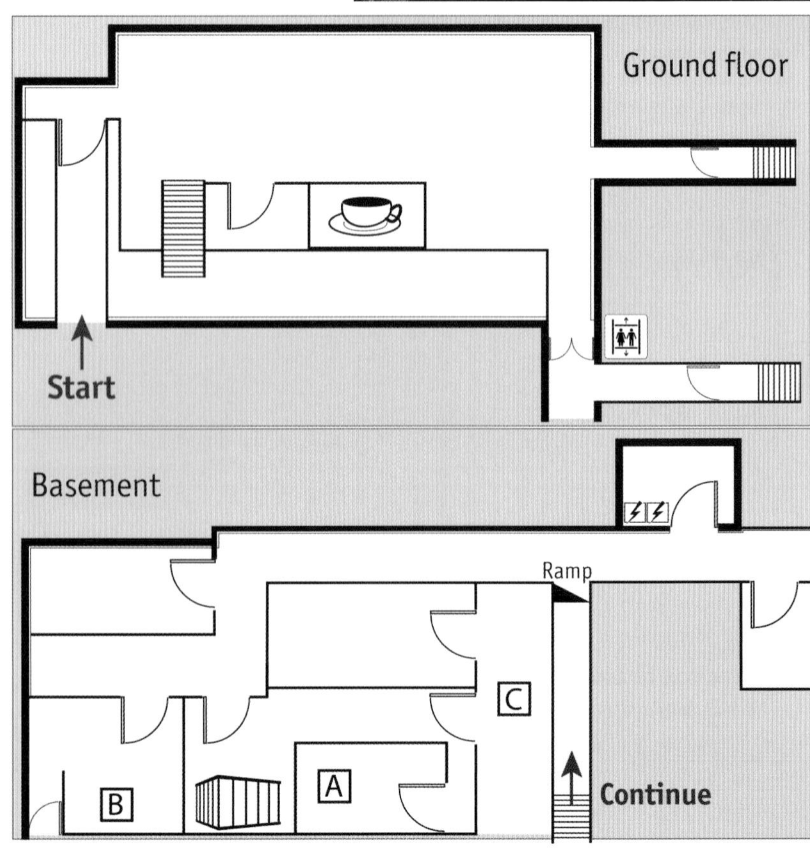

b Read the dialogue between Luke and Tom. Can you remember any of the missing words? Watch or listen again and check.

Luke OK, go to the end of the corridor, go ________ the door and turn ________.
Tom We're in a large open area.
Luke That's right. Now, go ________ ahead. You should see some stairs on your right. Go ________ the stairs and a coffee bar. Turn right. ________ on and you should see a set of double doors.
Tom Should we go through?
Luke Yes. Now, you should see some stairs on your ________.
Tom Yeah, I see them.
Luke Right. Go ________ the stairs, continue straight on, and walk down the ramp.
Tom We're at the end of the ramp. Which ________ now?
Luke ________ right and carry on straight ________ the corridor. Go past a maintenance room and two fuse boxes, and try the next door on your right.
Tom The door's locked. Is there ________ way?
Luke Hold on. OK. Turn ________ and go ________ down the corridor.
Tom Should we go back up the ramp?
Luke No. Go straight to the end of the corridor and turn left.
Tom We're here. There are two doors. Which ________ should we take?
Luke ________ the one on your left.
Tom It's open!
Luke What can you see?
Tom There are three big safes and cages full of documents. Are you sure this is the ________ way?
Luke Yes, you're in the store room. Can you hear a generator?
Tom Yes! It's coming from the end of the corridor.
Luke Head ________ it. But watch out for guards!
Tom There's a door here and a narrow corridor to the right. What should we do?
Luke I don't know!
Tom Wait. I can hear voices. There are people in there.
Police Inspector That must be the room.
Tom OK. We're going in.

c 5 21 Watch or listen and repeat the highlighted sentences. Copy the rhythm.

d In pairs, practise giving directions in a building. **A** choose a place on the plan but don't tell **B**. **A** give **B** directions to the place. **B** check with **A** that you are going the right way, and anything else you don't understand.

e Swap roles.

3 VIDEO A HAPPY ENDING?

a 5 22 What do you think the police officers found? What do you think happens to all the characters? Watch or listen. Were your predictions correct?

b Watch or listen again. Mark the sentences **T** (true) or **F** (false). Correct the **F** sentences.

1 The news report says that Andrew Page is getting better.
2 Selina and Grant managed to escape.
3 Rob thinks the clue was very difficult.
4 Henry is very grateful for all their help.
5 They go out for a meal to celebrate.
6 Rob thinks it is still worth coming to the UK.
7 Jenny wants to stay longer in the UK.

c Look at the **Social English phrases**. Can you remember any of the missing words?

Social English phrases

Henry I must ________, I was beginning to lose hope.
Henry Goodness ________ what would have happened if you hadn't found me in time.
Henry Could you ________ the glasses, Luke?
Rob It's ________ to have you back, Dad.
Henry I just ________ you were here, Rob.
Jenny I can't ________ to get back to the peace and quiet of New York!

d 5 23 Watch or listen and complete the phrases.

e Watch or listen again and repeat the phrases. How do you say them in your language?

Can you...?

- [ ] give directions inside a building
- [ ] check that you understand the directions
- [ ] express relief and gratitude

G *be, do,* and *have*: auxiliary and main verbs
V British and American English
P sentence stress

How often do you have American fast food?

Hardly ever. I'm not very keen on fast food.

10A America and the world

1 GRAMMAR
be, do, and *have*: auxiliary and main verbs

a Which of these statements about America are true? Why do you think so? Discuss them with a partner.

How much do you know about the USA?

Are these statements true or false?

1 The US **has** a higher percentage of millionaires than any other country.

2 In the US, *colour, honour,* and *favour* **aren't** spelt with a *u*; words ending *-tre* (*centre, litre*) **are** spelt *-ter.*

3 Over 90% of Americans **don't** own a passport.

4 The average American husband **does** 50% of the housework.

5 The world's first skyscraper **was** in New York.

6 In 1950, only 22% of American adults **were** single; now the figure **is** about 50%.

7 English **has** always **been** the official language of the United States.

8 Texas used **to be** part of Mexico and **didn't** join the US until the year 1845.

9 The US **had** the world's biggest economy until it **was** overtaken by China in 2013.

10 In the US, football **is** known as *soccer*, the name which the sport **had** originally **been** called at British public schools.

b 5 24))) Listen and check your answers. Correct the false statements.

c Look at the **bold** verbs in the questions. With a partner, circle the ones which are **auxiliary** verbs.

d ➤ **p.150 Grammar Bank 10A.** Learn more about *be, do,* and *have* and practise them.

2 PRONUNCIATION
sentence stress

a 5 28))) Listen and repeat the sentences. Copy the rhythm.

1 The **capital** of the **USA** is **Washington DC**.
2 It **isn't New York**.
3 **When** are your **friends arriving**?
4 I **have** a **house** in **New Jersey**.
5 **How long** have you **known** your **best friend**?
6 I **haven't seen** my **grandparents** for **ages**.
7 **Anne does Pilates twice** a **week**.
8 **Where** does your **sister live**?
9 **My brother doesn't like animals**.

b Listen again. What vowel sound do *are, have,* and *does* have when they are unstressed?

c Complete the rules with a partner. Circle the right word.

When are *be, do,* and *have* stressed?

be

1 is usually *stressed* | *unstressed* in positive sentences or in questions.
2 is *stressed* | *unstressed* in negative sentences.

do* and *have

3 are *stressed* | *unstressed* when they are main verbs.
4 are usually *stressed* | *unstressed* when they are positive auxiliary verbs.
5 are *stressed* | *unstressed* when they are negative auxiliary verbs in questions.

d ➤ **Communication** *More facts about the USA?* **A** *p.111*, **B** *p.112*. Say sentences to your partner, who must decide if they are true or false.

3 SPEAKING & READING

a Talk to a partner. Are the following aspects of American culture important in your country? What do you think of them? Do you prefer them to ones from your country? Why (not)?

- films and TV programmes
- music
- food
- chain stores, coffee shops, etc.
- fashion
- technology

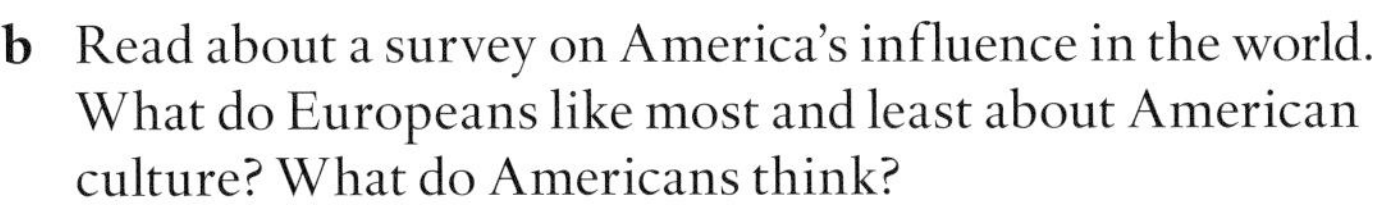

b Read about a survey on America's influence in the world. What do Europeans like most and least about American culture? What do Americans think?

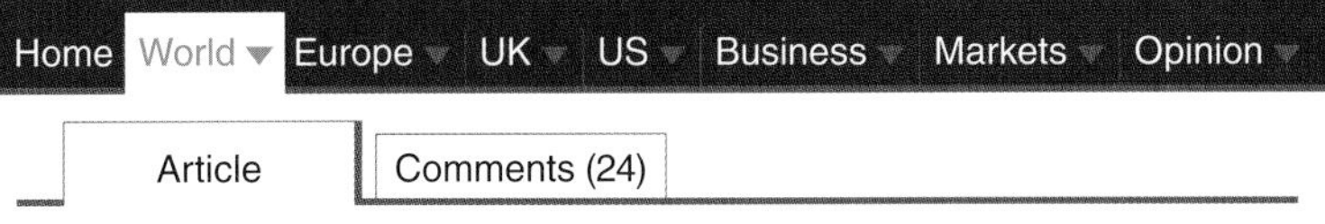

Who's negative about American culture? You'd be surprised…

In a recent survey *The Wall Street Journal* asked more than 18,000 people in 18 countries (16 European nations, plus the US and Russia) to identify the best and worst parts of US cultural influence in the world.

What Europeans think

Among Europeans, 32% said US influence was negative, while 26% gave a positive response. 40% said American films and television programmes were the best contribution, making this the most popular category overall. All of the European countries said American food was the worst contribution. 65% of French people gave this answer, the highest in the group.

What Americans think

Surprisingly, many Americans view their own country more negatively than Europeans do. 46% of Americans said the US has a negative influence in the world, while only 33% described it as positive. Americans named a number of different things as their country's best contribution to world culture, including the food at 11%. When asked to identify America's worst contribution, 32% of Americans pointed to film and television, much higher than in any other country.

4 LISTENING & SPEAKING

a 5 29 Listen to three Americans talking about what they think are their country's best and worst contribution. Fill in as much of the chart as you can.

	Best	Worst
1 Andy		
2 Molly		
3 Jenny		

b Compare answers with a partner. Then listen again and complete the chart.

c Is there anything that surprised you? Who do you agree with more?

d In pairs, talk about ways in which *your* country has had an influence in the world. Which influences are the most positive? Are any negative?

5 VOCABULARY

British and American English

a What do these American English words mean? Write the British word with the same meaning.

	British	American
1	________	cookie
2	________	cell phone
3	________	restroom
4	________	movie
5	________	movie theater
6	________	high school
7	________	vacation
8	________	garbage
9	________	parking lot
10	________	fries

b 5 30 Listen and check.

c Now match some more British and American words.

	British			American
1	lift	☐	a	apartment
2	sweets	☐	b	stand in line
3	flat	☐	c	faucet
4	petrol	☐	d	check
5	queue *verb*	☐	e	subway
6	trainers	☐	f	gas
7	underground	☐	g	elevator
8	pavement	☐	h	candy
9	(restaurant) bill	☐	i	sidewalk
10	tap	☐	j	sneakers

d 5 31 Listen and check.

e Do you know any other words that are American English? Do you know what they are in British English?

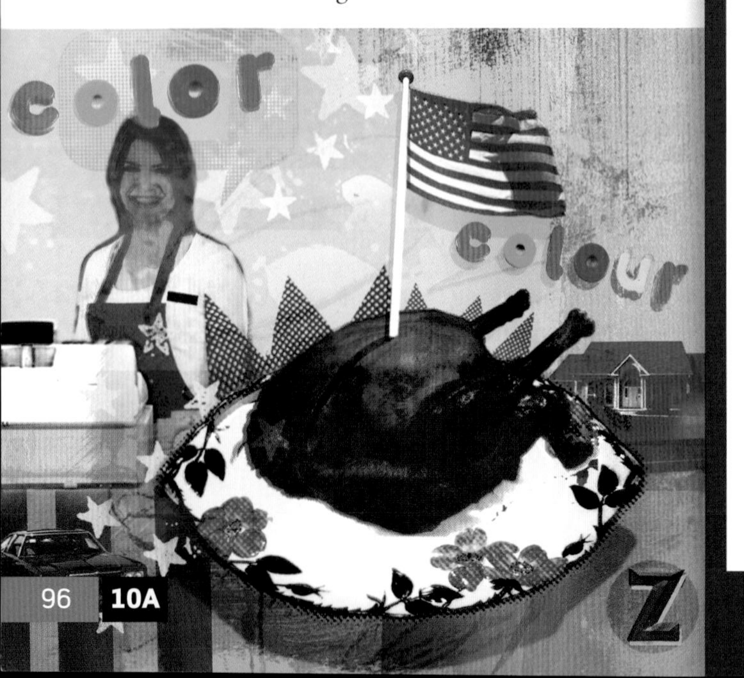

6 READING

a Look at the title and the first paragraph of each article. Which writer is British? Which is American?

b Read the articles. Write the headings in the correct place. There is one heading you don't need to use.

A Being unfriendly
B Thinking we're stupid
C Not knowing how to spell words...or pronounce them
D Being a bit stingy
E Paying for health care
F Being such patriots
G Being too nice
H Believing the stereotypes
I Flying to clear the table

HOME NEWS CONTACT VIDEOS **BLOG** LOG IN

6 Things Americans Do That Drive Brits Crazy

By Ruth Margolis

American people are some of the friendliest you'll ever meet. But occasionally they do things that we find a bit... eccentric?

1 Saying 'I love your accent!'
Before I moved to the USA, I never imagined that my London accent made me sound intelligent. At first the compliments were nice, but then a New York mum asked me to teach her two-year-old how to talk like me. A bit too much, I thought.

2 ________________
In America, people in shops say things like 'Ma'am, you have been an awesome customer today' just because I bought some toilet paper. I do not want that.

3 ________________
American waiters love to please, but sometimes they're too helpful. Overenthusiastic waiters take away your plate the second it's empty, even if no one else at the table has finished.

4 Insisting that turkey is tasty
There's a good reason why Brits only eat this bird at Christmas. Turkey meat is dry and tasteless. But Americans put it in everything – burgers, meatballs, lasagna – everything!

5 ________________
We get it, you're proud to be an American. We Brits like our country too, but to your average Brit, hanging a giant flag from your house is a little bit creepy.

6 ________________
Having to remove 'u's from words like 'colour' and change 're' to 'er' in words like 'theatre' is a headache. And Americans, please note: saying 'erb' instead of 'herb' and pronouncing 'fillet' as 'fillay' (without the 't') is not clever or sophisticated. You are not French.

Search

6 Things Brits Do That Drive Americans Crazy

By Maria Roth

We Americans love Brits. They're so charming and smart! But there are some things about them that we don't quite understand.

1 ________________

When strangers in stores and people on the street make eye contact, nod, or say 'Hi!' it's OK to smile and say hello back. We won't bite!

2 Overcooking vegetables

The authentic British way to prepare vegetables is to put them in boiling water for a fortnight. We Americans think this is weird and unpleasant.

3 ________________

Oh, we fat Americans with our big cars and flags! Too many Brits are convinced that this inaccurate picture of us is true, and we are not amused.

4 ________________

It seems that some Brits would rather not leave a 15 to 20 per cent tip for their waitress. They may not realize that waiters in the US are paid very low wages and depend on tips to survive.

5 ________________

We get it, in British English 'trousers' means pants and 'pants' are really underwear. And the letter z is 'zee' to Americans, but 'zed' to Brits. We Americans just have a different way of speaking and writing. It doesn't mean we're stupid, and I promise we're not trying to offend you.

6 Not wanting to 'share'

Brits are famous for being reserved – they never complain or discuss their problems. But that's not the way we do things here. We're more open with our friends, and even with strangers, and when people don't share we find it strange.

Adapted from www.bbcamercia.com

c Read the articles again. Find words which mean:

Text 1

1 ________ *noun* something people say to express admiration e.g. *He paid me a ~ and said I looked lovely.*
2 ________ *adj* (esp. NAmE) fantastic, great
3 ________ *noun* a bird similar to a very large chicken
4 ________ *verb* (informal) understand
5 ________ *adj* (informal) causing you to feel nervous and frightened

Text 2

6 ________ *verb* move your head up and down, e.g. to say yes or to say hello
7 ________ *noun* two weeks
8 ________ *adj* very strange
9 ________ *adj* not correct
10 ________ *verb* would prefer

d 5 32 Listen and check.

e Do you find any of these things about Americans or the British annoying? Are there any customs in your country that might drive foreigners crazy?

7 5 33 **SONG** *Living in America* ♫

G revision of verb forms
V exams
P revision of sounds

What's the hardest exam you've ever done?

Probably my driving test!

10B Exam time

1 VOCABULARY exams

a Look at the pictures of people doing exams. Which person is…?

1 a candidate doing an oral exam
2 a candidate taking a written exam
3 a candidate cheating in an exam
4 an invigilator
5 an examiner

b Complete the statements about exams with a word or phrase from the box.

cram fail marks
multiple-choice papers take

1 I never get nervous when I ____________ an exam.
2 I usually get good ____________ in exams if I revise enough for them.
3 I find reading past ____________ is a good way to revise for an exam.
4 I find ____________ questions very easy because you can always guess one of the options.
5 It's a bad idea to stay up late and ____________ the night before an exam.
6 If you ____________ your driving test, you have to wait three months before you can retake it.

Verbs + *exam*
We often use the verb *take* with *exam*, e.g. *to take an exam*, but we can also say *do an exam* or *sit an exam*.

c 5 34 Listen and under<u>line</u> the stressed syllable.

can|di|date e|xam e|xa|mi|ner
in|vi|gi|la|tor mul|ti|ple-choice o|ral

d Discuss the statements in **b** with a partner. Which are true for you? Why (not)?

2 PRONUNCIATION
revision of sounds

a Which word has a different sound? Say the three words aloud, and then circle the one you think is different.

1	revises	prepares	gives
2	failed	learned	cheated
3	marks	grant	cram
4	work	oral	report
5	wrong	diploma	college
6	thesis	degree	science
7	school	good	childhood
8	written	idea	result
9	guess	test	before

b 5 35 Listen and check

3 LISTENING & SPEAKING

a Tell a partner about the last time you took an exam or test. How hard was it? Did you pass or fail? Why?

b Read about exams in the UK. Do you have similar exams in your country?

Article Talk | Read Edit View history

Exams in the UK

Eleven-plus exam: An exam taken in some parts of the UK at the end of primary school (age 11). The results are used to decide what sort of secondary school a child can attend.

GCSEs: Exams in different subjects taken at secondary school (approximately age 16). Before 1988, students did similar exams called O-levels.

A-levels: Final school exams (approximately age 18). You need good results in A-levels to attend university.

c 5 36 Listen to four people talk about their experiences with exams or tests. Which speakers...?

- mention an exam or test that they failed
- used to find exams stressful

d Listen again. Choose a, b, or c.

Tip: Multiple-choice listening
- Remember to read the questions carefully before you listen.
- Remember to make sure that all of the information is correct in the option you choose. Don't choose it just because it contains a word or phrase that you heard in the recording.

1 Mark had problems with his history O-level because...
 a he didn't have time to finish the questions.
 b he hadn't prepared the right questions.
 c he had drunk too much coffee the night before.

2 Sophie failed her driving test the first time because...
 a she didn't follow the examiner's instructions.
 b she didn't realize that what the examiner asked her to do was a trick.
 c she stopped somewhere where it wasn't safe.

3 When Kate had an exam she...
 a prepared with other students the day before.
 b stayed up late studying the night before.
 c made sure she slept well the night before.

4 Paul did badly in his GCSE chemistry...
 a because he'd done very little work for it.
 b because his memory failed.
 c although he thought he'd done well.

e Ask and answer the questions with a partner.

- What's the hardest exam you've ever taken?
- Have you ever done an exam where everything went wrong?
- How do you usually prepare for a big exam?
- Do exams make you feel stressed? If so, what do you do about it?

4 READING

a Is there a university entrance exam in your country? How difficult is it considered?

b Read the article about the *gaokao* (/gaʊ kaʊ/), China's national university entrance exam. How does it compare with university entrance exams in your country?

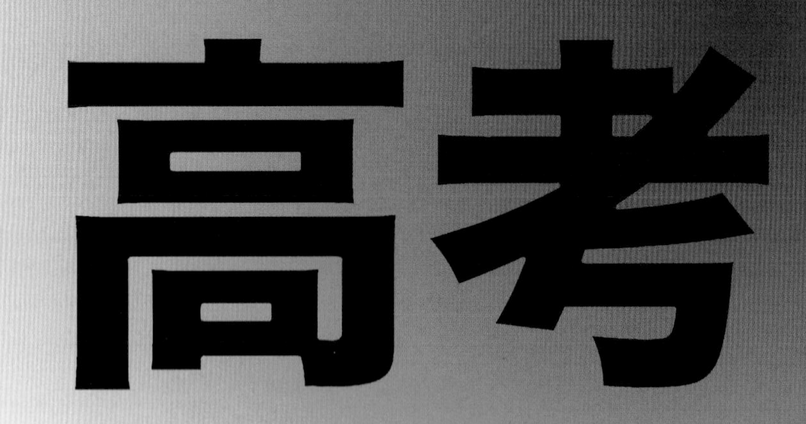

News | Sport | Comment | Culture | Business | Money | Life & style | Travel | Environment | Tech | TV | Video

A nation prepares for the dreaded *gaokao*

SHANGHAI, 5 June – Tomorrow cities throughout China [1] will close roads near schools, prohibit the hooting of car horns, and even change some aeroplane flight paths, so that nine million students can concentrate on the *gaokao*, the three-day-long national university entrance exam.

University places are scarce in China, and most students [2] are not going to have a chance if they do not do well on the *gaokao*, a name which means 'high exam' in Mandarin Chinese. The stakes are very high indeed: a place in a top university will almost always lead to a high-paid job after graduation. For millions of Chinese, the exam is an important chance to improve their lives, and because most Chinese families [3] have only one child, the pressure on candidates is intense.

We spoke to students who [4] hadn't been out with their friends for many months, and who [5] were studying all the time that they weren't sleeping. And while some cram, others cheat. Each year, candidates [6] are caught with high-tech devices such as wireless earphones, as well as pens and watches with tiny scanners. James Bond would be proud.

Teachers' lives are difficult, too. One *gaokao* tutor [7] explained her schedule: morning exercises start at 6.10 a.m.; evening classes end at 10.00 p.m.; students get only one day off a month – and teachers must spend that day marking practice exams.

To prepare for the exam, students memorize past exam papers and try to guess what questions [8] will be asked this year. All candidates answer questions in Chinese, Maths, and English, then choose two additional subjects: History, Geography, Physics, Biology, Chemistry, or Political Ideology. Some of the unusual essay questions that [9] have appeared on past papers include:

- 'An Englishman dreams of living in Western China in another era. Write a story based on this.'
- 'Why chase mice when there are fish to eat?'
- 'Talk about water.'
- 'Why do we want to return to our childhood?'

The exam [10] has been criticized for testing endurance rather than intelligence. Small reforms [11] were made to the exam a few years ago, but little has changed overall. More and more Chinese students [12] have been moving overseas for university or even secondary school, just to avoid the *gaokao*. The number of candidates who sit the exam has fallen dramatically in recent years, from 10.2 million in 2009 to nine million this year.

However, at the same time, the *gaokao* [13] is beginning to be more widely recognized abroad. The University of Sydney has said it will accept *gaokao* scores from Chinese students in place of its own entrance exam. China may not need to reform the *gaokao* after all – it will reform the rest of us.

Adapted from the Financial Times

c Read the article again. Mark the statements **T** (true) or **F** (false).

> **Tip: True / False reading**
> - Quickly read the text for the main ideas, then read the statements carefully.
> - Re-read the text carefully and look for information that shows whether each statement is true or false.

1 During the *gaokao* nobody is allowed to drive in cities where the exam is being held.
2 Unless you do well in the *gaokao*, you probably won't get a place at university.
3 The exam gives young people the opportunity to do better in life.
4 Students preparing for the exam still have time for a social life.
5 Students are always finding different ways to cheat.
6 The *gaokao* was mentioned in a recent James Bond film.
7 *Gaokao* tutors only have one day a month when they don't have to work.
8 Science subjects are optional in the *gaokao*.
9 Some people don't like the exam because they don't think it shows how intelligent you are.
10 More Chinese students are taking the *gaokao* now than ever before.

d What do you think of the *gaokao*? What do you think is the best way to decide whether someone should get a place at university or not?

5 GRAMMAR revision of verb forms

a Look at the numbered verbs in the text and match them with the tenses and forms below.

- ☐ present simple (*I make…*)
- ☐ present continuous (*I'm making…*)
- ☐ present simple passive (*It is made…*)
- ☐ past simple (*I made…*)
- ☐ past continuous (*I was making…*)
- ☐ past simple passive (*It was made…*)
- ☐ future simple (*I will make…*)
- ☐ future with *going to* (*I'm going to make…*)
- ☐ future simple passive (*It will be made…*)
- ☐ present perfect simple (*I've made…*)
- ☐ present perfect continuous (*I've been making…*)
- ☐ present perfect passive (*It's been made…*)
- ☐ past perfect simple (*I had made…*)

b ➤ **p.151 Grammar Bank 10B.** Practise the main verb forms in English.

6 LISTENING & SPEAKING

a You're going to hear an examiner giving advice for doing well in oral exams. Before you listen, look at the tips below. With a partner, try to guess the missing words (but don't write them in yet).

> **Tip: Filling in missing information**
> - Read the text first so you understand the topic, and to help you predict what the missing information is.
> - You may need to write more than one word in each space.
> - Try to spell the words correctly.

Exam tips: doing well in oral exams

1 *Arrive at the examination centre at least* ________________ *before the exam begins.*
2 *Make* ________________ *contact with the examiners and* ________________.
3 *Try to look* ________________ *in what the other candidate is saying.*
4 *Give your partner the opportunity to* ________________ *too. Ask for your partner's* ________________ *after you've given your own.*
5 *If you can't think of a word, don't 'freeze' and say* ________________. ________________ *(use other words).*
6 *Don't use* ________________ *speeches.*

b **5 37** Listen and check. Complete the tips.

c Now try a speaking exam task with a partner. ➤ **Communication** *An exam task p.112.*

7 WRITING

➤ **p.121 Writing** *An exam task.*

9&10 Revise and Check

GRAMMAR

a Circle a, b, or c.

1 They asked us how long ______.
   a did we live there b we'd lived there
   c had we lived there
2 She ______ she couldn't remember my name.
   a said b told c said me
3 He asked whether ______ British or American.
   a I was b was I c I am
4 We told them ______ make so much noise, but they didn't turn the music down.
   a not to b don't c that they didn't
5 I said that I ______ be late.
   a wouldn't to b won't c wouldn't

b Complete the sentences with the correct form of the verb in brackets.

1 He wouldn't have passed the exam if he ______ so hard. (not study)
2 If we'd had a smaller wedding, we ______ less money. (spend)
3 He ______ go to university if he'd had better exam results. (be able to)
4 I ______ much last weekend. (not do)
5 ______ you ______ your grandparents recently? (visit)
6 **A** I went on holiday to Turkey last month.
   B ______ you ______ there before? (be)
7 She ______ too hard lately – she looks exhausted. (work)
8 We got to the reception late and the speeches ______. (finish)
9 Work on the new bridge ______ by the end of next year. (complete)
10 I ran to the bank but it ______ already ______. (close)
11 Over 10 million tablets ______ since 2005. (sell)
12 Why ______ you ______ biscuits? It's nearly lunchtime. (eat)
13 Alex ______ us his holiday photos when the boss came in! (show)
14 It's only 9.00 but she ______ already ______ at work for two hours. (be)
15 The film ______ in Japan in the 1960s. (make)

VOCABULARY

a Complete the words.

1 My **mem**______ is terrible.
2 He finds it hard to **mem**______ new vocabulary.
3 Her **mem**______ were published last year.
4 It was a very **mem**______ wedding.
5 There's a **mem**______ to the Unknown Soldier.

b Write words for the definitions.

1 a woman on her wedding day ______
2 a formal talk that a person gives to an audience ______
3 a male friend or relative who helps the groom ______ ______
4 a formal social occasion to celebrate something ______
5 a party that a man has with his male friends just before he gets married ______ ______

c Write *Br* or *Am*, and give the British or American alternative.

1 ☐	movie theater	______	6 ☐	holiday	______
2 ☐	biscuit	______	7 ☐	apartment	______
3 ☐	sneakers	______	8 ☐	lift	______
4 ☐	garbage	______	9 ☐	pavement	______
5 ☐	toilet	______	10 ☐	gas	______

d Complete the words.

1 Most of my friends passed the exam, but I **f**______.
2 The questions were all **m**______-choice.
3 You lose **m**______ if you make spelling mistakes.
4 I passed my driving **t**______ the first time I took it.
5 He **ch**______ in the exam, so they gave him 0%.

PRONUNCIATION

a Circle the word with a different sound.

1 e	guest	forget	memory	exam
2 æ	marry	pageboy	tap	cram
3 eɪ	pass	bridesmaid	holiday	pavement
4 /ɪd/	reported	failed	decided	waited
5 z	memoirs	trainers	lifts	papers

b Underline the stressed syllable.

1 me|mo|rize
2 un|for|get|ta|ble
3 ce|re|mo|ny
4 bride|groom
5 can|di|date

CAN YOU UNDERSTAND THIS TEXT?

a Read the article once. If you were going to study in the US, which considerations would be most important to you?

How overseas students can choose a US university

Selecting a university thousands of miles away, perhaps without the opportunity to visit beforehand, will worry even those overseas students most enthusiastic about an American education. Fortunately, thanks to the internet, you can get a good feel for an institution without multiple transatlantic flights. Many universities provide online tours of their campuses and give you a clear description of student life and the services available to international students. Investigate each university and be honest about where you might [1]______ best.

Academic considerations

What is it you really want to study? If you have specific requirements, will the university you are looking at be able to satisfy [2]______ needs?

If you plan on studying for a professional qualification in the US, [3]______ the UK professional organization if your qualification will be accepted when you get home. Usually there aren't any problems, but you [4]______ be required to take additional coursework or sit an examination, and it is best to know this in advance.

City or country?

Do you prefer an urban or rural setting? While it may be exciting to think of yourself in a large, glamorous city, the cost of living is often much higher – will your [5]______ be big enough? Also bear in mind that students in cities may feel more socially isolated than those who choose a rural or suburban university.

Conversely, a college that is miles away from any city might have more campus-based activities, but you may find it frustrating if you can't escape. Relying exclusively on your university for socializing can be too restrictive.

Beach or snow?

The United States is geographically diverse. Before choosing a university, it is important for you to consider what type of climate suits you best. You may have [6]______ your Easter break in Florida, but are you prepared for the summer heat or lack of a winter? You may think you like snow, but are you prepared to deal with temperatures of –40 degrees while studying in Buffalo, New York?

Small or large?

If you attend a very small college, will you get tired of seeing the same 500 people every week? Or will you feel lost if you are one of 60,000 at a large public university? [7]______ many enjoy being the only 'foreigner', [8]______ find comfort in having a well-run place to go when they're homesick or confused and need to share their problems.

Adapted from uniintheusa.com

b Read the article again and choose the best words to fill the gaps.

1	a set up	b fit in	c put up
2	a your	b their	c its
3	a tell	b say	c ask
4	a may	b will	c must
5	a studies	b budget	c qualifications
6	a hated	b experienced	c enjoyed
7	a Although	b But	c Because
8	a they	b others	c people

VIDEO CAN YOU UNDERSTAND THESE PEOPLE?

5 38 **In the street** Watch or listen to five people and answer the questions.

Yasuko

Robin

Sean

Mairi

Pranjal

1 Yasuko is better at remembering ______.
 a names than faces b people than dogs
 c dogs than people

2 Robin's wedding took place ______.
 a in a registry office b a short time after she got engaged
 c just three weeks ago

3 Sean ______.
 a is positive about the opportunity to make money in the US
 b thinks some music considered American actually came from other places
 c thinks that American music dominates too much worldwide

4 One of the reasons Mairi doesn't go to American fast food restaurants is because ______.
 a she doesn't like the atmosphere
 b she thinks they are not good value for money
 c there aren't any in her neighbourhood

5 Pranjal has sometimes ______.
 a expected to get better results in exams
 b done really badly in exams
 c not prepared for an exam

CAN YOU SAY THIS IN ENGLISH?

Do the tasks with a partner. Tick (✓) the box if you can do them.

Can you...?

1 ☐ describe a wedding you've been to, or talk about the kind of wedding you'd like to have
2 ☐ talk about the influence of American culture in your country, and say what you think about it
3 ☐ talk about an exam you took that didn't go well
4 ☐ ask and answer these questions:

- Do you think you have a good memory? What things do you find it easy / hard to remember?
- Do / Did you find exams stressful at school? How do / did you prepare for them?

Short films A wedding planner
Watch and enjoy a film on iTutor.

1A HOW WAS IT NAMED?
Student B

f Read about how the iMac was named. Find answers to the questions below.

1. Who named the product?
2. What instructions did the company's founder give for choosing a name?
3. What does the name mean?
4. Were any other names considered?

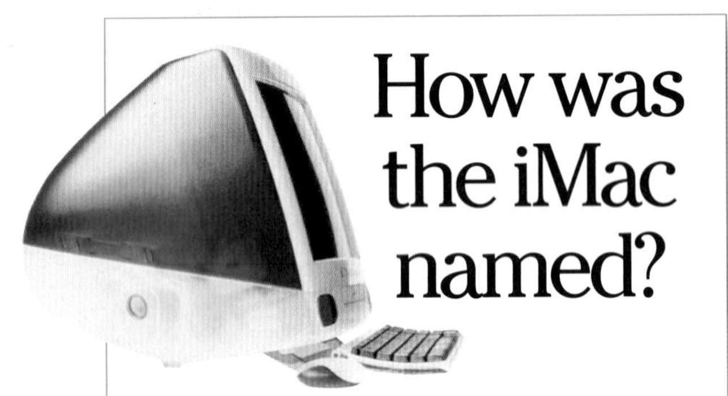

How was the iMac named?

First produced in 1998, the bright turquoise iMac computer was a huge success for Apple and started a range of other 'i' products like the iPod, the iPad, and the iPhone. But who put the 'i' in iMac?

The answer is Ken Segall, an advertising executive in New York City. He had known Steve Jobs, the founder of Apple, for many years before he named the iMac. There was already a range of Macintosh computers, so Jobs asked Segall for a new name that had 'Mac' or 'Macintosh' in it. He also wanted the name to show people that they could go online more easily with the new computer.

Segall and his team thought of dozens of names before they chose 'iMac'. The 'i' was for 'internet', but it could also mean 'individual' or 'imagination'. A few days after coming up with the name, Segall went to Jobs and suggested it to him, together with four other names. Unfortunately, Jobs hated all of them. He preferred a name that he had thought of on his own: 'MacMan'.

A week later, Segall suggested more names to Jobs, including 'iMac' again. 'Well,' said Jobs, 'I don't hate it this week.' The rest is history.

g Listen to **A** tell you about how the Kindle was named.

h Now tell **A** about how the iMac was named, using questions 1–4 to help you.

1B COLOUR AND PERSONALITY

a Read about the colours you have chosen in first and second place, and in seventh and eighth place. Underline the things that apply to you.

Colour personality test

RED: If you put red in 1st or 2nd place, you are energetic and assertive – you say what you think, and people listen to you. However, you are also impulsive, and sometimes make decisions without thinking enough. If you put red in 7th or 8th place, you have lost some of your enthusiasm for life.

YELLOW: If you put yellow in 1st or 2nd place, you are hard-working and ambitious. You are often good at business, and are optimistic about the future. If you put yellow in 7th or 8th place, you may feel a bit isolated at the moment. You need to make an effort to meet new people.

BLUE: If you put blue in 1st or 2nd place, you are very loyal and reliable. You never panic, and are in control of your life. You are also sensitive, however, and your feelings can be easily hurt. If you put blue in 7th or 8th place, you may feel unsatisfied with your life, and want to make changes.

GREEN: If you put green in 1st or 2nd place, you are persistent, and don't give up easily. You want to be recognized, and you probably don't like change. However, you can also be selfish and quite possessive. If you put green in 7th or 8th place, you are probably quite stubborn, and can be very critical of other people.

PURPLE: If you put purple in 1st or 2nd place, you are a bit immature, and can be moody. You dream of the perfect relationship or the perfect job. If you put purple in 7th or 8th place, you are mature and responsible.

BLACK: If you put black in 1st or 2nd place, which is unusual, you are rebellious, and don't accept your current situation. If you put black in 7th or 8th place, you feel in control of your life, and are calm and self-confident.

BROWN: If you put brown in 1st or 2nd place, you are restless and insecure. You worry about your health, and may be a bit of a hypochondriac. Security is very important to you. If you put brown in 7th or 8th place, it means you don't look after yourself enough, and may have health problems.

GREY: If you put grey in 1st or 2nd place, you are very independent and afraid of commitment. You don't like doing things in groups, and prefer watching to doing. If you put grey in 7th or 8th place, you are sociable and ambitious.

Adapted from http://www.colorquiz.com

b Tell your partner about the results. What do you agree with? What don't you agree with?

Talking about findings and results

According to the personality test, I'm...
It says that I'm...
That's quite accurate. / That's definitely me.
That's not me. / That isn't accurate at all.

2A CAROLINE'S HOLIDAY PLANS Student A

a Ask and answer questions with **B** to complete Caroline's holiday itinerary. Use the information in the calendar and the correct form of the verb, present simple or present continuous.

A What time does she leave London?

B At five past eleven in the morning. What time does she arrive in Palma?

A At two forty in the afternoon.

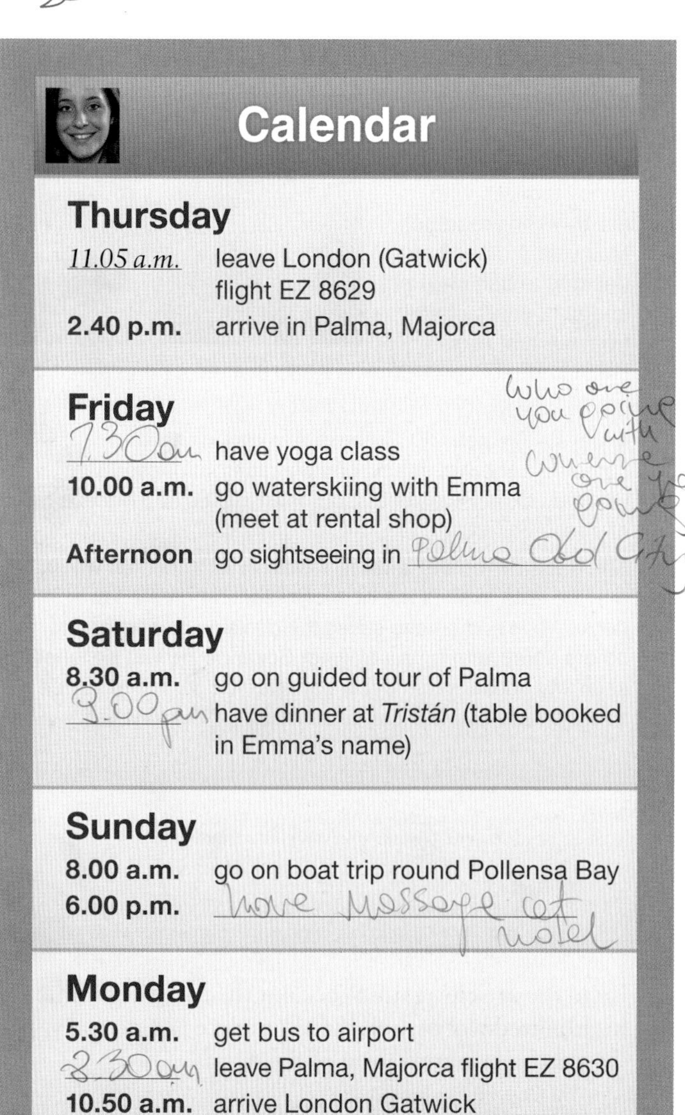

Calendar

Thursday

11.05 a.m.	leave London (Gatwick) flight EZ 8629
2.40 p.m.	arrive in Palma, Majorca

Friday

7.30am	have yoga class
10.00 a.m.	go waterskiing with Emma (meet at rental shop)
Afternoon	go sightseeing in Palma Old City

who are you going with
where are you going

Saturday

8.30 a.m.	go on guided tour of Palma
8.00pm	have dinner at *Tristán* (table booked in Emma's name)

Sunday

8.00 a.m.	go on boat trip round Pollensa Bay
6.00 p.m.	have massage at hotel

Monday

5.30 a.m.	get bus to airport
8.30am	leave Palma, Majorca flight EZ 8630
10.50 a.m.	arrive London Gatwick

b Check your answers by comparing your calendars.

3A NEWS STORIES Student B

c Read *Babies at the movies*. Find answers to the questions below.

1 What new idea is being tried? Where?
2 What problem is this idea meant to solve?
3 Who will be affected by it?
4 What good points about this idea are mentioned?
5 What problems with the idea are mentioned?

Home | News | Sport | TV&Showbiz | Health | Science | Travel | Money

Babies at the movies

In family-friendly Brooklyn, New York, where going for a walk involves pavements full of mothers pushing buggies and toddlers on scooters, cinemas have now also become a part of baby culture.

Three cinemas in the area have agreed to put on early afternoon sessions so that parents can watch the latest films with their young children and avoid calling the babysitter.

The cinemas are open to anyone at these times, though the experience may not be suitable for the average film fan. To avoid waking up sleeping babies, the sound of the films is softer than usual. Films with loud, surprising noises, such as gunshots, are usually not shown.

One mother, Rhonda Walsh, 32, described her visit with her four-month-old daughter, Madeleine. 'There was a chorus of crying,' she remembered.

But in spite of the screaming babies, she managed to enjoy the experience. 'Of course I don't remember what the movie was,' she added.

Adapted from the Daily Mail

Glossary

1 __________ /ˈskuːtəz/ *noun* child's toys with two wheels that you stand on and move by pushing one foot against the ground
2 __________ /ˈskriːmɪŋ/ *verb* crying loudly in a high voice
3 __________ /ˈbʌgiz/ *noun* chairs on wheels that you use for pushing a baby or young child in
4 __________ /ˈgʌnʃɒts/ *noun* sounds of a gun being fired

d Read the article again. Work out the meaning of the highlighted words, and then complete the glossary. Check the pronunciation of the words.

e Work in groups with **A** and **C**. Tell each other your stories. Try to use the words from the glossary and explain them to **A** and **C** if necessary.

Communication

2A CAROLINE'S HOLIDAY PLANS Student B

a Ask and answer questions with **A** to complete Caroline's holiday itinerary. Use the information in the calendar and the correct form of the verb, present simple or present continuous.

A What time does she leave London?

B At five past eleven in the morning. What time does she arrive in Palma?

A At two forty in the afternoon.

Calendar

Thursday

11.05 a.m.	leave London (Gatwick) flight EZ 8629
2.40 p.m.	arrive in Palma, Majorca

Friday

7.30 a.m.	have yoga class
10.00 a.m.	go water skiing with ______________ (meet at rental shop)
Afternoon	go sightseeing in Palma Old City

Saturday

8.30 a.m.	______________
9.00 p.m.	have dinner at *Tristán* (table booked in Emma's name)

Sunday

8.00 a.m.	______________
6.00 p.m.	have massage at hotel spa

Monday

________	get bus to airport
8.30 a.m.	leave Palma, Majorca flight EZ 8630
________	arrive London Gatwick

b Check your answers by comparing your calendars.

3A NEWS STORIES Student C

c Read *Airline's new child rules cause controversy*. Find answers to the questions below.

1 What new idea is being tried? Where?
2 What problem is this idea meant to solve?
3 Who will be affected by it?
4 What good points about this idea are mentioned?
5 What problems with the idea are mentioned?

Home | News | Sport | TV&Showbiz | Health | Science | Travel | Money

Airline's new child rules cause controversy

It is a decision that adult air passengers will love – but it could annoy families who are travelling together. Malaysia Airlines has decided to ban children under 12 years of age from the first class cabin and the top deck of its A380 planes, so that adult travellers can relax without hearing crying and screaming.

Malaysia Airlines CEO Tengku Azmil said that the company received 'many' complaints from passengers who buy expensive tickets, but then can't sleep because of crying children.

The decision means families travelling with children will only be able to sit in the economy section on the lower deck. While some have called the decision discriminatory, others agree with it. Travel writer Suzanne Rowan Kelleher said: 'My guess is that many parents would opt for kid-free zones on planes when they're travelling without their children.'

Adapted from the Daily Mail

Glossary
1 __________ /'skriːmɪŋ/ *verb* crying loudly in a high voice
2 __________ /dɪ'skrɪmɪnətəri/ *adj* unfair; in a way that treats one group of people worse than others
3 __________ /dek/ *noun* one of the floors of a ship, bus, or plane
4 __________ /bæn/ *verb* say officially that something is not allowed

d Read the article again. Work out the meaning of the highlighted words, and then complete the glossary. Check the pronunciation of the words.

e Work in groups with **A** and **B**. Tell each other your stories. Try to use the words from the glossary and explain them to **A** and **B** if necessary.

3B SPOT THE DIFFERENCES Student A

Describe the photo to your partner. Your partner has a very similar photo. Find ten differences between the photos.

A *In my photo, there's a... in the foreground.*

B *There isn't one in my photo.*

7B GOING OUT OR STAYING IN? Student A

Read about the situation below and talk about it with your partner. Try to agree on a plan for Saturday evening at the end of the conversation.

You and a friend are planning to meet on Saturday evening, but you haven't decided what to do. You are quite tired as you have had a hard week. **You would like to stay at home and watch a DVD together.**
Plan exactly how you want to spend the evening (which DVD, what you would have to eat and drink, whose house you would go to, etc.)
B is your friend. Try to convince him / her to agree with your plan. Give reasons.

Making suggestions

Why don't we...?	*Let's...*
I think we should...	*Maybe we could....*

PRACTICAL ENGLISH 3 REPORTING A MISSING PERSON Student A

a You are going to report a missing person. Read your role and decide on the details.

You are sharing a flat in London with a friend from your country. The address is 23 Barrow Street, London W2 7EG.
- *Decide which of your friends it is.*

You saw each other in the morning.
- *Decide what time and where.*

You had arranged to have dinner together at home.
You got home at 5 o'clock, but it is now 10.00 p.m. and he / she hasn't turned up, and isn't answering his / her phone.
You are worried and go to the police.
- *Decide what your friend's normal routine is.*

b **B** is a police officer. He / She will ask you questions about your friend, and make a report. **B** will start.

c Swap roles. You are now a police officer. **B** is going to report a missing person. First, think what questions you need to ask.

MISSING PERSON INFORMATION

Reported by
Name
Address
Phone

Missing person
Name
Address
Description
(age and appearance)
Last seen
Wearing
Expected to see at for
Plans for rest of day
Normal routine

d Interview **B** and fill in the form. Finally, tell **B** not to worry and that you are sure the person will turn up soon. You start:

Come in and take a seat. Now, you want to report a missing person, is that right?

e Together decide what happened to your friends!

Communication

3B SPOT THE DIFFERENCES Student B

Describe the photo to your partner. Your partner has a very similar photo. Find ten differences between the photos.

A In my photo, there's a... in the foreground.

B There isn't one in my photo.

7B GOING OUT OR STAYING IN? Student B

Read about the situation below and talk about it with your partner. Try to agree on a plan for Saturday evening at the end of the conversation.

You and a friend are planning to meet on Saturday evening, but you haven't decided what to do. You haven't been out for ages. **You would like to go out somewhere, e.g. to a show or a restaurant.**
Plan exactly how you want to spend the evening (where you would like to go and when) .
A is your friend. Try to convince him / her to agree with your plan. Give reasons.

Making suggestions

Why don't we...?	*Let's...*
I think we should...	*Maybe we could....*

PRACTICAL ENGLISH 3 REPORTING A MISSING PERSON Student B

a You are a police officer. **A** is going to report a missing person. First, think what questions you need to ask.

MISSING PERSON INFORMATION

Reported by Name
Address
Phone

Missing person
Name
Address
Description (age and appearance)
Last seen
Wearing
Expected to see at ______ for ______
Plans for rest of day
Normal routine

b Interview **A** and fill in the form. Finally, tell **A** not to worry and that you are sure the person will turn up soon. You start:

Come in and take a seat. Now, you want to report a missing person, is that right?

c Swap roles. Now you are going to report a missing person. Read your role and decide on the details.

You are sharing a flat in London with a friend from your country. The address is 15 Vine Road, London EC1 9AJ.
- *Decide which of your friends it is.*

You saw each other at lunchtime.
- *Decide what time and where.*

You had arranged to go to the cinema together.
The film started at 7.00 but your friend didn't turn up.
It is now 11.00 p.m., and he / she isn't answering his / her phone. You are worried and go to the police.
- *Decide what your friend's normal routine is.*

d **A** is a police officer. He / She will ask you questions about your friend, and make a report. **A** will start.

e Together decide what happened to your friends!

6A WHAT'S IT CALLED? Student A

a You are a customer at a DIY store. You want to buy the things below, but you don't know the word. **B** is a shop assistant. Have a conversation with **B**, explaining what you want. He / She will tell you the names of the things you want to buy and where to find them. **B** will start.

______ ______ ______

Paraphrasing
Sorry, but **I can't remember the word.**
I'm looking for **a thing that you use for** + verb + *ing*
It's a kind of... It looks like...

b Now you are the shop assistant. Listen to **B** explaining what he / she wants to buy. Ask questions and decide which of the things below they are. Tell **B** what they are called (and spell the words if necessary), and where to find them. You start: *Can I help you?*

PRACTICAL ENGLISH 4
RENTING A ROOM Student A

a You have a two-bedroom flat and you want to share it with someone. **B** would like to rent the other room. He / She is coming to see you. First, look at your house rules and decide if there is anything you'd like to add.

House rules
- No smoking
- Share kitchen – keep food on 2nd shelf of fridge
- Don't use washing machine or dryer after 10.00 p.m.
- Make sure to lock door (two keys) when going out
- ______

b Greet **B** and tell him / her about the house rules, and answer any questions. You start.

Hi, come in. Nice to meet you... If you don't mind, I'm going to start by telling you about the house rules...

c Decide whether you would like to rent the room to **B**.

d Swap roles. You are looking for a room to rent. **B** has a room in his / her flat. You are going to meet **B**. **B** will tell you about the house rules. You also have some questions to ask. Decide if there is anything you'd like to add.

- Wi-fi?
- OK if you practise your electric guitar?
- What's public transport like?
- ______?

e Go to meet **B** and talk about the flat. **B** will start.

f Decide if you want to rent the room.

6A WHAT'S IT CALLED? Student B

a You are a shop assistant at a DIY store. Listen to **A** explaining what he / she wants to buy. Ask questions, and decide which of the things below they are. Tell **A** what they are called (and spell the words if necessary), and where to find them. You start: *Can I help you?*

broom /bruːm/ | mop /mɒp/ | drawing pins /ˈdrɔːɪŋ pɪnz/

velcro /ˈvelkrəʊ/ | saw /sɔː/ | drill /drɪl/

b Now you are a customer. You want to buy the things below, but you don't know the word. **A** is a shop assistant. Have a conversation with **A**, explaining what you want. He / She will tell you the names of the things you want to buy and where to find them. **A** will start.

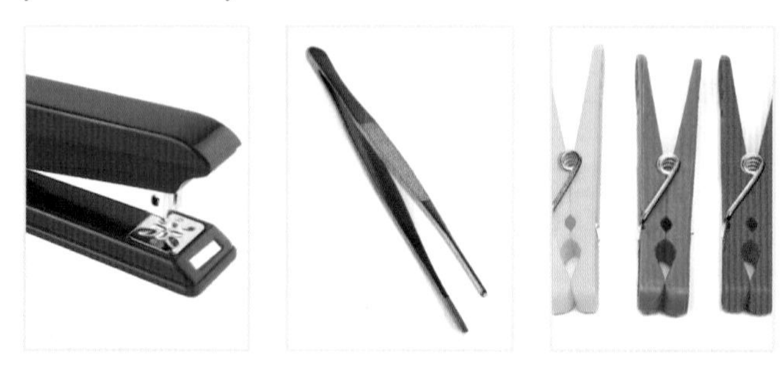

________ ________ ________

Paraphrasing
Sorry, but **I can't remember the word.**
I'm looking for **a thing that you use for** + verb + *ing*
It's a kind of... It looks like...

PRACTICAL ENGLISH 4
RENTING A ROOM Student B

a You are looking for a room to rent. **A** has a room in his / her flat. You are going to meet **A**. **A** will tell you about the house rules. You also have some questions to ask. Decide if there is anything you'd like to add.

- You have a cat. OK to bring it?
- You have a motorbike. Where can you park it?
- You have to leave for class / work very early. OK to have a shower about 6.30 every morning?
- ________________________?

b Go to meet **A** and talk about the flat. **A** will start.

c Decide if you want to rent the room.

d Swap roles. You have a two-bedroom flat and you want to share it with someone. **A** would like to rent the other room. He / She is coming to see you. First, look at your house rules and decide if there is anything you'd like to add.

House rules
- No smoking
- No pets
- Share kitchen – use recycling bins, one for glass, one for paper, one for all other rubbish. Don't leave washing-up overnight.
- No showers after 10.00 p.m.
- ________________

e Greet **A** and tell him / her about the house rules, and answer any questions. You start.

Hi, come in. Nice to meet you... If you don't mind, I'm going to start by telling you about the house rules...

f Decide if you would like to rent the room to **A**.

8A HOT OR COLD? Student B

c Read the article on p.111 about a spa treatment and find answers to the questions below.

1 What's the treatment called?
2 Where does it come from?
3 What is it supposed to be good for?
4 In what sort of room do you have the treatment?
5 What is the temperature of the treatment?
6 How long does the treatment last?
7 Are there any safety precautions?
8 How did the journalist feel afterwards?

Big chill: the medical benefits of cryotherapy

I've come to a spa in Austria to experience temperatures more than 100 degrees below zero – and while wearing just shorts and a T-shirt.

The reason? Because experts say that spending a short time in an enormous freezer – or cryotherapy, as it's called – can help people with chronic pain or skin problems, and can even improve sporting performance.

Cryotherapy was invented in Japan and later perfected in Poland. It is also good for anyone suffering from stress, depression, or insomnia. This was the part that appealed to me most. Nearly 40 and a mother of three, I haven't slept well for the whole night since the birth of our first child nine years ago.

The treatment lasts only three minutes. (Any longer than eight minutes in the –110°C room and you'd be dead.) When the time comes to enter the chamber, I'm truly terrified. First I have to put on a pair of special trainers and socks, because if you fall over during cryotherapy, you'll stick to the floor. Then I open the door.

My first feeling is relief. It's deeply freezing – my arms sting immediately – but somehow it's bearable. It's not like any cold I've ever experienced before – nothing like a really cold day, for example. There's no wind, and the air is dry. It's easier to put up with than a cold shower.

After just two minutes 40 seconds, I'm finished. The next morning, I'm looking forward to doing it again. After three sessions, my skin looks really healthy and I feel energized. I also sleep deeply for the first time in years.

Glossary

1 __________ /ˈtʃeɪmbə(r)/ *noun* a small room used for a special purpose
2 __________ /pʊt ˈʌp wɪð/ *phrasal verb* accept something that is annoying or unpleasant
3 __________ /rɪˈliːf/ *noun* a feeling of happiness that you have when something unpleasant stops or doesn't happen
4 __________ /stɪŋ/ *verb* make someone feel a sudden, sharp pain, e.g. after being bitten by an insect
5 __________ /ˈbeərəbl/ *adj* that can be accepted or tolerated

Adapted from www.telegraph.co.uk

d Read the article again. Work out the meaning of the highlighted words and phrases, and then complete the glossary. Check the pronunciation of the words and phrases.

e Listen to **A**'s story and ask about any new words.

f Imagine you had the treatment in the article. Think about how you felt before, during, and afterwards. Describe the experience to **A** in your own words. Use your answers in **c** to help you. Explain the words in the glossary if necessary.

I was on holiday in Austria and I had a really amazing treatment called...

8B LOCAL HISTORY Student A

a On a piece of paper, write down the information below. Write the names or places only – not the questions. Don't try to translate place names or names of festivals, etc.

1 a famous person who's buried in or near your town
2 a building or monument in your town that you think is ugly and should be pulled down
3 something that used to be made or grown in or near your town, but isn't any more
4 a festival that is celebrated in your town
5 a typical dish which has been made and eaten by local people for many years

b Give your paper to **B**. **B** is a tourist in your town. He / She will ask you about the names and places. Give as much information as you can.

c Now you are a tourist in **B**'s town. Ask **B** about the names and places on his / her list.

A *What's the Ponte della Constituzione?*

B *It's a new bridge which was finished in 2008. It was designed by Calatrava...*

10A MORE FACTS ABOUT THE USA? Student A

a Read sentence 1 to **B**. Try to get the right rhythm. **B** will guess if it's true or false.

b Tell **B** if he / she is right, and explain why. Continue with sentence 2.

A *Alaska is larger than Spain, France, and Germany combined. True or false?*

B *True.*

A *That's right. Alaska has an area of 1,718,000 km² and Spain, France, and Germany have an area of 1,538,000 km².*

Are these statements true or false?

1 **Alaska is larger than Spain, France, and Germany combined** ***True.*** *Alaska has an area of 1,718,000 km² and Spain, France, and Germany have an area of 1,538,000 km².*

2 **50% of Americans speak another language at home.** ***False.*** *20% speak a language other than English at home, and about 8% don't speak any English at all.*

3 **American workers have less paid holiday than workers in other countries.** ***True.*** *Most Americans have 10–20 days of paid holiday a year.*

4 **The top holiday destination abroad for Americans is Cuba.** ***False.*** *Although Cuba is less than 200 km from the US, Americans are not allowed to travel there unless they get a licence.*

5 **No American has ever won the Nobel Peace Prize.** ***False.*** *Over 20 Americans have won the prize, including Martin Luther King, Jr. and Barack Obama.*

c Now listen to **B**'s sentences and say if you think they're true or false.

Communication

8B LOCAL HISTORY Student B

a On a piece of paper, write down the information below. Write the names or places only – not the questions. Don't try to translate place names or names of festivals, etc.

1. a building, bridge, or monument that has recently been built in or near your town
2. a famous person who was born in or near your town
3. an event that will be celebrated in your town soon
4. typical souvenirs that are made or sold in your town
5. a place in or near your town that is visited by a lot of tourists

b You are a tourist in **A**'s town. Look at **A**'s list of places and names, and ask **A** about them.

B Who's Juan Belmonte?

A He's a famous bullfighter who's buried in... He died...

c Give your paper to **A**. **A** is a tourist in your town. He / She will ask you about the names and places. Give as much information as you can.

10A MORE FACTS ABOUT THE USA? Student B

a Listen to **A** reading you some sentences about the USA. Say if you think they're true or false.

b Now read your sentence 6 to **A**. Try to get the right rhythm. **A** will guess if it's true or false.

c Tell **A** if he / she is right, and explain why. Continue with sentence 7.

B *The US has more national parks than Europe. True or false?*

A *I think that's false.*

B *That's right. The US has 59 national parks, and Europe has 366.*

Are these statements true or false?

6 The US has more national parks than Europe.
False. *The US has 59 national parks, and Europe has a total of 366, but the US parks cover 210,000 km^2, a larger area than all the European parks.*

7 Americans buy more Mexican salsa per year than ketchup.
True. *This has been true since 1992; $680 million was spent on salsa last year, compared to $420 million for ketchup.*

8 The USA has 5% of the world's population but 25% of the world's prisoners.
True. *The prison population has increased by 700% since 1971 to almost 2.2 million.*

9 The Declaration of Independence was signed in 1876.
False. *It was signed in 1776.*

10 Häagen-Dazs is an American company.
True. *It was started by the Mattus brothers in New York in 1976. They chose the name, which doesn't actually mean anything, because they thought it sounded Danish and they admired Denmark and its culture.*

10B EXAM TASK

Try a speaking exam task with a partner.

Read the situation and discuss it with your partner for 2–3 minutes. Try to use some of the tips you heard in **6b**.

Your teacher has asked you for ideas to improve your school. Look at the picture. Talk about what improvements you think would be most useful.

Writing

1 DESCRIBING A ROOM

a Read Ana's description of her room. Does it sound comfortable to you? Why (not)?

b Read the description again. Number the topics in the order she mentions them.

- [ ] The colour of the walls, door, etc.
- [ ] What furniture there is
- [ ] Where the room is
- [ ] Why she likes it

c Complete the gaps in the text with a preposition from the list. Some prepositions are used more than once.

above ~~at~~ from in inside on with

d You're going to write a description of your favourite room. **Plan** the description.

1. Say which room it is and where.
2. Describe the room, the furniture, and the decoration.
3. Say if the room has changed at all.
4. Explain why it is your favourite room.

e **Write** the description of the room, in **four** paragraphs. Use **Vocabulary Bank** *Adjective suffixes p.152* to help you with vocabulary.

f **Check** your description for mistakes (grammar, vocabulary, punctuation, and spelling).

◄ *p.11*

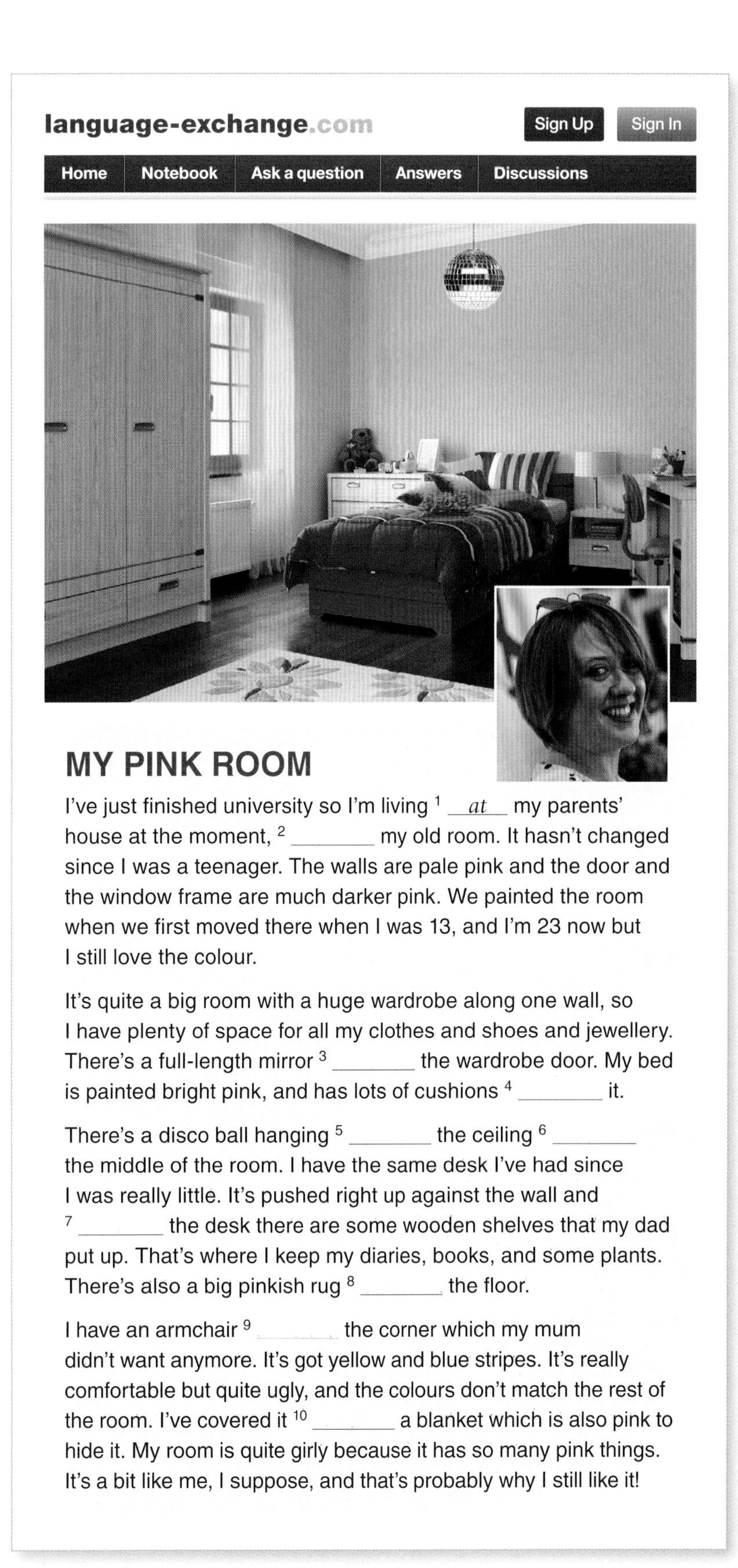

MY PINK ROOM

I've just finished university so I'm living [1] *at* my parents' house at the moment, [2] ________ my old room. It hasn't changed since I was a teenager. The walls are pale pink and the door and the window frame are much darker pink. We painted the room when we first moved there when I was 13, and I'm 23 now but I still love the colour.

It's quite a big room with a huge wardrobe along one wall, so I have plenty of space for all my clothes and shoes and jewellery. There's a full-length mirror [3] ________ the wardrobe door. My bed is painted bright pink, and has lots of cushions [4] ________ it.

There's a disco ball hanging [5] ________ the ceiling [6] ________ the middle of the room. I have the same desk I've had since I was really little. It's pushed right up against the wall and [7] ________ the desk there are some wooden shelves that my dad put up. That's where I keep my diaries, books, and some plants. There's also a big pinkish rug [8] ________ the floor.

I have an armchair [9] ________ the corner which my mum didn't want anymore. It's got yellow and blue stripes. It's really comfortable but quite ugly, and the colours don't match the rest of the room. I've covered it [10] ________ a blanket which is also pink to hide it. My room is quite girly because it has so many pink things. It's a bit like me, I suppose, and that's probably why I still like it!

Writing

2 HOLIDAY TWEETS

a Read the holiday tweets once. Who is on holiday now? Who is going to have a holiday soon? Who has just finished a holiday?

Caroline
Having the most amazing experience in Majorca! Met fantastic people but have put on 3 kilos in 4 days!

Mark
Another hard day: reading, having a nap by the pool, eating, and sunbathing. ☺

Haylee
48 hours until I'll be in Rio sipping a piña colada – or is it a caipirinha? Can't wait!

Michael
Oh no! 3 noisy children sitting behind me on my plane to LA. This is going to be the longest flight of my life.

Sheila
Just got to Uganda! So beautiful here! After 13 hours on bus, am ready for a shower!

Andrew
Packing bags. Holidays so stressful! Not sure I want to go!

Danielle
Got back an hour ago – plants dead and no milk in fridge. ☹
Send me back to the beach.

Sam
Making the most of last glorious morning in sun. Going home this p.m. and to work tomorrow.

b Read the tweets again. How does each person feel? What words and phrases or symbols do they use to express their feelings?

c Read the **Useful language** box. Then rewrite the last four tweets using full sentences.

Useful language: writing tweets

Because tweets are short messages and can only have a maximum of 140 characters (including letters, spaces, icons, and punctuation), people frequently leave out words in sentences, often pronouns and auxiliary verbs like *I'm*, *I've*, *it's*, and *there is / are*. This is acceptable in tweets and text messages but not in formal writing.

Having the most amazing experience = I'm having the most amazing experience

Another hard day = It's been another hard day

3 noisy children sitting behind me = There are three noisy children sitting behind me

d Imagine you're having a four-day holiday. **Write** a tweet for each of the situations below. Use the **Useful language** and **Vocabulary Bank** *Holidays p.153* to help you with vocabulary.

- the evening before your holiday
- the first morning of your holiday
- the second and third days
- the last evening of your holiday
- the day after your holiday is over

e **Check** your tweets to make sure they are not more than 140 characters.

◄ *p.17*

3 AN ARTICLE

a Look at the photos in the article from a photography magazine. Which of them do you like? How are they different from ordinary portraits of people?

b Read the article and write the headings in the correct place. (There are two headings you don't need to use.) Which tip do you think is the most useful? Have you ever used any of these tips yourself?

Don't make them pose
Try different angles
Move away from the centre
Take a close-up
Don't look at me!

c You are going to write three tips for how to take good holiday photos. With a partner, **plan** the content of each tip and think of three headings.

Use the **Useful language** and **Vocabulary Bank** *Photography p.155* to help you with vocabulary.

> **Useful language: tips and instructions**
>
> **Imperatives**
> ***Get*** *up high and look down on your subject.*
> ***Don't make*** *people pose.*
>
> **Possibilities**
> ***You could*** *sit on the floor...*
> ***You might*** *ask the person to look at something outside the photo.*
> ***One good idea is to*** *photograph people while they are working...*
> ***Another possibility is to...***

d **Write** your article explaining why each tip is useful.

e **Check** your article for mistakes (grammar, vocabulary, punctuation, and spelling).

◀ p.29

THREE TIPS FOR TAKING GREAT PORTRAIT PHOTOS

1 ______________

In most photos, the subject is looking at the camera. This is often a good idea, but there are other things you can try. You might ask the person to look at something outside the photo. This can make a photo more interesting – viewers want to know what the person is looking at. Or the person could be looking at something (or someone) that is in the picture.

2 ______________

Many people are very uncomfortable when people are taking photos of them and don't know how to relax. One good idea to help them is to photograph them while they are doing something, for example, working, or with their friends or family, or doing something that they enjoy. This will help them relax, and you will get better pictures. This is an especially good idea if you are taking pictures of children.

3 ______________

If you change the angle or the perspective of your photos, you can make them more interesting and unusual. Get up high, for example, stand on a table or chair, and look down on your subject. Or you could sit on the floor and look up. Both of these angles will make the photo more original.

Writing

4 A LINKEDIN PROFILE

a LinkedIn is a website where you can connect with colleagues and former school or university friends, who might be able to help you to find a new job. Read the beginning of Kate Lewis's profile. What kind of company do you think Shopping Spy is? What do you think Kate is studying?

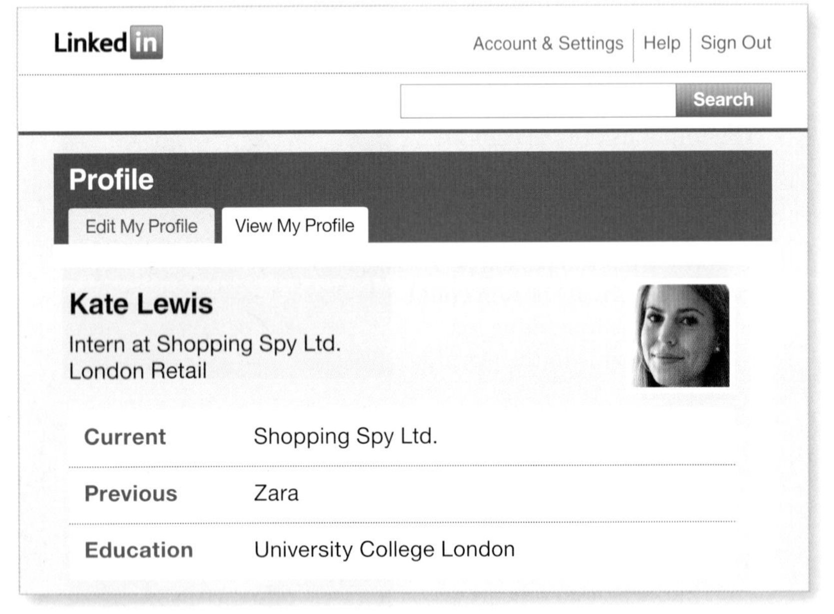
Linked in
Account & Settings | Help | Sign Out
Search

Profile
Edit My Profile | View My Profile

Kate Lewis
Intern at Shopping Spy Ltd.
London Retail

Current	Shopping Spy Ltd.
Previous	Zara
Education	University College London

b Now read the rest of Kate's profile and check if you were right.

c Read the profile again. The computer has found eight spelling mistakes. Can you correct them?

Summary

I am currantly studying at University College London and will gradaute in June with a degree in Comunications and Marketing. I am looking for a position in retail or marketing in the fashion industry. I am enthusiastic and hard-working, and keen to start in my new profesion.

I already have some expierence working in fashion. At present, I am working part-time as an intern at Shopping Spy Ltd., which is a website that helps shoppers find great shops and sales in London. I work in the online team, which provides essential information to customers and collegues. I have direct contact with customers.

I have also had a part-time sales job at the Zara store in Covent Garden.

Experience

Intern
Shopping Spy Ltd., London
September – present (9 months)

Sales assistant and cashier
Zara, London
June – September 2013 (4 months)
I greeted customers and asisted them with purchases. I brouhgt out new stock, and worked at the till.

d **Plan** your own profile. Use the **Useful language** and **Vocabulary Bank** *Study and work p.157* to help you.

1 Include a summary of your present situation.
2 Give details about your education and previous work experience.

e **Write** your profile for a site like LinkedIn. (Or go to linkedin.com and create a profile.)

Useful language: writing a CV, covering letter, or LinkedIn profile

I am currently working at / a student at...
I am seeking a position in the... industry
I have... years' experience -ing

Punctuation

Use Capital letters for company names, countries, cities, languages, and school subjects.
Use a full stop (.) after company abbreviations like Ltd. and Inc.

f **Check** your profile for mistakes (grammar, vocabulary, punctuation, and spelling).

◀ p.41

5 AN INFORMAL EMAIL

a Read an email from Louisa to her daughter, Maria, who is studying in Boston. What is the main subject of her email? How does she feel about it?

b Read the email again and complete it with a verb from the list in the present perfect continuous. Use contractions.

clear do (x2) watch read snow study

c Imagine you are replying to a similar email from a friend or family member. **Plan** what you're going to write.

1. Thank him / her for writing, and react to the news in his / her email.
2. Say what you've been doing lately.
3. Think of at least three questions to ask in your email.
4. Ask him / her to reply to the email.

d **Write** the email. Use the **Useful language** to help you, and follow 1–4 in **c** above.

Useful language: informal emails

Thanking someone for an email
Thanks for your email / message.
It was great to hear from you.
Glad to hear you're well.

Mentioning previous emails
I'm so pleased / happy / sad / sorry to hear that...

Asking someone to reply
Write (back) soon!
Looking forward to hearing all your news.
I can't wait to hear from you.

e **Check** your email for mistakes (grammar, vocabulary, punctuation, and spelling).

 p.51

From: Louisa and Eric Barton
To: Maria Barton
Subject: May 1st – what happened to spring?

Hi Maria,

Thanks for your email. Glad you're well, and hope that it's not too cold in Boston.

When your father and I woke up this morning, this is what we saw! The calendar says it is May 1st, but the weather doesn't agree. It [1] ________ for about 12 hours non-stop now. Your poor father [2] ________ the snow all morning so that we can drive to the supermarket and buy some food. I [3] ________ the news on TV. They say the storm will be over by tomorrow, so don't worry too much about us.

Besides the weather, nothing is new here. Dad [4] ________ a lot of repairs around the house over the past few weeks. He finally fixed the freezer – just in time for the snowstorm!

I [5] ________ a great novel for the book club: It's 'The Bostonians' by Henry James. It made me think of you there in Boston – have you read it? I'm sure you'd enjoy it.

Well, good luck with your exams. [6] ________ you ________ hard? I hope so.

Miss you lots. What [7] ________ you ________? Write soon!

Much love

Mom

6 A RESTAURANT REVIEW

a Read the two reviews of the same restaurant. What do they agree about? What do they disagree about?

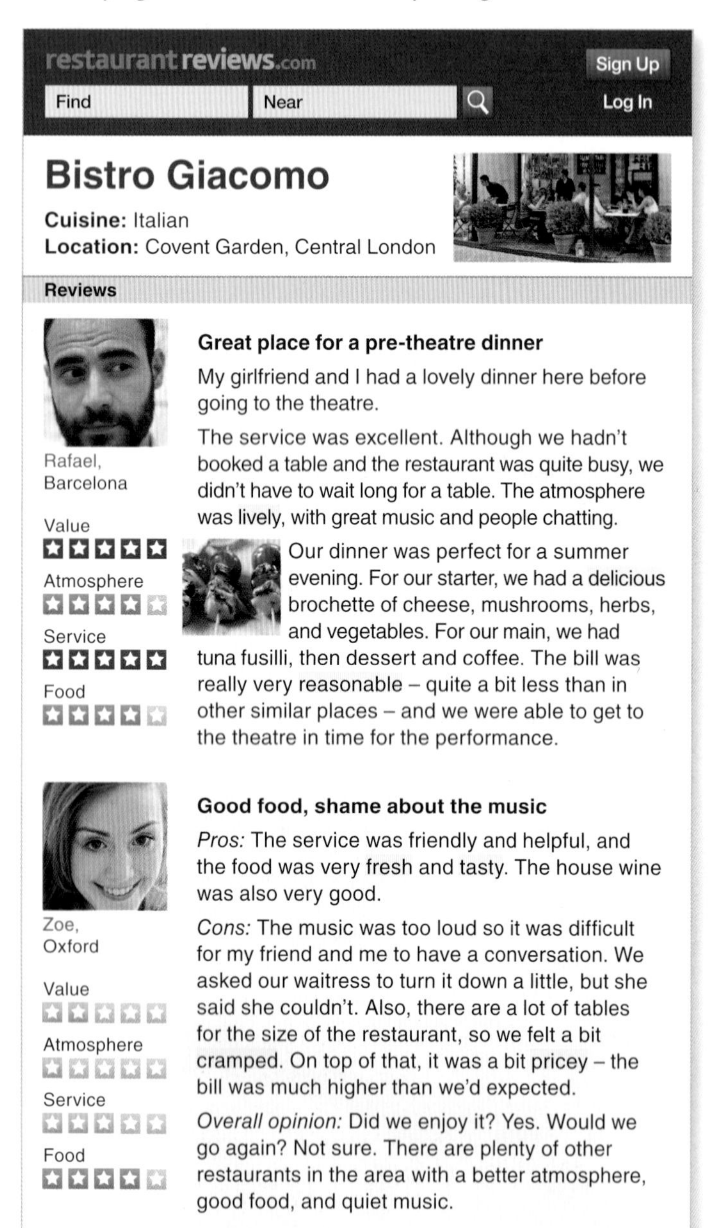

restaurantreviews.com

Sign Up

Find | Near

Log In

Bistro Giacomo

Cuisine: Italian
Location: Covent Garden, Central London

Reviews

Rafael, Barcelona

Value ★★★★★
Atmosphere ★★★★☆
Service ★★★★★
Food ★★★★☆

Great place for a pre-theatre dinner

My girlfriend and I had a lovely dinner here before going to the theatre.

The service was excellent. Although we hadn't booked a table and the restaurant was quite busy, we didn't have to wait long for a table. The atmosphere was lively, with great music and people chatting.

Our dinner was perfect for a summer evening. For our starter, we had a delicious brochette of cheese, mushrooms, herbs, and vegetables. For our main, we had tuna fusilli, then dessert and coffee. The bill was really very reasonable – quite a bit less than in other similar places – and we were able to get to the theatre in time for the performance.

Zoe, Oxford

Value ☆☆☆☆☆
Atmosphere ☆☆☆☆☆
Service ☆☆☆☆☆
Food ★★★★☆

Good food, shame about the music

Pros: The service was friendly and helpful, and the food was very fresh and tasty. The house wine was also very good.

Cons: The music was too loud so it was difficult for my friend and me to have a conversation. We asked our waitress to turn it down a little, but she said she couldn't. Also, there are a lot of tables for the size of the restaurant, so we felt a bit cramped. On top of that, it was a bit pricey – the bill was much higher than we'd expected.

Overall opinion: Did we enjoy it? Yes. Would we go again? Not sure. There are plenty of other restaurants in the area with a better atmosphere, good food, and quiet music.

b Read the reviews again. Which person...?

1 organizes their review into good points and then bad points
2 gives more details about what they had to eat
3 says it was good value for money
4 summarizes their opinion
5 do you think gives the most useful information
6 will probably go to the restaurant again

c Look at the highlighted words in the text and work out their meanings. Then put the words in the right place in the **Useful language** box.

Useful language: describing restaurants

	positive 🙂	negative ☹
the service	friendly helpful efficient	rude slow unfriendly dreadful
the room and the atmosphere	1 *lively* cosy romantic	2 crowped noisy cold
the food	3 fresh 4 tasty 5 delicious	overcooked small portions nothing special
the prices	good value for money 6 reasonable	expensive 7 pricey

d You're going to write a review of a café, bar, or restaurant you've been to recently for a website. **Plan** your review.

Either follow the style of the first review and give the following information:

1 Say which place you went to, and who with.
2 Say why you decided to go there.
3 Describe the food.
4 Describe the service and atmosphere.
5 Say what you think about the prices.
6 Say whether you would go back or not, and if not, why?

Or follow the style of the second review and use the following headings:

Pros
Cons
Overall opinion

Use the **Useful language** and **Vocabulary Bank** *At a restaurant p.161* to help you.

e **Write** your review.

f **Check** your review for mistakes (grammar, vocabulary, punctuation, and spelling).

◀ p.61

7 DESCRIBING A BUILDING

a Read the description of the Hagia Sofia. Match the highlighted words with the pictures.

b Read the description again and match the questions with paragraphs 1–5.

a How much does it cost to go in? ____
b What does it look like outside? ____
c What does it look like inside? ____
d What's the most beautiful building in your town? Where is it? ____
e Who was it built by? When was it built? ____

c There are five places where the writer has used the wrong word. Can you correct them?

d You're going to write a description of a building in your town or city for a tourism website. **Plan** what you're going to write. Answer the questions in **b** in the right order. You may need to research some of the information.

e **Write** your description. Use the **Useful language** to help you.

> **Useful language: describing a famous building**
> *It is situated in...*
> *It was designed / built by...*
> *Construction began / was completed in...*
> *Inside, you can see...*
> *There is / are...*
> *It is famous for...*

f **Check** your description for mistakes (grammar, vocabulary, punctuation, and spelling).

◀ p.81

1 I think the most beautiful building in my town is the Hagia Sophia. Its situated in a historic part of Istanbul called Sultanahmet.

2 The Roman emperor Justinian built the Hagia Sophia on the spot were two other churches had burned down. Construction began in 532 and the building was completed in 537. In 1453 it became a mosque, and it's been a museum since 1935.

3 It was the world's largest cathedral for nearly a thousand years and it is famous for it's large **dome**. It is surrounded by four tall **minarets**, each of which is different. There is also a lovely park in front of the building.

4 Inside the Hagia Sophia you can look up at the dome, which has beautiful Arabic writing in the centre. On the second floor, their are beautiful **mosaics** on the walls. Some of them are more than a thousand years old. In the north-west of the building there is a **column** with a hole in the middle called the Wishing Column which people think has special powers.

5 If your over 18, you must pay an entrance fee of 25 Turkish lira (about 10 euros). The building is open from 9.00 a.m. to 5.00 p.m. (7.00 p.m. in summer) but is closed on Mondays.

Writing

8 A STORY

a Read Matt's story about his wedding. What problems were there?

The most important day of my life

I think the most important day of my life was my wedding day. My wife and I got married in a little church in the countryside and we have about 20 gests. It wasn't a very big wedding but it was very beautiful. The weather was perfect – sunny and warm. However, there was one problem. We were hired a woman to play the violin at the wedding ceremony but [1] __________ she lost and never arrived. That was a stressed situation for all of us. [2] __________, there was a piano in the church and one of the bridesmaids, my wife's niece, was an excellent piano player. She was prepared to play for us, but she really didn't know any wedding music. [3] __________, my brother had his iPad so we downloaded the score for some wedding music, and [4] __________, our niece played the music very good. [5] __________, I think she was better than a proffessional musician because she was part of our family, and of corse now it is a great story. That was five years ago, and now we have two small children who love to here the story of our wedding music.

b Complete the story with an adverb or adverbial phrase from the list. (Some can go in more than one place.)

in fact   in the end   fortunately   luckily   unfortunately

c There are ten mistakes (grammar, vocabulary, punctuation, and spelling). Can you correct them?

d Look at the exam question below.

- Your English teacher has asked you to write a story.
- Your story must have one of the following titles:
  I won the prize!
  It was so embarrassing!
  A day I'd like to forget!
- Write your story.

You are going to choose a title and write a story. **Plan** your story. Choose your title and think of some ideas for your topic.

e Now make notes for the story. Think about:

1. where and when the event / moment happened
2. who was there, and why they were there
3. what actually happened on that day
4. how you felt about it then, and how you feel now

f **Write** your story. Use the **Useful language** to help you.

Useful language: telling a story with sentence adverbs
__Unfortunately / Sadly__, there was a big traffic jam before our wedding.
__Fortunately / Luckily__, we had a map and found a faster way.
__Eventually / Finally / In the end__, we arrived at the church just before the ceremony.
__Surprisingly / Amazingly / Interestingly,__ we were the first people to arrive at the church.
__In fact / Actually__ I thought she played beautifully.

g **Check** your description for mistakes (grammar, vocabulary, punctuation, and spelling).

◀ p.91

9 AN EXAM TASK

a Read the essay topic and the student essay. Does the writer agree or disagree with the statement?

Your class has just had a discussion about exams and education. Your teacher has asked you to write an essay on the topic below. Write about 200 words.

Exams are not a good way of testing what students know. Do you agree or disagree?

1 In most countries around the world, students are tested on what they know through exams, both at school and at university.

2 In general, I think testing through exams is a good thing. Firstly, it is a fair system [1] ________ all students have to do the same thing in the same period of time with no help. Secondly, having exams makes students work harder. It is well known that many students only really work hard [2] ________ they know they have an exam in the near future. Thirdly, the only real alternative is continuous assessment. This system benefits young people whose parents are closely involved in their education and help them with projects, [3] ________ it isn't as fair as an exam. In continuous assessment it is also much more difficult to stop students from cheating by using other people's work from the internet [4] ________ their own.

3 The only real disadvantage of exams is that some students get very nervous and don't do their best, [5] ________ learning relaxation techniques is a good way of helping with this problem.

4 In conclusion, [6] ________ the exam system is not perfect, I think that it is the best way there is of testing students' knowledge.

b Read the essay again. In which paragraph does the writer...?

Paragraph ☐	give his / her opinion and three reasons for it
Paragraph ☐	give a summary of the essay
Paragraph ☐	give an introduction to the topic
Paragraph ☐	give a contrasting opinion

c Read the essay again and complete it with a connecting word or phrase from the list.

although because but instead of so when

Useful language: essays for exams

Generalizing
In general,...
It is well known that...
Generally speaking,...
In most countries around the world...

Giving your opinion
I think...
In my opinion,...

Organizing points
Firstly / Secondly / Thirdly...

Contrasting opinions
One disadvantage of... is that...
On the other hand,...

Conclusions
In conclusion,...

d You're going to write an essay for an exam. The topic is: *It is not a good idea to cram the evening before an exam.* Think about whether you agree or disagree with the statement. **Plan** your essay in four paragraphs.

1 Introduce the topic.
2 Give your opinion and two or three reasons for why you think that.
3 Give a contrasting opinion.
4 Summarize your opinion in the conclusion.

e **Write** your essay. Use the **Useful language** to help you.

f **Check** your essay for mistakes (grammar, vocabulary, punctuation, and spelling).

◀ p.101

Listening

1.2

Interviewer Excuse me, I'm doing a survey. Can I ask you some questions about your name?
Sean OK.
Interviewer So, what's your name?
Sean Sean Gibson.
Interviewer Is that S-E-A-N or S-H-A-U-N?
Sean S-E-A-N.
Interviewer Why did your parents call you that?
Sean I think I'm named after the actor Sean Connery, who played James Bond in the 60s. He was very famous at the time when I was born.
Interviewer Do you have a nickname?
Sean Actually, at school they used to call me 'Brains'. Um, it was meant to be a joke, I think, because I wasn't a particularly good student.
Interviewer And are you happy with your name?
Sean Mmm, I like it. I was usually the only Sean at school, which I think was quite a good thing. But people find it quite difficult to spell, especially as there are two possible spellings, and most foreign people find it really difficult to pronounce.
Interviewer Would you like to change it?
Sean No, I definitely wouldn't change it.
Interviewer So, what's your name?
Deborah Deborah.
Interviewer Is that with an h at the end?
Deborah Yes, D-E-B-O-R-A-H.
Interviewer Why did your parents call you that?
Deborah Ah, I'm actually named after the hospital where I was born, Deborah Hospital in New Jersey – near New York. My dad thought of that.
Interviewer Do you have a nickname?
Deborah No, but everyone calls me Debbie or Deb.
Interviewer Are you happy with your name?
Deborah Not really.
Interviewer Would you like to change it?
Deborah I don't know. When I was little, I renamed myself April and then Caroline, but now I don't like those names either.
Interviewer So what's your name?
James James.
Interviewer Is that spelt in the usual way?
James Yes. J-A-M-E-S.
Interviewer Why did your parents call you that?
James I'm not sure. I think they just liked the name. I'm not named after anyone or anything like that.
Interviewer Do you have a nickname?
James Not exactly. At university some of my friends called me Jim for short, but I didn't like it very much. I've always introduced myself as James.
Interviewer Are you happy with your name?
James Yes. I've always liked it.
Interviewer Would you like to change it?
James No. I can't imagine being called something different. But I don't think it really matters anyway – a name is just a name.
Interviewer So what's your name?
Philippa Philippa.
Interviewer How do you spell it?
Philippa P-H-I-L-I-P-P-A.
Interviewer Why did your parents call you that?
Philippa My parents are Scottish, but they were living in England when I was born. They heard the name Philippa – it isn't a common name in Scotland – and they decided that they liked it.
Interviewer Do you have a nickname?
Philippa Well, when I was growing up everyone called me Pippa for short, which I didn't like at all!
Interviewer Are you happy with your name?
Philippa I hated it when I was growing up because it was different. And not one single person spells it right! But now I don't mind it, because it is a bit different.
Interviewer Would you like to change it?
Philippa No, I like it for me.

1.7

Interviewer Good afternoon. This is *Uncommon Knowledge*, the programme that looks at everyday things from unusual angles. Today we're talking to the Creative Director of a company that names companies and products. Welcome, John.
John Hello, Sarah.
Interviewer Now, tell us. How do companies choose their names? Are they usually named after the people who start them?
John Well, sometimes. Many companies are named after their founders, for example the Swedish furniture company IKEA. The first two letters in IKEA – the I and the K – are the initials of Ingvar Kamprad, the company's founder.
Interviewer And what about the last two letters, the E and the A? What do they stand for?
John The E is for Elmtaryd, which is the name of the farm where Ingvar Kamprad grew up.
Interviewer And the A?
John The A is for the name of a village near his hometown, called Agunnaryd. I'm not quite sure exactly why this village was important to him, but obviously it was.
Interviewer I always assumed that 'ikea' was a Swedish word with some sort of special meaning.
John Ah, I'm afraid not. But many other companies choose names which have specific meanings. For example, Samsung, the big Korean electronics company.
Interviewer What does Samsung mean?
John In Korean, Samsung means 'three stars'. The name was chosen back in the year 1938, and at that time three stars was the most impressive rating that people could imagine for hotels and things like that.
Interviewer So if they'd started the company today they would probably have called it 'five stars' – whatever that is in Korean.
John Absolutely. In any case the company was very different in its early days. For instance, in the beginning, in 1938, Samsung wasn't an electronics company. It was a company which sold fish, vegetables, and fruit to China. It didn't start selling electronics until the 1970s.
Interviewer Oh really? I didn't know that.
John And another brand name with a special meaning is Nike, the American company which is famous for its trainers and sports clothes.
Interviewer I think I know this one. Nike is the Greek goddess of victory. Is that right?
John Yes, that's right. What's interesting is that 'Nike' wasn't the company's original name. When it started in 1964, its original name was Blue Ribbon Sports. They changed their name to Nike a few years later in 1971.
Interviewer Very interesting.
John Yes. And another company with an interesting name is Sony, the Japanese electronics company. Sony is a combination of 'sonus', the Latin word for sound, and 'sonny', an American slang term that means 'boy'.
Interviewer 'Sound' plus 'boy'.
John That's right. They chose it because it has an interesting meaning and it's easy for people all over the world to pronounce. Obviously that's an important thing for a business name.
Interviewer One more question, this time about the American internet company, Google. The name has something to do with numbers, I think.
John That's right. 'Googol' is a word for a very large number: a one followed by 100 zeroes.
Interviewer Really? That's quite hard to visualize!
John The name shows that there is a huge amount of information online, and you can find it all by Googling it.
Interviewer Yes. It's a really good name for a search engine.
John Yes, indeed. Now, of course, the spelling is different. 'Google' the company is G-O-O-G-L-E, but the number is spelled G-O-O-G-O-L. But that's where the name comes from.
Interviewer Fascinating. Thanks very much for speaking with us this afternoon.
John You're very welcome.

1.15

Interviewer Why did you decide to try colour analysis, Wendy?
Wendy Well, I was sharing an office with a lady who always looked incredibly stylish and well-dressed. And when I asked her what her secret was, she told me that she'd done colour analysis. Another reason was that I was really bored with black. I felt like I wore black too often, and I wanted to wear new colours that were more suitable for me. I didn't know what was wrong with the way I dressed, but I wasn't happy about it. So I brought two friends along and we went to see a colour consultant.
Interviewer What was she like? It was a woman?
Wendy Yes, she was a woman. Just wonderful, very friendly and helpful. She put loads of scarves on me that were in different colours and shades. They just drape the scarves around the front of you, like when you go to the hairdresser's, and see which ones look best for your skin tone. Once she'd done all the colours for me, then she put me in the right make-up as well.
Interviewer What colours did she say were best for you?
Wendy Well, I learned that I'm a 'winter person'. There are four sorts of people: spring, summer, autumn, and winter. The winter colours are all very strong, for example dark purple, a dark blue, fuchsia, and a light purple colour called lobelia, which is named after a flower. Another colour winter people should wear a lot is emerald green. And she said I shouldn't wear yellow or orange, or shades of colours which have a lot of yellow in them, like lime green.
Interviewer Do you still wear black?
Wendy Yes. Winter people are the ones who can wear black. I still do wear it once or twice a week.
Interviewer What changes did you make after your colour analysis?
Wendy The first thing I did was get a couple of affordable T-shirts in my new colours, to sort of try it out. I've got a little book with a set of swatches in my colours that I carry with me, absolutely everywhere, so I can be sure I'm buying the right colours. Also, my two friends were both autumn people, so we did a big clothes swap. I gave them all of my autumn colours and they gave me all of their winter colours.

Interviewer Did people notice a change in you?
Wendy They definitely noticed. And the most frequently used word was 'glamorous'. 'Wendy, you look so glamorous!' And after a while I really felt more glamorous. I might just be wearing a T-shirt and a pair of jeans, but in the right colour, and it makes a great difference. Now I feel more confident as a person, in the workplace, and socially. I feel more confident when I go shopping too – before I never knew what to buy and was just hopeless, really.
Interviewer Would you recommend colour analysis to others?
Wendy Absolutely. In fact, about four or five people in the office saw me and did the same thing. My mother's done it too. I told my husband to do it – they do it for guys as well – but he hasn't agreed yet. But he will!

1 19

Andrew Are you all right? I'll carry that for you.
Jenny Oh yeah, that'd be great. Thank you.
Grant We've just arrived on the flight from New York. He's talking to someone. I'll follow them.
Andrew And have you been to the UK before?
Jenny A few times, actually. I work for a magazine in the States – *New York 24seven* – and we have a sister company in London.
Andrew I see. And are you here on business this time?
Jenny Sort of. I'm here for a few meetings, but I have a couple of days off beforehand. I'm visiting my father-in-law in the countryside. How about you? How was your holiday in New York?
Andrew It wasn't really a holiday. I was doing some research there.
Jenny That sounds interesting.
Andrew It was, but I didn't have much time for sightseeing! Is your husband coming too?
Jenny No, he's working.
Andrew What does he do?
Jenny He's a journalist. He's on assignment in Alaska at the moment.
Andrew In Alaska? Wow!
Jenny I know, right? I've never been, but he says it's incredible.
Andrew I can imagine. A bit different from the English countryside!
Jenny That's true.
Andrew I'd better go. Oh, before I forget, here's your laptop.
Jenny Oh yeah! Thanks a lot. Sorry, I didn't ask your name.
Andrew Andrew Page. And yours?
Jenny Jenny Zielinski. It was nice meeting you.
Andrew You too.
Jenny And thanks again for helping with my bags.
Andrew No problem. Have a great time at your father-in-law's.
Jenny I will... if I ever get through here!
Andrew Bye then.
Jenny Yeah bye. Take care.
Jenny Henry?... Hi, yeah, I'm here at last. The flight was late taking off... I'm so sorry you've had to wait for me... I know, I know. And you won't believe this – it looks like my suitcase didn't get here... I'm not sure, it's turning out to be a nightmare! I can't wait to just get back to your house and – oh, hang on, I have to go – it's my turn. Bye.

1 22

Jenny ...and we landed on time but then I couldn't find my suitcase so then I had to go to lost luggage and report it missing.
Henry You poor thing! What a journey!
Jenny Well, I'm here now.
Henry And it's lovely to see you.
Jenny It's great to see you too.
Henry No, no, no, let me take that.
Jenny It's OK.
Henry You've had a hard journey. Allow me.
Jenny Thanks, Henry.
Grant We've got a problem.
Rob I can't believe I'm not there with you, Jenny.
Jenny Neither can I. It's weird, isn't it?
Rob I really miss you.
Jenny Me too. How's Alaska?
Rob Not great. It's been snowing all day! I haven't left the hotel.
Jenny Oh no! That's awful.
Rob What are you drinking? Is that coffee?
Jenny No, it's tea.
Rob Tea?
Jenny It's good. Really!
Rob Where's Dad now?
Jenny I think he's getting me something. I'm not sure what.
Rob So why are you using his computer?
Jenny Oh, it's crazy. You know my laptop?
Rob Yeah?
Jenny This screen keeps popping up and asking me for a password. I've never seen it before. I'm worried I have a virus.
Rob It's not your day, is it? First your suitcase and then your laptop!
Jenny No, but your dad's being so nice. And he says your cousin Luke will be able to fix my computer for me. Apparently he's kind of a computer geek.
Rob Kind of? He's a genius. If he can't do it, nobody can.
Jenny Well, I'm going to go see him tomorrow.
Henry Here's a pair of my pyjamas you can use, Jenny.
Rob Oh wow! You'll look great in those, Jenny!
Selina Selina Lavelle.
Grant Selina? It's Grant. She's in the house, but she isn't alone. I could come back tomorrow with...
Selina No. Stay there. All night if you have to.
Grant Yes, boss.

1 27

So, in reverse order, the list of things that the British most often leave behind when they go on holiday.

At number ten we have – their passports. Yes, believe it or not many Brits only realize when they get to the airport that they've left their passports at home.

At number nine, flip flops. An easy solution there – they can buy some new ones at their holiday destination.

Number eight, their mobile phone. This is bad news, as it's not easy to replace when you're on holiday, but maybe it's a good thing as it makes it easier to really disconnect, without calls or emails.

At number seven, toothbrushes, and at number six, toothpaste. Another easy thing to buy though, at any local chemist's.

At number five, sunglasses. Yes, Brits have them, but because we don't use them very often we forget to pack them, and we end up buying another pair, which we will then forget again next time.

Number four, a good book. But nowadays if you've forgotten a book but you have a Kindle or iPad, it's easy to buy some more wherever you are.

At number three, sunscreen. This is something we really ought to try to remember to take, because sunscreen is often much more expensive in holiday resorts. And you really can't sunbathe or do water sports without putting some on.

At number two, phone chargers. So you remembered your phone – but you forgot the charger. Well, it is possible to buy chargers when you're away, or you might even be able to buy one online and get it delivered to wherever you're staying.

Finally, the number one thing people forget to bring is... comfortable shoes! We seem to forget that when you go sightseeing or even shopping, not to mention going for walks, comfortable shoes are a must. So next time you pack, make sure all these things are on your checklist!

1 32

Interviewer How long have you been an airport screener?
Screener Two years.
Interviewer What's the most difficult part of the job?
Screener Definitely the repetition. You say and do the same things again and again... and again. I mean, it's so boring. It eats away at you. I also don't like taking and throwing away people's things. But there are certain things you can't bring through security. I often have to take away big bottles of sunscreen and expensive perfume, home-made food, uh, also, you know, razors and scissors and other things and throw them in the trash, usually in front of the passenger. They look so sad and confused. It makes me feel a little sad for them, too.
Interviewer What do you like about the job?
Screener The only thing that keeps it interesting is the variety of people you meet. I enjoy talking with people and wondering where they're travelling to and things like that. It really tells you something about society.
Interviewer What are your colleagues like?
Screener Um, some are great, but some are terrible. Like, if a passenger is moving too slowly, they can be really unkind. Even if it's an elderly traveller, or just a businessman with too many electronic gadgets. The bad ones, um, they shout at people to push their bags through the belt. I mean, they don't have to be rude about it. One of my colleagues refuses to say 'please' and 'thank you'. Can you believe that? He tells people to lift their arms, show their feet, take off their belt, and things like that, in a very unkind way.
Interviewer Why do you think some screeners are so unfriendly?
Screener Well, I think that it really is, as I said before, because of the repetition. I mean, you try standing in the same place and repeating the same instructions to people and watch them make the same mistakes again and again. It's emotionally exhausting.
Interviewer What are some things that annoy you about passengers?
Screener I always find it surprising when people don't know they have to take off their coats or boots, or take out their laptops, or that they can't take bottles of water through. Sure, not everyone has the opportunity to travel, but I mean, have these people not picked up a newspaper, or watched TV, or spoken with someone else who has flown in the last ten years?
Interviewer How do passengers treat you generally?
Screener Some are nice and courteous. Especially in the morning, people seem either cheery and warm or, you know, simply tired and indifferent. They're rarely rude in the morning. By the afternoon, people become more stressed, and they become less friendly and sometimes angry. They get so upset at us personally. But, I mean, we don't make the rules. Someone else does.

1 40

Harry I live in Hereford, which is a small town in the UK very near Wales, and our local shopping street, our high street, it has all the normal chains like McDonald's and WHSmith the stationer's. There are also some smaller shops that are independently owned – there's a butcher's, a hardware store, things like that. There used to be a department store that was owned by a local family, but it closed down last year.

The local shops are already having problems, I'd say. And now they're going to develop a new shopping centre outside town, and that'll kill the high street. Also, more people are shopping online now. It worries me because if there are no shops, then the centre of town will just die and become really depressing, maybe just with pound shops or empty stores.

Kate In Toronto, where I live in Canada, the shopping street near my house has everything, from delicatessens and pharmacies to restaurants and clothing stores. There are also corner shops, grocery stores, and chains like Starbucks as well.

The smaller, independently owned shops are definitely struggling because people are going to big indoor shopping malls or supermarkets, especially in winter when it's too cold to be walking around outdoors. Online shopping is still not very common due to the long distances between cities and towns in Canada. Postal delivery and overnight delivery aren't really practical.

Ken I'm from Kobe, a city in Japan, and near the train station we have little shops like a baker's, a café, a greengrocer's, and lots of corner shops.

But people there shop at department stores, mainly. You know, Japanese department stores have everything – clothes, TVs, fruit, and vegetables. I don't often go to small, independent shops, because I usually need to buy a lot of different things. So it's a lot more convenient to go to a department store. I know the small shops are disappearing and that's a little sad, but better things are replacing them. They're just responding to the customers' needs. It's what the shoppers want.

Bea I live in the centre of Valencia in Spain, and my nearest big shopping street is called *Calle Colón*. I almost always go shopping there as it's so close. It has pretty much all the shops I like and a big department store too called *El Corte Inglés* – it's a Spanish institution!

I'd say the small local shops are doing quite well. Of course some places close down, but then new ones open up – a Japanese chain called Muji, for example, that sells stuff for your house. There are quite a few shopping centres round Valencia but I never go to them, as they tend to be out of town, so you need a car or bus to get there, and I think the same is true for a lot of people round here, and also tourists like the small shops. Even though I do use them, for me there are two problems with small shops in Spain. One is that they often close at lunchtime, which I find really impractical. The other thing is that small shops don't offer the same sort of service that a big store can. For example, it's more difficult to have things delivered, or to change something and get your money back.

2 10

Interviewer Welcome back. Up next, age and the generation gap. We know how hard it can be to tell someone's age, but in fact it turns out there may be a way that's quite simple. It's called the 'Mosquito Tone Test', and Mark is here to tell us more.

Mark Thanks, Sue. The Mosquito Tone is a sound – a very high pitched, very annoying sound, which is why it's named after the insect. What's interesting is that apparently as we age, we slowly lose our ability to hear this sound. According to scientists, almost everyone under the age of 25 can hear the Mosquito Tone, but almost no one over 25 can hear it!

Interviewer Really! Is that right?

Mark Yes. And to test this out, I actually played the tone for my family last night. My wife and I heard absolutely nothing at all, but our teenage daughters could hear it, and in fact they complained that it was an irritating sound that was quite painful to hear.

Interviewer Oh no! Well, at the risk of irritating some of our younger listeners' ears, why don't we play the tone briefly now?

Mark OK, here goes. I'm playing the tone in 3, 2, 1...

Interviewer Have you played the tone yet?

Mark I just did. Or, at least, I think I did.

Interviewer Well, I suppose that just confirms that neither of us are under 25!

2 11

Interviewer Now Mark, apart from testing a person's age, what is the Mosquito Tone being used for?

Mark This has actually become an interesting controversy. Because the sound is so annoying, and because only the young can hear it, the Mosquito Tone is being used to keep teenagers away from certain places.

Interviewer What kinds of places?

Mark Well, for example, from shopping centres. As you know in some towns you get large groups of young people hanging around shopping centres and causing trouble. And some shop owners say that these gangs can annoy other customers, or frighten them away, which is obviously not good for business. So now these centres can play the Mosquito Tone over their audio system, and the groups of teenagers will feel uncomfortable and leave the area. But of course the sound won't annoy the other customers at all, as they don't hear it.

Interviewer Have you spoken to any of these shop owners?

Mark Yes, I have, and they said that the Mosquito Tone has worked very well for them. And they also said that although it's true that the Mosquito Tone is certainly very annoying, it doesn't hurt the teenagers.

Interviewer It sounds like rather a good idea to me. But you said this was a controversy. Who's against it?

Mark Well, there are some groups of people who are trying to ban the Mosquito Tone. They've pointed out a number of problems with it. Firstly, they worry that the sound really is harmful, but more to the point they say that the Mosquito Tone affects all young people, some of whom are well-behaved and just want to go shopping. And finally they say that the Mosquito Tone doesn't actually stop the problem of teenage gangs, it just drives them from one place to another.

Interviewer Those do seem like good points.

Mark Yes, indeed. And there's also an interesting twist. Some teenagers have discovered an advantage to the Mosquito Tone.

Interviewer Oh yes?

Mark Well, the Mosquito Tone has also been released as a ringtone for your mobile. So in secondary schools that don't permit mobile phones, teens can use their phones in class. They can receive calls and messages during lessons and teachers don't have any idea what is happening.

Interviewer Because the teacher can't hear it! That must really annoy them.

Mark That's right. And if they can't hear it, they can't...

2 18

Interviewer What inspired you to become a photographer?

Brian My cousin, who was ten years older than me, built a darkroom in his house which I used to visit. From the moment I saw a developing photograph appearing like magic on a piece of paper under the red light, I was completely hooked. At the same time my school started a photography club, so I joined it. I soon knew it was what I wanted to do, and later I went on to study photography and film-making at university.

Interviewer What sort of people do you usually photograph, and where?

Brian I've mainly photographed classical musicians and their ensembles and orchestras. I usually photograph them at work and they often perform in wonderful buildings, which are also great for photography, so I've had the chance to work in palaces and churches in Rome, Vienna, Salzburg, Paris, and other places.

Interviewer Have you had any other famous clients?

Brian Yes, several. I was once asked to photograph Prince Charles, for example.

Interviewer Oh, and how did that go?

Brian In fact, it was a bit embarrassing. He was visiting a mosque, and though there were many other press photographers there, I was the only one who was given permission to enter the mosque at the same time as the Prince. When I got to the door, I was asked to take my shoes off, and I realized that I had an enormous hole in one of my socks! I was so embarrassed, all I could think about was this hole as I tried to get shots of Prince Charles. And then he left through a different door, and I had to follow him, still in my socks.

Interviewer Do you have a favourite portrait of a celebrity?

Brian I have lots, but for example there's a portrait of Meryl Streep by Annie Leibovitz, where she's wearing a face-mask. It's absolutely wonderful.

2 19

Interviewer What are some tricks to taking a good portrait?

Brian Each situation is different and what works for one person may not work for another. The most important thing is to get people to relax. Being photographed makes most people nervous and insecure, so, assuming they're not professional models, generally it's best not to have other people around, watching the photo shoot. Once people relax they can even enjoy the process but it does take a long time, so another important thing if you want to have a good photo taken of you is not to be in a hurry. I often need between three and four hours.

Interviewer What else can the person who is being photographed do to improve the picture?

Brian To start with they should wear comfortable clothes, and if they can, if it's a studio photo, bring some different clothes with them – things that they feel good in.

Interviewer What about make-up?

Brian If people are used to wearing make-up, then they should use it, because again it will make them feel good. Actually make-up is often a good thing – and in fact, even for men, a little powder can make them look better under studio lights.

Interviewer What about how to pose?

Brian Well, standing up straight isn't usually a good pose. You can get much more interesting pictures of people, for example, sitting on the floor, leaning against the back of a chair, or sitting just on the edge of a chair. Interestingly, sometimes it's a good thing for people to feel a bit uncomfortable, because the more uncomfortable people are the less they think about their expression and the better the pictures can be. It also helps if people look away and only turn to the camera at the last moment.

Interviewer Brian, thank you very much, and I'll try to remember those tips.

2 23

1 I really love this photo, even though I look a bit strange in a dress that was obviously too big and a coat that was too small! But it's the way that my grandfather and I are looking at each other that I love about it. We were about to go for a walk, and are standing just in front of the door of his house, on the steps. It was a really cold day so he'd lent me his fur hat. I don't know who took the photo, probably my grandmother, but it's a lovely reminder of my grandfather, who died a few years ago. I have it in a frame on my desk, and both my mother and my grandmother have a framed copy of the same photo – we all love it.

2 My favourite photo ever – not just from my childhood but in my whole life – is this one that my dad took when we went camping. I'm standing in the mountains and on a rock in front of me

is this animal called a marmot – it's like a big mouse, and they're quite common round here. The marmot was standing incredibly close to me and it almost looks as if it's smiling at the camera! It wasn't shy at all. A strange thing is, I always remembered the day the photo was taken, but I actually didn't see the photo with my own eyes until last year, when I turned 35. My parents found a load of old photos and scanned them for me so that I'd have them in digital form. I wanted to enlarge this one and make it into a poster, but the file wasn't big enough.

3 Er, there are loads of childhood photos to choose from, but one of my favourites is this one which was taken by my dad – he was always the family photographer – and I think it was a day when we went for a picnic with my brothers and cousins. In the picture, I'm the little blonde one in the front. I think I was about seven or eight, er, and the two boys on the right are my brothers, and the rest are my cousins.

It reminds me of how close I am to my extended family. So, er, I look at it when I miss home – and it cheers me up. I used to have it stuck on my fridge but now it's packed away in a box somewhere. But my mum uploaded it onto Facebook so now I can look at it any time.

2 24

Jenny Hello?... Yes, it is... Oh, that's great news. Thank you... Later today? Great. Now I won't have to buy new clothes... Yeah, that's the right address. Bye.
Henry Good news?
Jenny Great news! They found my suitcase, and they're bringing it over later today.
Henry Excellent. Right, I'll take you to my nephew's house so he can fix your computer.
Jenny I'm looking forward to meeting Luke.
Henry You'll like him. He's a bright boy. Not that I understand a word he says.
Jenny I'll bet he doesn't know much about Greek mythology either!
Henry You're probably right.
Henry That's funny.
Jenny What's wrong?
Henry The tyre's flat.
Jenny Do you have a spare?
Henry Well, yes, but it shouldn't be flat, it's new and...
Henry I don't believe it!
Jenny What is it?
Henry They're both flat! They've been punctured!
Jenny What? Somebody did that on purpose? In the English countryside?
Henry You get vandals everywhere these days. Well, I'll just have to stay here and see if I can get the AA to bring out another spare tyre. I'll call you a taxi.
Jenny Isn't there a bus I could catch?
Henry Well, there's a bus stop on the main road. You could get the bus to Oxford from there, I suppose.
Jenny How do I get to the bus stop?
Henry The quickest way is the footpath at the back of the house.
Jenny I think I'll do that then.
Henry Are you sure you want to get the bus? How will you find Luke's house?
Jenny You gave me the address. I can look it up on my phone if I get lost.
Henry Yes, of course. But, this is really inconvenient for you. You were going to borrow my car, weren't you?
Jenny No, don't worry, Henry. I'd actually decided to rent a car anyway. I'll need it for work and it'll probably be cheaper to rent here than in London. I can get one while Luke is working his magic.
Henry Well, if you're absolutely sure. Just go to the back door and you'll see the path. Follow that – takes you to the bus stop.
Jenny OK. Oh, and I'd like to cook dinner this evening to thank you for having me.
Henry You don't need to do that!
Jenny I want to.
Henry Well, if you're sure. What time?
Jenny How about seven o'clock?
Henry Great! And I'll keep my phone on in case you need me.
Jenny See you later, Henry.
Henry Bye!
Henry Who's that?
Jenny Luke?
Luke You must be Jenny. Hi.
Jenny Nice to meet you.
Luke You too. Come in. Would you like some coffee? I've just made some.
Jenny I'd love to, but I'm running a bit late. We had trouble with the car and then the bus took forever. And I really need to get to a car rental place. I'm really sorry, but could I just leave the computer with you?
Luke Yeah, no problem.
Jenny That's great. I feel awful just leaving it here like this.
Luke Honestly, don't worry about it.
Jenny Are you sure?
Luke Yeah, it's cool. I love doing this kind of thing. I'll send you a text and let you know how I'm getting on.
Jenny That's nice of you, Luke. Thanks. See you later.
Luke See you later.

2 27

Jenny Henry? Henry? Henry?
Henry This is Henry Walker. I'm afraid I can't take your call at the moment. Please leave your message after the tone.
Jenny Hi, Henry, it's Jenny here. I just wanted to let you know everything went fine. I got my car and I'm back home. Remember I'm making dinner. See you soon.
Jenny Hi Luke, it's Jenny.
Luke Hi Jenny, what's up?
Jenny I just wanted to apologize for running off this morning.
Luke You really don't need to! I should apologize, actually. It's going to take me longer than I thought to unlock your computer. It's like there's an extra security code or something.
Jenny That's really weird.
Luke Don't worry, I'm sure I can crack it.
Jenny I just have no idea how it got there. Oh, hang on.
Luke What is it?
Jenny My suitcase has arrived!
Luke Hey, that's great!
Jenny Oh, look at that. The lock's broken.
Luke Must have been the baggage handlers!
Jenny Well, at least it's back.
Luke So, how's uncle Henry?
Jenny He isn't here. I called him but he didn't answer.
Luke He probably went for a walk. He often does that. He thinks about his research and stuff.
Jenny Well, I hope he's back in time for dinner!
Luke He will be. He's always on time.
Jenny Yeah, Rob told me Henry's very punctual.
Luke Unlike Rob!
Jenny Exactly.
Luke Is that the jet lag catching up with you?
Jenny Yeah, I'm pretty tired.
Luke You should have a nap. Don't worry, I'll get this computer working as soon as I can.
Jenny Thanks, Luke. See you later.
Luke Bye!
Jenny Oh no, dinner! Henry? Henry? That's strange.
Henry This is Henry Walker. I'm afraid I can't take your call at the moment. Please leave your message after the tone.
Newsreader The victim of last night's assault at Heathrow Airport has been named as Andrew Page. Mr Page is a research scientist from Oxford. Police believe he was attacked as he left the airport. He is now in hospital in a critical condition. Police are appealing to anyone who may have seen Mr Page to contact them immediately. Mr Page had just returned from New York where he was conducting research on renewable energy.
Rob Hi, Jenny.
Jenny Rob, I need to talk to you.

2 29

Sunday
Liz Dave and I meet Ash and Ross, two London freegans who will train us how to find food in the rubbish. Ash is 21, and his friend Ross is 46. This is Ash.
Ash First, you need the right equipment. Take gloves and a torch. Also, you have to know where to go. Small to medium size shops are probably best. The larger shops lock their bins.
Liz We're in the car park behind a supermarket. It's 5.00 p.m. and dark, so people don't notice us. Ash and Ross walk confidently to the bins, lift the lids, and start looking for food.

The first bin bag we open contains frozen meals, including chicken curry and chilli con carne. The meals haven't been opened and the sell-by date is today. Underneath are ten tubs of ice cream, with the same sell-by date. At the bottom is a carton of eggs. The sell-by date is next week. Ross says this isn't surprising.

Ross We get a lot of eggs. Sometimes, if one breaks, they just throw away all of them. But, er, you know, just be careful when choosing what to eat. If the packaging is open or it's past the sell-by date, don't take it. Oh, and wash everything you find before you eat it.

Monday
Liz Now it's time for Dave and me to try freeganism on our own. As we begin, it's freezing cold. After an hour and a half of searching, we still haven't found one unlocked bin. Eventually, we go behind a smaller supermarket and... success! The bins are open. There's a plastic bag full of vegetables at the bottom. So, while Dave holds the lid open, I reach in. A couple of people are watching us, and I'm so embarrassed. But the bag's full of potatoes, apples, and carrots, and there's nothing wrong with them. We'll make a nice soup with them. Now, we just need bread. We look inside a coffee shop's bin and there is some. But we're right outside the station and it's rush hour. We're too embarrassed to take it. So we go to the bins outside a nearby supermarket, where we find a plastic bag of sliced bread. The bag is unbroken and the sell-by date is today. At home, after washing the vegetables, we cook a delicious soup, which we have with the bread. Dessert is baked apples. Wonderful.

2 30

Tuesday
Liz I don't feel ill – a good start – so we enjoy a freegan breakfast of avocados, which were a present from Ash and Ross, and we have the rest of yesterday's bread. We decide to visit the bins by the supermarket where we found the vegetables yesterday. Again, we find lots of vegetables and fruit – potatoes, peppers, a melon, and some salad. The salad is close to the sell-by date, but if it were in your fridge, you'd eat it. Other sell-by dates are not for another week. I don't understand why they were thrown away. After a lunch of yesterday's soup, we search at bakeries but find nothing. Luckily, we've found enough food this morning for dinner and tomorrow's breakfast.

We've decided that it's OK to use a few shop-bought ingredients such as pasta, so on the menu tonight is a spicy pasta soup with green peppers and the carrots from yesterday. For dessert we have another baked apple.

Wednesday
Liz Today, after a breakfast of melon, we head off to check out the bins in the market, which smell terrible compared with the supermarket rubbish. We find enough food to eat like kings: sausages,

cabbage, lemons, and some onions. Although three days is a short time to live as a freegan, I've already learned that a lot of food is thrown away for no good reason. Perhaps I should continue with my freegan lifestyle? After all, the food we found, after a good wash, was the same as the food you buy in a shop. Except, of course, it was free.

2 43

Rosie In the fashion industry, it's almost impossible to get a job unless you do an internship first. Companies get so many applications for internships that they don't need to pay you. The most I got was about £15 a day for lunch and transport.

It's slave labour, but it teaches you a lot. I learned loads about making and designing clothes. I sometimes worked beyond 11.00 p.m., and that wasn't easy, but then you look in the newspapers and see a model who's wearing a hat that you helped to make. It's so exciting.

I'm in a lot of debt after doing three months' unpaid work in London. My parents were able to help me a bit, but I had to earn money by working in a bar as well.

Overall, I think internships are brilliant. I'd definitely advise someone to do an internship – despite the hard work and the debt, you learn so much that it's worth it.

Joe I had an internship in the music industry for a few months when I was in my early twenties. The positive side was having a job. An internship is a position in an organization like any other job, so you feel that you've taken a step in the right direction. And I enjoyed working in the music industry – I liked the office environment and my colleagues.

The downside was that I was paid very little – the minimum wage – and it all went on food and travel. And the job itself wasn't very interesting, to be honest. There were boring, repetitive tasks like writing the company newsletter or managing their social media channels.

But all in all it was positive. I think the best experience was sometimes being in the same room as the boss and listening to his phone calls – that was first-hand experience of how to run a business. And of course the internship went straight onto my CV. Any experience is better than no experience from an employer's perspective.

Lauren I've done four internships in publicity. My last one was two months at a small PR agency. They paid for my travel expenses and lunch, and I learned a lot. That really helped me when I applied for jobs because I knew what I was talking about.

But in the other three I worked ten-hour days, six days a week, and I got no money at all, so I also had to work in a pub to support myself. Each time I was told, 'Do well and there'll be a job at the end of it.' But then you realize there is no job. It makes you angry.

During one of those internships, the manager went on holiday for a month and I had to manage everything. In another one, I worked from home, using my own phone, and wasn't paid a penny, not even to cover the phone bill. I only met the boss once – it was all done by email. She promised me a job after three months, but it never happened.

3 8

Interviewer Welcome back. My next guests are two sisters who write scripts for *Bob's Burgers*, an animated series which will be shown next month on Sunday evenings. Please welcome Wendy and Lizzie Molyneux! Lizzie, Wendy, thanks so much for joining us.

Wendy / Lizzie Thanks, it's great to be here, our pleasure.

Interviewer Now, tell us a bit about *Bob's Burgers*.

Wendy Well, like *The Simpsons*, it's meant for adults and older kids even though obviously it's a cartoon.

Lizzie It's a comedy – it's about a funny guy who owns a hamburger restaurant, and his weird kids and weird wife. They all work in the restaurant and live in the apartment above, and they have lots of problems keeping the restaurant in business.

Interviewer So, how did you get the job as writers?

Wendy A few years ago we wrote a script for another animated series that the network decided not to make. But people read our script and they liked it.

Lizzie Yeah. So later we had an interview with the producers of *Bob's Burgers*. We loved the show and the producers, so we were sure we would never get the job.

Wendy But then we did!

Lizzie Happy ending!

Interviewer What's it like to be a TV writer? I mean, what's your daily routine?

Lizzie Er, we start work at about 10.00 in the morning. Most weekdays we are either working on a story or coming up with some new jokes for scripts that have already been written. Then in the afternoon it's more of the same.

Interviewer How long does it take to actually write and create an episode?

Wendy Actually, it takes a really long time – about six to eight months from the idea to recording. First, you come up with an idea for a story. Then, you work with a bunch of other writers to create an outline for the story.

Lizzie There are about ten full-time writers on the show.

Wendy Right. Then, you go write a full script. That script gets read aloud by the actors, then we record their voices in a studio. Once we have the recording, the artists create an animatic, which is like a rough draft of the cartoon, in black and white.

Lizzie And after that, the rough drawings are sent to a studio in Korea where the colour animation is created.

3 9

Interviewer Who do you think is most important to the show: the actors, the writers, or the director? Or someone else?

Lizzie Well, on our show it is definitely the creator of the show, Loren Bouchard. He's always at the office. He manages the writers, the directors, the actors, and pretty much everything else.

Wendy Yeah. He barely even has time to eat, but when he does he pretty much only eats baked potatoes.

Interviewer Sounds like a strange guy. Do you have guest stars on *Bob's Burgers*?

Wendy Actually yes, we've had a lot of amazing guest stars on our show, like Jon Hamm from *Mad Men*.

Interviewer What's it like being sisters and co-writers? Did you write things together when you were children?

Lizzie We probably collaborated on making fun of our other sisters, but we didn't actually write together until we were adults.

Interviewer Apart from *Bob's Burgers*, what TV programmes do you like?

Wendy Actually, I love watching dramas like *Game Of Thrones* or *Homeland*. I don't always want to watch other comedies, because then I'd be thinking about work. I will watch anything with zombies as well!

Lizzie I also enjoy terrible reality shows like *The Real Housewives of Beverly Hills*.

Interviewer One last question. What are your future ambitions?

Wendy To write more TV!

Interviewer Wendy, Lizzie, thank you for coming on the programme.

Wendy / Lizzie Thank you. Our pleasure.

3 15

Melisa I live in Istanbul now, in Turkey, but I used to live in the country in the province of Sakarya. It was an amazing place to live – just so beautiful. There's a large lake nearby and the hills are covered with pine trees – people go to picnic there. The coast is also not far away. When I lived there it was as if time had stood still. There was no water or electricity – we had our own well and generator – and there was only one shop. We had to wait for a minibus from the nearest town to bring fresh bread and the newspapers every morning! I worked in a school in a nearby town – in fact the one that sent the bread and papers – and in my free time I played tennis, went for walks, and played the piano. I made my own entertainment. In the end I had to move to Istanbul for work, but I really miss the fresh food and fresh fish, the peace. I sometimes used to think when I was living there that there wasn't enough choice of things to do, things to buy, but now I think I have too much choice.

Eric A few years ago my wife and I retired and we moved to a little town in the mountains here in Colorado. It's gorgeous. We have a house on a hill, and we're surrounded by mountains, which we can see from our window, as well as the woods and a very pretty lake. There are lots of paths and we walk every morning with our dog, er, who loves chasing after sticks and things.

There's so much to do. In the summer we go hiking and we have a little canoe we take on the lake, and of course in the winter we go skiing. We have lots of friends here and we often have dinner parties or we have our book club meetings. There's a joke here that we only have three seasons: summer, winter, and 'mud season'. That's after the snow has melted and everything, I mean everything, is covered in mud. That's the only bad time to be here. And the other problem is that we don't have a supermarket. The nearest one's about 20 miles from here.

3 19

Interviewer How long have you been on *The Archers*?

Tim Well, I celebrated 30 years on *The Archers* this June.

Interviewer Which character do you play?

Tim I play a character called David Archer, who is a farmer, who's the son of Phil Archer, who in turn was the son of Dan Archer, who was the very first Mr Archer back in 1951, when the programme started.

Interviewer What kind of person is David Archer?

Tim Well, David is some..., some might say he's a bit thick, 'thick' meaning stupid. He's not. He's a simple soul. He's extremely honourable, he's extremely hard-working, he's honest, he's dependable. But he's a farmer, and that's the most important thing in his life, is making the farm work and keeping his family together.

Interviewer How much did you know about life on a farm before you joined the cast?

Tim Well, unusually, I actually knew a bit because I'd worked on farms when I was a child. And I was in fact born on a sheep station in Tasmania. And so when I was a boy I used to go and work casually at the local farm. And then also my father in the 1970s gave up being an advertising executive and went off down to Devon to live off the land, and so he started this ten-acre organic smallholding in Devon. And my wife and I went down and helped him to get that going, so I've got quite a lot of practical experience on the farm.

Interviewer Is that an exception on *The Archers*?

Tim Yes, yes, most of the actors don't know one end of a cow from the other, to be honest.

Interviewer Do you think that country and city people react to *The Archers* in a different way?

Tim Yes, they do. City people look at Ambridge, which is the village that we live in, as a kind of an English ideal of the countryside. It's an old-fashioned England where everybody's nice to each other. There's not much crime. There aren't any yellow lines so that you can't park. And that's, I think, what they love about it. And from the country people, what they tend to like is the fact that they all say, 'That's exactly like the village that I live in.' There's the vicar, there's the doctor, there's the person who runs the pub – and there's the bossy woman who runs around trying to organize everybody, you know.
Interviewer Would you actually like to live on a farm yourself – or do you?
Tim We've got a cottage in Norfolk, so we're – I'm up in the country every weekend. And also I was brought up in the country. Until I was 21, we lived just north of London, in Hertfordshire. So I'm a country boy at heart and, er, you know...
Interviewer Have you ever lived in a city?
Tim Yeah, we do now. I mean, I've lived in London since – well, for 30 years. So I'm a country boy who's kind of ended up in the town because that's where the work is.
Interviewer Thank you very much.
Tim My great pleasure.

3 21
Rob He was attacked?
Jenny That's right. The police found him at the airport.
Rob You're sure it's the same person?
Jenny Definitely. I saw his picture. His name's Andrew Page and he's a scientist.
Rob And you spoke to him?
Jenny He helped carry my bags! I mean, I could have been the last person to see him before it happened.
Rob I think you should go to the police.
Jenny I know. And Rob, there's something else.
Rob What is it?
Jenny Well, I don't want to worry you, but your dad hasn't come home. We were supposed to have dinner at seven.
Rob What time is it now?
Jenny It's a little after nine.
Rob What? That is worrying. Dad's usually really punctual.
Jenny Should I call the police?
Rob I think you should. It's really not like him.
Jenny OK, and Rob?
Rob Yeah?
Jenny Oh, it's nothing.
Rob What is it?
Jenny I know this seems odd but the house feels strange.
Rob What do you mean?
Jenny I don't know, but I don't like being alone here.
Rob Well, it's late and you're tired.
Jenny That's true. But I don't think I'll be able to sleep here.
Rob Why don't you ring Luke? You could stay with him, and you could go to the police together and tell them about Dad.
Jenny OK, I think I'll do that.
Rob I'll ring you later.
Jenny OK. Rob, I'll be fine. Don't worry. Bye.

3 24
Jenny Good morning.
Luke Hi.
Jenny Thanks for letting me stay. I feel a lot safer here.
Luke What? Oh, no problem.
Jenny I tried Henry again. Still no answer. I wonder if...
Luke Yes! I've done it! I'm in.
Jenny What?
Luke I've cracked the security code on your computer.
Jenny That's great, Luke, but Henry...
Luke Wait a minute, that's not right. The username says A. Page... and all the files are encrypted.
Jenny A. Page? Are you sure?
Luke Let me just see if I can open the files. What the...? Jenny, take a look at this. It's a formula or something.
Jenny What does it mean?
Luke I have no idea.
Jenny It's a message from Henry!
Luke What? What does it say?
Jenny It's a video. Hang on.
Henry Hello, Jenny. As you can see, I'm all right. I can't tell you where I am. But listen carefully. These people want some documents on your computer. They want you to leave it at the house. To prove that I'm OK, here's a copy of this morning's paper.
Henry There's one last thing that they want me to tell you. Don't go to the police again. If you go to the police, you know what'll happen. Now, Jenny, please don't worry. Tell Rob his old man will be in his study again soon.
Jenny We need to call Rob.

3 31
1 I love IKEA. Especially the bookshelves. We have several. And I'm usually pretty good at putting their stuff together. But I have had a few problems over the years. I remember I once had some trouble with a wardrobe. After hours and hours, and a lot of swearing, I finally managed to put it together. But I'd assembled it in my study, next to the bedroom, which was where the wardrobe was going, because I had more space there. And when my husband and I tried to move it into the bedroom we couldn't get it to fit through the door. So I had to take it to pieces, move all the bits into the bedroom, and start all over again. I suppose it was my fault though, not IKEA's. And the wardrobe looked very nice and has lasted for ages.
2 About three years ago, my girlfriend and I went to IKEA to buy a kitchen. The units were cheap and cheerful, but they also looked quite well-designed, and we were very excited by how good it was all going to look. The guy in the store said they were easy to put up, that it wouldn't take long, etc., etc. and I'm quite handy, quite practical, so I thought no problem, though I admit my girlfriend was a bit sceptical. Anyway when we got home I thought I'd assemble one cupboard, just to see how easy it was going to be. It was a nightmare. The instructions were incomprehensible – it took me the whole afternoon just to do this one cupboard and when it was finished I realized I'd put the door handle on the wrong way round. In the end, we had to pay someone to come and do it all for us.
3 I have lots of things from IKEA – it's great for students because generally speaking it's pretty cheap. Anyway, I bought a table there with my boyfriend not long ago. We started putting the table together and at one point we had three legs screwed in. Then we reached for the screws to attach the fourth leg – and realized there were no more screws. We had to take off the other three legs, take one screw off every one of them and reassemble the table. It's wobbly, but at least it has four legs! But it does annoy me when they don't give you the right number of nails or screws or whatever, and it's not the first time it's happened to me. Now I always check before I bring stuff home.

3 43
Presenter Welcome back to *Breakfast*, and now's the time when we talk about what was on TV last night with our TV critic, Ryan. We're going to start with *Service*, Michel Roux's series, which had its final episode last night. Ryan, you watched the whole series, didn't you?
TV critic Yes, I did. For those of you that haven't watched it, *Service* took eight young people with no real background in service or restaurant work, and tried to convert them into great waiters, capable of working in a top restaurant in the UK, or indeed anywhere in the world.
Presenter Tell us a bit about what they were like at the beginning.
TV critic Well, in the first episode, after just a few hours of training, the group had to manage the dinner service at a pizza restaurant, and almost everything went wrong. Customers waited ages for their food, then got the wrong orders, and the team all fought with each other. One of the trainees, Nikkita, started to cry, and Ashley – well, when the pressure got too much, he simply disappeared and left the others to it!
Presenter But by the end, I'm assuming they'd all improved enormously?
TV critic Yes. In later episodes, the trainees gained massively in confidence, mainly thanks to Michel Roux's encouragement and his positive attitude, and also his great colleagues who helped to train them. They served in all sorts of different settings, including an elegant Paris restaurant – the first trip to France for most of them – and a five-star hotel. They learned to handle really demanding situations, for example, by the end Brooke was able to cook *crêpes Suzette* – at the table for her customers – that's crêpes flambéed with orange juice and alcohol. That was a moment which really boosted her confidence.
Presenter So tell us about last night's final episode.
TV critic Right. In the final episode, Chef Michel let the trainees handle the dinner service at his own Michelin-starred restaurant, Le Gavroche. He admitted that he was quite terrified, but in the end, in his own words, they did superbly well.
Presenter And the big question last night, of course, was: who were the two winners?
TV critic The two winners were Danielle, the former hairdresser, who won a scholarship to become a wine waiter. And Ashley, the young man who used to be in trouble with the law, who won the scholarship in service and waiting. But in addition, Michel Roux was so impressed with the trainees' progress that he decided to award one extra scholarship, and that went to the former salesperson James, the oldest of the group at 24.
Presenter It's an inspiring story, and we wish them all the best.
TV critic And it made great television. Next, I'm going to talk about a new sitcom that was...

4 3
Story 1
Welcome back to the evening news. It's quarter past seven, which means it's time for 'odd news', our round-up of strange and unusual stories from around the world.

Starting close to home, ATM customers in Glasgow were pleasantly surprised this afternoon when a cash machine started giving out free money. The Bank of Scotland ATM was giving out double the amount requested by customers – if you asked for £20, you got £40. The news spread quickly over social networks, and soon over a hundred people were queuing, looking for free money. Eventually, police arrived and stood guard over the machine until the bank was able to switch it off remotely. The bank said it was unlikely to take action because of the difficulty of tracing all the payments made.

This is not the first time a cash machine has broken down in this way. A similar malfunction took place in London about six months ago, and some years ago cash machines in Coventry gave away more than £850,000 in error.

If you were one of the lucky ones who got an extra £20 note, be warned: keeping the extra money is considered a crime, and the law expects you to give it back. During the incident in Coventry, three family members were sent to prison for a year for collecting over £134,000 from the faulty machines.

Our next odd story takes us to the other side of the world, where...

Story 2

And now the news. If you've taken money out recently at an ATM in New York City, you might want to check your wallet for fake notes. They should be easy to spot because they'll be blank on one side and printed on ordinary paper.

Police have warned customers and shops to look out for the fakes after they were found in two ATMs on Monday. They were never supposed to fool any customers, police say. But they were meant to make the machines think they were full of cash when, in fact, they were missing about $110,000.

So who did this, and why? According to police, it was a man who worked for a company that repairs the cash machines. He filled the machine with the fake notes and kept the real money for himself. The man went on holiday to the Dominican Republic to enjoy the stolen cash, but he was immediately arrested when he came back ten days later.

For our next story, we're going over to our reporter in...

4.12

1 Hi... Yeah, not bad... Yeah, it's half time... One-all. Yeah, there's a really good crowd. The stadium's packed... No, no trouble. The Liverpool fans are making a bit of noise, but nothing major... OK, I'll call you when it's over. With a bit of luck we'll be in the semi-final in an hour's time.

2 **A** So, tell me all about it!
B It was absolutely brilliant. We were in the second row, just near the stage, and when he was singing I swear a few times he looked right at me!
A Did he sing *Baby Baby*?
B Of course! All the best songs. It was just an amazing performance.
A Were Sandy and Annette there?
B Yeah, we met for a drink in the interval.
A Gosh, you're so lucky you got tickets!

3 **A** OK, I'm looking for tickets now... There's a matinee at 3.00 p.m. and then an evening performance at 8.00 p.m.
B Let's go at 8.00 if we can get seats.
A Well, there aren't any in the stalls, but there are two upstairs in the circle, in the second row.
B OK. Go for it. It's a small theatre anyway, so we should have a good view wherever we sit.
A OK. Right, we've got them. We can pick them up at the box office.

4.17

Presenter Next on *Arts Week* is Jill who has been to see a really exciting new theatre production, *Sleep No More*, that's on in New York.
Critic Thanks, Peter. By now you've probably heard that *Sleep No More* is one of the hottest tickets in theatre here, and the performances were sold out months ago. Well, I was lucky enough to get a ticket for last night's performance. It was a thrilling, creepy murder mystery – sometimes scary, but also a lot of fun.
Presenter I've heard that it's not like any other play anyone's ever been to.
Critic That's right. It takes place in an empty six-floor building which has been transformed, just for this play, into the McKittrick Hotel. And in *Sleep No More*, the members of the audience don't have normal seats. Instead, you walk freely through the 'hotel', going into all the different rooms. While you're walking and watching, you see different parts of the play.
Presenter How many rooms are there in the 'hotel'?
Critic More than 100, and each one is completely different. For example, my favourite room was a dark, mysterious sweet shop full of candy jars. You could touch anything in the rooms, so you could open a jar and eat something if you wanted to.
The sweet shop was fun, but in fact most of the rooms were pretty spooky. For example, there was also a dark old-fashioned pharmacy. It was full of plants and herbs and collections of strange little things. Another room I liked was an empty hospital. There were about 50 drawers in this room, and every single one of them contained about a hundred samples of people's hair.
Presenter Spooky. So, what was happening while you were wandering through these rooms? Are there actors there?
Critic That's right. The members of the audience all have to wear white masks, so that you know who's the audience and who are the actors, and the actors are all wearing 1930s-style costumes. An actor might interact with you. It happened to me three times, and it was very exciting!
Presenter How long does it take to see the performance?
Critic Well, you have a few hours. The best thing is to spend the first hour or so exploring the rooms. After that, try to follow some of the characters. You may think you're just wandering around freely, but in fact the directors make sure that you end up exactly where they want you to be. And somehow, I don't understand how, we – the audience – all ended up in the same room for the final scene, and that's when you realize how many people have been walking around the, the hotel.
Presenter But what exactly is the play about?
Critic Er, that's a difficult question to answer. It's a murder mystery, I know that much. And it's a very artistic and interesting experience to walk through all the rooms. To be honest, even by the end I wasn't that certain about the plot.
Presenter So not a typical theatre performance.
Critic No, but it was a very enjoyable evening.
Presenter Thanks very much, Jill. So, now you know, if you are planning a trip to New York, try to get tickets. Next, we'll learn more about an unusual new art gallery...

4.22

Jenny Rob, are you OK?
Rob Yes... no... I don't know.
Jenny What are you going to do?
Rob I need to get to England as soon as possible. I wish I was there with you now.
Jenny Me too. I just don't know what to do. Should we go back to the police?
Rob I don't think so. You heard what they said. They're obviously watching you and I don't want them to hurt Dad!
Luke And we can't just give them the laptop. We know what they're capable of.
Rob You're right. You know, there's something bothering me about Dad's message. It's the words he used.
Jenny What do you mean?
Rob I'm not sure. Can you play the end of the message again for me?
Henry Please don't worry. Tell Rob his old man will be in his study again soon.
Rob That sounds strange.
Luke What sounds strange?
Rob 'His old man.'
Luke Why is that strange? He is your dad!
Rob But he'd never call himself my 'old man'. It's just not like him.
Jenny So what are you saying? That he said it deliberately?
Rob I think it could be a clue.
Jenny But 'old man'? What on earth can that mean?
Rob I don't know. But I'm sure it means something.
Jenny You know, there was something else. I could hear something in the background.
Luke Like a generator or something.
Jenny Not just that. At the beginning of the video. It sounded like a church bell ringing.
Luke That could be anywhere.
Jenny You're right.
Rob Anyway, I need to try and get a flight to London.
Jenny OK. Good luck. We'll call you later.
Rob Bye, guys.
Jenny Bye.
Luke Well, you definitely can't go back to Henry's house now.
Jenny You're right. I'll need to find a room in a hotel or a B&B.
Luke Don't be silly. You can stay here as long as you like.
Jenny Won't Simon mind?
Luke Simon? No, he'll understand. And we've got the spare room.
Jenny Are you sure?
Luke Of course I'm sure.
Jenny Thanks, Luke. That's very nice of you.
Luke No worries. I'll tell you about the house.

4.25

Jenny Oh, I hope we're doing the right thing.
Luke What do you mean?
Jenny Maybe we should just go to the police.
Luke We can't. You heard what the kidnappers said.
Jenny I know, I know... but it's all such a mess. What will we do if we can't find him?
Luke We will!
Jenny I hope so. I just don't know.
Luke Is that Rob?
Jenny Yes. Rob, hi!
Rob Hi, Jenny.
Jenny Any news?
Rob It's snowing really heavily and there aren't any flights to London. I don't know when I'm going to get back.
Jenny Oh, Rob, that's terrible!
Rob I know, but I'll keep trying.
Jenny Is there anything we can do?
Rob Yes, actually. I've been thinking about Dad's message – that 'old man' business.
Jenny What about it?
Rob He must be telling us where he is. It's the only explanation.
Jenny But what can we do about it? We don't know what it means.
Rob Well, Dad also mentioned something about his study, didn't he?
Jenny Yeah, but...
Rob I'm sure I remember something about an old man. It's the name of a book or a painting or something, and I think it's in the study.
Jenny Henry's study?
Rob Yeah. Listen Jenny, I think you'll have to go back there.
Jenny Back to Henry's house? But we know they're watching.
Rob I know, and I'm really sorry, but it's our only chance.
Jenny You're right. Luke and I will figure something out.
Rob Thanks, Jenny. I wish I was there to help.
Jenny Don't worry, we'll be OK. Talk to you soon.
Rob Bye Jenny. And be really careful!
Jenny Did you get that?
Luke Yes, but we can't go to the house now. If they're there, they'll see us immediately.
Jenny We'll have to go when it's dark.
Luke But they still might see us.
Jenny We can sneak in the back way. There's a footpath.
Luke Good idea. I know that way really well. I used to play around there when I was a kid.
Jenny We'll need flashlights though.
Luke I've got some.
Jenny OK. We'll have to be careful, but we just might be able to do this!

4 32

Interviewer Dino, what made you choose hairdressing?

Dino Hm, I always liked it from when I was child. I remember being taken to the barber's by my dad when I was a child in Greece, and I really loved the atmosphere there.

Interviewer He wasn't a barber himself though?

Dino No, but my aunt was a hairdresser.

Interviewer What sort of training did you do?

Dino When I came to London I went to the Vidal Sassoon Academy. It was a two-year course – absolutely fantastic, very intense. I loved it!

Interviewer What sort of things do you love or hate doing in hairdressing?

Dino I love everything. There really isn't anything I don't like. And I do everything: cut, colour, highlights, straightening. Nowadays some hairdressers specialize in maybe just colour, or just styling, but I think it's important to do everything.

Interviewer So do you think that's an important quality for a hairdresser?

Dino Very important. I don't believe in specializing in just one area.

Interviewer Any other important qualities?

Dino I think you need to be sociable, to be able to talk to people, calm them down if they're stressed, listen to them if they want to talk.

Interviewer Do you enjoy that?

Dino Yes, I do. The sociable side of hairdressing was one of the things that attracted me to it. Even women who want to tell me all their problems – I don't mind it at all, it doesn't distract me.

Interviewer Are women clients very different from men?

Dino Yes, definitely. They are normally the ones who want to talk, and they are much more worried – stressed – about their hair. Men are more quiet and relaxed, and they're not normally very fussy about their hair.

Interviewer What do you do if a client doesn't like the results?

Dino I try to correct it immediately. That's easy if it's the colour, less easy if it's a cut.

Interviewer Have you ever had a really bad experience where you couldn't correct it?

Dino Only once, when I was still at college. I cut a woman's hair shorter than she was expecting it – not much, only about one centimetre shorter, but she burst into tears – and I couldn't correct that.

Interviewer I often feel that hairdressers always want to cut off more hair than their clients want – is that true?

Dino I think maybe it is. Many hairdressers want to make the hair healthier, and cut of all the parts that are, you know, damaged. Or sometimes they have a style in mind and they just want to do it. But obviously, normally I try to do what the customer wants. You have to be flexible. That's another important quality in a hairdresser.

Interviewer So, if you completely disagreed with what a client wanted, would you still do it?

Dino Well, if a client wanted a treatment that I thought was going to damage her hair, for example, if she wanted to have her hair bleached when it was already in bad condition, then I would say no. But if it was a question of style – for example, a woman who wanted to have her head shaved completely – I would try to convince her that it wasn't a good idea, but if she insisted, I would do it. It's her choice after all.

Interviewer Do you have any tips for having good hair?

Dino Yes – use good products, ones which are right for your type of hair. I notice that a lot of people take a lot of trouble choosing the right face cream – you know for dry skin, or problem skin, for day, for night, and so on. But with shampoo they just buy the first one they see in the supermarket.

4 37

Verger Good afternoon, everyone, and welcome to Westminster Abbey, which as you know is one of the most important and historic churches in Britain. Over 1,000 years of British history are contained within these walls and, indeed, under the floors.

We are now standing in front of the High Altar. Many of you will recognize this as the place where Prince William and Kate Middleton stood at their wedding in 2011, and of course many other royal weddings have taken place here. It's also where Princess Diana's coffin was placed during her funeral, although as you probably know she is not buried in Westminster Abbey. You may notice that although the part of the building where we are is obviously very old, the altar is relatively modern. In fact it was designed in the 19th century. Now, if I can direct your attention…

Right. Let's continue, shall we? The area where we are now is called the Shrine of St. Edward the Confessor, who was king from the year 1042 to 1066, and was the first king to be buried in the Abbey. You can see his tomb here. These tombs here are of an early king, Edward I, and his wife Eleanor, who was the daughter of the Spanish king, Ferdinand of Castile. There's an interesting story here, that when Queen Eleanor died in 1290, the King and Queen were in Lincoln, about 145 miles from London. Edward followed her body to Westminster Abbey, and at each place where they stopped overnight on the way, he erected a memorial cross. They came to be called the Eleanor crosses, and three of them still exist today. In fact…

Let's move on to see some other royal tombs. We are now in the beautiful Lady Chapel, or chapel of Henry VII as it's also called. Many other kings and queens are buried here including Queen Elizabeth I, and her half-sister Queen Mary, the daughter of Catherine of Aragon. Now, you'll notice…

We are now standing in an area called Poets' Corner, which is probably one of the most famous spots in Westminster Abbey. The first writer who was buried here was Geoffrey Chaucer in the year 1400. Charles Dickens was also buried here. And although Shakespeare is not buried here, there is a plaque for him. Jane Austen has a plaque as well, although, again, she is not actually buried here in the Abbey. If I can bring you along…

We are now in an area called the Quire. These seats are where the Westminster Abbey choir sings during church services. As you can see, there is a tall and very lovely screen here, and on the other side of the screen is a monument to Sir Isaac Newton, the scientist. A number of prominent British scientists are buried in this area, including Charles Darwin, and also famous English composers. Moving on in this direction, we can see how…

The simple wooden chair that you see here is the Coronation Chair. It may look simple, but for hundreds of years, nearly every English monarch has been crowned here, including our present queen, Elizabeth II.

There's also a funny story about this chair. In the 18th century, there was a school for boys in Westminster Abbey. And if you look at the back of the Coronation Chair, you can see graffiti – I mean places where schoolboys have carved their names and written messages on the chair. Look here – one boy has written, 'I slept the night in the Coronation Chair'.

5 2

Presenter And now Brian is here to tell us about a fascinating project that's recording the life stories of people throughout the United States.

Brian That's right, Liz. It's called the StoryCorps project, and they've already recorded the stories of over 45,000 people. These are everyday ordinary people – friends, older relatives with memory loss, also veterans and immigrants with powerful stories to tell. Everyone who participates receives a free CD with their story on it, and many stories are also online for everyone to enjoy.

Presenter Wow! Can you tell us about some of the people who have recorded their stories?

Brian There are so many great ones. As I said, some of the people who have recorded their stories are people with memory problems.

Presenter OK.

Brian For instance, there was a very interesting story from a woman named Gweneviere Mann, a young woman who has no short-term memory.

Presenter Oh? So she can't remember things that have just happened?

Brian Yes, that's right. She was there with her boyfriend, Yasir Salem, and they talk about the things she does to help with her problem. For example, she always has a notecard in her pocket with the date on it. And even things like meals. She has to write down every meal she's had.

Before she started doing that, she would sometimes have lunch three times in a day because she didn't remember she'd eaten already.

Presenter Has she always had this condition?

Brian No. She went to hospital for an operation and she had a stroke, and that's when her problem started. The doctors told her that her condition would improve in a couple of years. But unfortunately, it didn't.

Presenter That sounds so sad.

Brian Well, yes. And Gweneviere did say that she was afraid she would wake up one day at age 80 and not remember the last 40 years of her life. But she and Yasir actually have a very positive attitude to it overall. She's able to laugh at her situation, and she tells a lot of funny stories. For example, she lives in New York, but after her stroke she always used to say that she lived in San Francisco. Yasir would have to correct her every time. And she often used to ask him if one of her colleagues was her mother.

Presenter But she wasn't.

Brian No, in fact they look completely different. Gweneviere's mum is dark-haired, but her colleague was blonde.

Presenter Does she mention any positive aspects of her memory loss?

Brian Yes, for example she ran the New York City marathon with Yasir. And her memory loss actually helped her. She told Yasir not to let her look at any of the distance signs along the way.

Presenter So she didn't know how far she'd run?

Brian Right. And when she asked Yasir how long they'd been running, he always told her it had been only 10 or 15 minutes, so she never felt tired or discouraged.

Presenter And did she finish?

Brian Yes, absolutely. She said that finishing the marathon made her realize that although she had lost some things, she had gained others. It's a really inspiring story, like so many others. I really recommend you listen to some of them.

Presenter I will. Thank you very much for telling us about the project.

Brian No problem.

5 10

Part 2

When George arrived at Singapore he found a telegram waiting for him.

Quite understand. Don't worry. Love Mabel.

'My God, I believe she's following me,' he said. He checked the passenger list of the next ship on its way to Singapore, and sure enough her name was on it.

There was not a moment to lose. He jumped on the first train to Bangkok. But he was uneasy; she would have no difficulty in finding out that he had gone to Bangkok. Fortunately there was a French boat sailing the next day for Saigon. He took it. At Saigon he would be safe. It would never occur to her that he had gone there.

It was five days' journey from Bangkok to Saigon and the boat was dirty, crowded, and uncomfortable. He was glad to arrive and went straight to the hotel. A telegram was immediately handed to him. It contained only two words:

Love Mabel.

He started to tremble.

'When is the next boat for Hong Kong?' he asked. He sailed to Hong Kong but was afraid to stay there. Then he went to Manila, and from there he went on to Shanghai. Shanghai made him feel nervous; every time he went out of the hotel he expected to run straight into Mabel's arms. No, Shanghai would never do. The only thing was to go to Yokohama. At the Grand Hotel in Yokohama a telegram awaited him.

So sorry I missed you at Manila. Love Mabel.

Where was she now? He went back to Shanghai. This time he went straight to the club and asked if he had received any telegrams. One was handed to him.

Arriving soon. Love Mabel.

5.12

Part 4

One morning George and the consul were in the courtyard when there was a loud knock at the door. The doorman opened it. Mabel walked in. She was neat and cool and fresh. There was nothing in her appearance to suggest that she had just come in after two weeks on the road. George was terrified. He was as pale as death. She went up to him.

'Hello, George, I was so afraid that I'd missed you again.'

'Hello, Mabel,' he said.

He did not know what to say. He looked this way and that: she stood between him and the doorway. She looked at him with a smile in her blue eyes.

'You haven't changed at all,' she said.

'I was afraid you'd got fat and bald. I've been so nervous. It would have been terrible if I hadn't been able to marry you after all.'

She turned to George's host.

'Are you the consul?' she asked.

'I am.'

'Good. I'm ready to marry him as soon as I've had a bath.'

And she did.

5.19

Jenny Keats, *The Iliad*, poems by Byron, *The Complete Works of Shakespeare*... nothing about an old man!

Luke Not even a picture on the front cover.

Jenny What about those paintings? Anything there?

Luke I've already checked them. Nothing. Should we look through each book?

Jenny That could take forever and we don't have time. This is hopeless. It's OK, it's Rob. Rob.

Rob Jenny. Any luck?

Jenny No. We've been here for hours and we've looked everywhere. We haven't found a single thing about an old man. Look Rob, maybe the 'old man' thing wasn't a secret message at all.

Rob But it sounded so odd. And why would he mention his study?

Jenny Well, he's under a lot of pressure. He probably just...

Rob Wait!

Jenny What?

Rob Is there anything on top of the bookcase?

Luke Just a load of old books. We've already been through them.

Rob Isn't there anything else?

Luke Wait a second. Yeah, there are two small paperweights.

Rob Do they have anything written on them?

Luke This one says 'Apollo, god of music and poetry'.

Rob What about the other one?

Luke It says 'Proteus... the old man of the sea'!

Rob That must be what Dad meant!

Jenny What does it mean? Who's Proteus?

Luke You know, that name sounds familiar.

Rob I think he's a Greek god. Dad's got loads of stuff like that.

Luke No, no, not that. I'm sure I've seen it somewhere. I'll Google it.

Jenny Does it mean anything to you, Rob?

Rob No. I can't remember hearing it before. Maybe it's someone's name or...

Luke Got it! Proteus is a biochemical company. It's based in Oxford and... oh, I don't believe it!

Jenny What is it, Luke?

Luke It's right by St Bartholomew's church. You know, the one with the famous bells!

Jenny That must be where Henry is! Rob, we've got to go call the police.

Laing Laing speaking... Yes?... Oh, Jenny Zielinski... OK, slow down... Where? Proteus?... Yes, I know it... No, Jenny, you can't go down there... It's too dangerous... and it's illegal... I know but... OK, OK, but not on your own... we'll meet you there in ten minutes.

Jenny It was night time and we could hear a generator in the background.

Laing Right, so we're looking for a room with a generator. How are you doing, Luke?

Luke I'm just downloading the plans for the Proteus building now. That's it. Done. OK, there's only one room with a generator. It's in the basement.

Laing Excellent.

Laing Tom, where are you?

Tom We're approaching a side entrance. There's nobody around.

Laing OK, Tom. I'm going to hand you over to Luke. He's going to guide you to a room in the basement. That's where we think Henry's being held.

Tom Got it.

Laing Be careful.

Tom Don't worry. Come on.

5.22

Newsreader Police have arrested a man and a woman following a raid on the Proteus building in Oxford early this morning. They have been named locally as Selina Lavelle and Grant McFadden. Mr McFadden has been charged with assault following the brutal attack on research scientist Andrew Page, who is still recovering in hospital. Ms Lavelle has been charged with false imprisonment, extortion, blackmail, and industrial espionage. Police believe she organized the kidnapping of university lecturer Henry Walker. Mr Walker, who was rescued in the raid, told reporters he'd been through a terrible ordeal but hadn't been badly hurt. He wished Andrew Page a speedy recovery and said he would visit him in hospital. Mr Walker thanked the police for their hard work. He said that he was too tired to talk to reporters in detail and was just looking forward to returning home.

Jenny Well, Henry, you're kind of a star.

Henry I never expected to become a celebrity, not at my age.

Rob Well, next time you're kidnapped, Dad, try to set us an easier clue.

Henry I must admit, I was beginning to lose hope. It took you a long time to work it out.

Rob You can't blame us! Proteus – the 'old man' of the sea? How were we supposed to know that?

Henry You need to brush up on your classics.

Luke Oh come on, Henry, I think we did really well!

Henry I'm joking, I'm joking. You were great and I really have to thank you. Goodness knows what would have happened if you hadn't found me in time.

Jenny We're just glad we did.

Henry Now, I had been saving this for a special occasion and, I think this is it. Could you fetch the glasses, Luke?

Luke No worries.

Rob It's great to have you back, Dad.

Jenny It sure is.

Henry I just wish you were here, Rob.

Rob Well, it's just stopped snowing. I could get a flight now and maybe we could stay there for longer. What do you think, Jenny?

Jenny Oh, I don't know. The English countryside is a little too wild for me. I can't wait to get back to the peace and quiet of New York!

5.29

Andy I think one of the best contributions America has made has been the Hollywood film industry, especially pre-turn of this current century, so we're looking at films from the Marx brothers and Harold Lloyd, to films like *Gone with the Wind* then films from somebody like Martin Scorcese or Woody Allen. I think these Hollywood movies have brought American culture and made it a higher culture in many ways and made it very exciting. I definitely think that the American ability to consume food in such vast quantities, such big sizes and mega-sizes, it's been talked about in so many ways, 'supersizing' food, I think that's a bad contribution that America has made to the general things in the world.

Molly I think the best thing about America is the can-do spirit, that you can do anything you want if you work hard enough and you really believe in your dream. I think that's great. I think the downside of America is all the chains, the sort of global chains that are set up in all countries now, and so there's, there are shops that are the same everywhere. And I think that's really a bad thing.

Jenny I think one of America's best contributions worldwide would be our effect on people's positivity and energy. We really are a new country and I think that's helped us to have that kind of onwards, upwards, bigger, better kind of attitude. And I think that affects everyone and people look to America for that. But on the other hand, they look to us for other things, like not being very healthy, being kind of fat, in general, and not really having so much positivity when it comes to our bodies.

5.36

Interviewer What's the hardest exam you've ever taken?

Mark My A-level physics exam – I didn't understand at least half the questions.

Interviewer Have you ever done an exam where everything went wrong?

Mark I'm afraid so. For a history O-level there were five questions – all short essays. I'd prepared five questions from previous exam papers, but nothing else. So I was gambling that at least three of the questions would come up. But none of them did, so obviously I didn't pass it.

Interviewer How did you usually prepare for a big exam?

Mark I remember it generally involved a lot of coffee and late nights!

Interviewer Did you find exams stressful?

Mark I never got that stressed about them until it was too late – that may have had a negative effect on the results, come to think of it. I was never the world's best at exams. I usually passed, but the results were never brilliant.

Interviewer What's the hardest exam you've ever taken?

Sophie I guess the hardest exam was probably my driving test – the practical part. I just didn't know what to expect. In fact I failed three times before I finally passed.

Interviewer Have you ever done an exam where everything went wrong?

Sophie Yes, in the beginning of my first driving test, I refused to stop where the examiner asked me to stop. I just didn't think it looked safe and I thought it was a trick – I mean, I thought that he was asking me to do something dangerous, to test me. Anyway it wasn't a trick and he wasn't happy at all.

Interviewer How did you usually prepare for a big exam?

Sophie Um, I did a lot of revising. For some exams at school and university, I also remember eating a lot of fish as I was told it helped. It's supposed to be good for your brain.

Interviewer Did exams use to stress you out?

Sophie Yes. I hated exams and used to get very nervous and stressed beforehand. But once the exam had started I usually relaxed.

Interviewer What's the hardest exam you've ever taken?

Kate Definitely my eleven plus exam. It was the first exam I'd ever done in my life. I was shocked! I still remember one of the questions, it was: 'Who was the father of the son of William Shakespeare?' I couldn't work out the answer.

Interviewer Have you ever done an exam where everything went wrong?

Kate No, I revise too much to let anything like that happen to me.

Interviewer How did you usually prepare for a big exam?

Kate Well, despite being a teacher now and telling my students not to study the night before the exam, to have an early night… I didn't use to do that myself. I used to cram right up until the last minute. And even if I did have an early night I slept really badly.

Interviewer Did exams use to stress you out?

Kate Oh yes, because you can have a bad day and simply not be able to show your real ability in a subject. I always worried that that would happen to me.

Interviewer What's the hardest exam you've ever taken?

Paul Probably the exam at the end of the first year of my geography course at university. Not because the questions were very difficult but because I'd done so little work for it.

Interviewer Have you ever done an exam where everything went wrong?

Paul Oh yes. I thought I'd done quite well in my GCSE chemistry exam but I failed it. So something must have gone very wrong.

Interviewer How did you usually prepare for a big exam?

Paul I used to read notes over and over again, right up till the last possible minute. Yeah, I relied heavily on short-term memory, I think.

Interviewer Did exams use to stress you out?

Paul Not really, though they probably would now. When I was at school and university it was just part of life – so not particularly stressful.

5 37

The first tip may seem obvious, but it's vital. Get to the place where the oral exam is going to be held in plenty of time. You need to relax before the exam, and if you're late you'll be stressed, and that will make it much more difficult. Try to get there at least half an hour before your time.

Then, when you go into the exam, make eye contact with the examiner (or examiners) and smile. Examiners are human, too. Treat them in a polite but friendly way. Body language is important too. Sit up straight, and if you are doing the exam with another candidate, try to look interested in what he or she is saying.

Another important tip if you are doing the interview in pairs – and many of the oral exams nowadays are in pairs – is to make sure you give your partner the opportunity to speak too. Ask for your partner's opinion after you've given your own, and try to integrate him or her into the conversation as much as possible.

Finally, two tips for when it's your turn to speak. Firstly, if you can't think of the word for what you want to say, don't freeze and say nothing. Paraphrase, use other words to communicate what you want to say. Say 'I'm sorry, I can't remember the word, but it's…' Don't forget that this happens to people all the time, even if they're speaking their own language.

And my last tip is, don't use prepared speeches, rehearsed speeches. Examiners can spot them straight away, and they give a very bad impression. It's fine to prepare, and to memorize words and phrases that you might need, for example, to describe what you do. But don't try to memorize whole speeches.

Try to remember the tips, and good luck! I'm sure you'll do well!

1A

pronouns

Revise the basics

1 **I** live in London. NOT ~~i live~~
2 **My** name's Anna.
3 My parents don't visit **me** very often.
4 They have a flat in north London, but **mine** is in south London.

pronouns and possessive adjectives

subject pronouns	object pronouns	possessive adjectives	possessive pronouns
I	me	my	mine
you	you	your	yours
he / she / it	him / her / it	his / her / its	his / hers
we	us	our	ours
you	you	your	yours
they	them	their	theirs

each other
We use *each other* to talk about an action between two people or groups of people, e.g.
We gave each other our email addresses.
They send texts to each other all the time.

direct / indirect object pronouns and word order

1.8

1 He gave **me some money.**
I'm going to lend **her my camera.**
They've shown **their friends their new flat.**
I'll send **you an email.**
We bought **our father some books.**

2 He gave **it to me.**
I'm going to lend **it to her.**
They've shown **it to them.**
I'll send **it to you.**
We bought **them for him.**

1 Some verbs can have two objects, usually a thing (the **direct object**) and a person (the **indirect object**). If the direct object is a noun (*some money, a digital camera*, etc.), we usually use verb + indirect object + direct object.

2 If the direct object is a pronoun (*it, them*), we usually use verb + direct object + indirect object, with either *for* or *to* before the indirect object – it depends on the verb. Some common verbs which can have two objects are:

bring (for / to), buy (for), cook (for), find (for), get (for), make (for)

give (to), lend (to), offer (to), read (to), sell (to), send (to), show (to), take (to), write (to)

- If the indirect object is a pronoun, remember to use the object pronoun, not the subject pronoun:
I bought it for her. NOT ~~*I bought it for she.*~~
I gave them my number. NOT ~~*I gave they my number.*~~

a Circle the correct form.

Me / My middle name's Alexandra, but *I / me* never use it.

1 My sister doesn't have a tablet. *He / She* prefers *his / her* laptop.
2 **A** Are these *your / yours* books here?
B Yes, they're *my / mine.*
3 Most people are happy with *theirs / their* names, but Kim doesn't like *her / hers.*
4 **A** What are *hers / her* children called?
B I don't know, she's never told *me / my.*
5 I gave *them / their* my phone number, but they didn't give me *theirs / their.*
6 **A** Is this *ours / our* car key?
B No, *ours / our* says 'VW'.
7 This is *my / mine* pen, so that one must be *your / yours.*
8 She'll phone *us / we* when *her / hers* flight arrives.
9 You should send *he / him* some photos – this is *his / him* email address.
10 *It's / They're* a really good restaurant but I can never remember *his / its* name.

b Rewrite the highlighted phrases. Replace the **bold** words with a pronoun and use *to / for.*

I gave you **that pen**. *I gave it to you.*

1 They sent me **a new password** yesterday.
2 I gave my girlfriend **some flowers**, but she's still angry with me.
3 She found me **some hotels** online.
4 My sister wrote me **these letters** when she was living in Japan.
5 Will you lend him **the money**?
6 My son made me **a birthday card** at school.
7 They didn't have the keys so they couldn't show us **their new flat**.
8 We didn't buy our daughter **a computer** because we think she's too young.
9 I read the children **the first Harry Potter book** last week.
10 A friend at university sold me **these CDs** for 50p each.

adjectives

Revise the basics

1 It's a **poisonous snake**. NOT ~~*snake poisonous*~~
2 They're very **powerful people**. NOT ~~*powerfuls people*~~
3 I'm **older than** my brother. NOT ~~*more old that*~~
4 Rome isn't **as expensive as** Paris. NOT ~~*as expensive than*~~
5 It's **the most difficult** exercise in the book. NOT ~~*the difficultest*~~

comparative and superlative adjectives

adjective	comparative	superlative
tall hot	taller hotter	the tallest the hottest
modern busy	more modern busier	the most modern the busiest
dangerous interesting	more dangerous less interesting	the most dangerous the least interesting
good bad far	better worse further	the best the worst the furthest

adjective + *one* / *ones*

I've lost my suitcase. It's a **big, blue one**. 1 16
Expensive laptops are usually more reliable than **cheap ones**.

- We use *one* / *ones* after an adjective instead of repeating a singular or plural noun.
- We don't use *one* / *ones* with uncountable nouns.
  I'm looking for full-time work, but I'd be happy with part-time. NOT ~~*part-time one*~~

more rules for comparatives and superlatives

1 I feel **more tired** than I did yesterday. 1 17
She's **the most stressed** person in the office.
2 She's **the cleverest** girl in the class.
The old road was much **narrower** than the new one.
It would be **simpler** to go back to the beginning.

1 One-syllable adjectives which end in *-ed* always use *more* and *the most* for comparatives and superlatives, e.g. *bored, pleased, shocked, stressed, tired*.
2 Some two-syllable adjectives can make comparatives and superlatives with *-er* and *-est*. Common examples are *clever, narrow, polite, quiet, simple, stupid*.
- A good dictionary will tell you the usual comparative and superlative form for a two-syllable adjective.

a bit and *much* + comparative adjective

1 It's **a bit cloudier** today than yesterday. 1 18
This phone's **a bit more expensive** than that one.
2 Your job is **much more stressful** than mine.
The business is **much busier** than it was last year.

1 We use *a bit* + comparative adjective to say that a difference is small.
2 We use *much* + comparative adjective to say that a difference is large.

a Are the highlighted forms right (✓) or wrong (✗)? Correct the wrong ones.

He's happier than he was yesterday. ✓
She's a person very ambitious. ✗
She's a very ambitious person.
1 That's the baddest film I've ever seen.
2 I'm not as sporty than my brother.
3 Cats are more selfish than dogs.
4 Mexico is further to travel, but the hotels are less expensive.
5 I always lose my phone, so I bought a cheap one.
6 My husband's a more good driver than I am.
7 These shoes are the more comfortable ones I have.
8 My brothers and sisters are all very successfuls.
9 This exercise is easyer than the other one.
10 It's the biggest room in the house.

b Complete the sentences to mean the same thing.

Adam is friendlier than Chris.
Chris isn't *as friendly* as Adam.
1 Tom isn't as lucky as his brother.
Tom's brother is ______ than he is.
2 Their house is much bigger than ours.
Our house is ______ than theirs.
3 My new password is easier to memorize than my old one.
My old password was ______ to memorize than my new one.
4 This flat is nicer than the other two we've looked at.
This flat is ______ of the three we've looked at.
5 My sister's children are more helpful than mine.
My children aren't ______ as my sister's.
6 The weather wasn't as good as we'd expected.
The weather was ______ than we'd expected.
7 The film was much less exciting than the book.
The book was ______ than the film.
8 Yellow will look better than red for your kitchen.
Red won't look ______ as yellow for your kitchen.

2A

present tenses

Revise the basics

present simple and frequency

1 **She goes** abroad a lot. NOT ~~*She go*~~
2 **Does he know** how to ski? NOT ~~*Do he know*~~
3 **We don't like** camping. NOT ~~*We not like*~~
4 **They never go** swimming. NOT ~~*Never they go*~~
5 **He's always late**. NOT ~~*Always he's late*~~
6 **I go for a walk every morning.** NOT ~~*I go every morning for a walk.*~~

present continuous

7 **He's working** today. NOT ~~*He working*~~
8 **They aren't / They're not sunbathing.** NOT ~~*They not sunbathing.*~~
9 **Are you going away** this weekend? NOT ~~*Do you go*~~ / ~~*You are going*~~

action and non-action verbs

1 33

1 **A** What **are** the children **doing** now?
B Mark**'s playing** tennis and Anna**'s reading**.
A Hi, Marta. **Are** you **waiting** for someone?
B Yes, I**'m waiting** for Tim.
2 I **like** vegetables now, but I didn't use to.
Oh, now I **remember** where I left my glasses.

1 Many verbs describe actions. These verbs are used in the present continuous to talk about actions happening now or in the future.
2 Some verbs describe states and feelings, not actions. Examples are *agree, be, believe, belong, depend, forget, hate, hear, know, like, look like, love, matter, mean, need, prefer, realize, recognize, remember, seem, suppose, want*. These verbs are normally used in the present simple, not the continuous, even if we are referring to now.

verbs which can have action and non-action meanings

1 34

Do you **have** any sunscreen? = possession (non-action)
He**'s having** a shower at the moment. = an action
Do you **think** we should have lunch in the hotel? = opinion (non-action)
They**'re thinking** about going on a cruise. = an action
I **see** what you mean. = understand (non-action)
I**'m seeing** the hotel manager tomorrow morning. = an action

- Some verbs have two meanings, an action meaning and a non-action meaning, e.g. *have, think, see*.
  If they describe a state or feeling, not an action, they are not usually used in the present continuous.
  If they describe an action, they can be used in the present continuous.

present continuous for future arrangements

1 35

I**'m leaving** tomorrow.
We**'re seeing** our grandparents this weekend.
When **are** they **coming** to see us?
She **isn't going out** tonight. She**'s staying in**.

- We often use the present continuous for future arrangements.

present simple for 'timetable' future

1 36

The train **leaves** at 6.30 in the morning.
Our flight **doesn't stop** in Hong Kong. It **stops** in Singapore.
When **do** you **arrive** in New York?

- We can use the present simple to talk about things which will happen according to a timetable, especially travel times and arrangements. The present continuous is usually possible as well.

a Complete the sentences with the present simple or present continuous form of the verbs in brackets.

<u>Do</u> you <u>know</u> how to waterski? (know)
1 __________ you __________ camping or staying in cheap hotels? (prefer)
2 We __________ of going on a safari next year. (think)
3 __________ we __________ to take insect repellent? (need)
4 She __________ to Frankfurt for a business meeting next week. (fly)
5 **A** This hotel __________ Wi-fi. (not have)
B It __________, we can go to a café. (not matter)
6 **A** What __________ you __________? (do)
B I __________ the spare memory card for my camera. (look for)
7 Tanya __________ a massage at the moment, and I __________ for souvenirs. (have, shop)
8 **A** Where __________ you __________ this weekend? (go)
B We __________ at home. (stay)

b Circle the correct form of the verb. Tick (✓) if both are possible.

We're going / *We go* to New Zealand on Saturday. The flight [1] *leaves* / *is leaving* at 6.50 in the morning. [2] *We need* / *We're needing* to check in two hours ahead, so [3] *we go* / *we're going* to the airport the night before, and [4] *we stay* / *we're staying* in an airport hotel (£200 a night, but it's better than getting up at 2.00 a.m.!). The first part of the flight, to Singapore, [5] *takes* / *is taking* 14 hours, and [6] *we break* / *we're breaking* the journey there for a couple of days. Then it's on to Auckland. The flight [7] *gets in* / *is getting in* at nearly midnight, but our friends [8] *meet* / *are meeting* us at the airport, and [9] *they look after* / *they're looking after* us for a week or so. Then [10] *we travel* / *we're travelling* round North and South Island – [11] *we rent* / *we're renting* a camper van. [12] *We have* / *We're having* to be back in Auckland on 22 February, but I don't think I'll want to come home!

possessives

possessive 's

1 That's **Mark's** jacket. 1 41
Have you seen **Andrew's** phone?
He's my **sister's** boyfriend.
2 I asked **Chris'** advice. / I asked **Chris's** advice.
3 This is a photo of my **parents'** house.
That's the **children's** bedroom.
4 We spent the weekend at **Paul's**.
I went to **my grandmother's** yesterday.

1 We usually use possessive *'s* to show possession after the names of people, animals, and organizations: *Have you seen the dog's lead? What do you think of the government's plans for education reform?*
2 If a name ends with *-s*, we make the possessive with *'* or *'s*. Both are pronounced /ɪz/.
3 Possessives are different for regular and irregular plurals.
- After a plural noun ending in *-s*, we make the possessive with a final *'* (but no extra *s*).
- After an irregular plural not ending in *-s*, we make the possessive with *'s*.

4 We can use *name* / *person* + *'s* to mean that person's house or flat.

's after two names
We saw Tom and Mary's parents. = Tom and Mary are brother and sister. We saw their parents.
We saw Gill's and David's parents. = We saw Gill's parents and we saw David's parents.

of to show possession

1 What's **the name of the street** where you live? 1 42
They sat at **the back of the bus**.
I've found **the top of the shampoo bottle**.
2 That man over there is **a friend of mine**.
This is **an interesting book of Sarah's**.
Tell me about **this plan of theirs**.
Where's **that husband of yours**?

1 With other nouns (not people or animals), we often use *of*.
2 We often use noun + *of* + possessive pronoun or name / noun + *'s* after *a* / *an* or *this* / *that*, not *'s*.

own

I'd love to have **my own** business. 1 43
That's my magazine – you can get **your own**.
Our town is going to get **its own** shopping centre.
Small bakers often sell **their own** bread and cakes.

We can use *own* after a possessive adjective for emphasis:

a Complete the sentences with apostrophes (') where necessary (possession or contraction).

Mark's brother works in a chemist's.

1 There are lots of expensive womens clothes shops round here.
2 We went to James and Amandas party last night.
3 Thats the towns only bakers.
4 On Saturdays I often look round the shops.
5 Theres been a florists on that corner for years.
6 Two of my friends wives run small businesses from home.
7 Shes going to spend a few nights at her parents.
8 There are too many estate agents in this neighbourhood.
9 Charles sisters both live in flats in the centre.
10 The towns only greengrocers closed down last year.

b Circle the correct form.

What's *the name of the street* / *the street's name* where you live?

1 That's *the car of my friend* / *my friend's car* over there.
2 He's 95 years old but he still does *all his own* / *all their own* shopping.
3 I live in the flat at *the building's top* / *the top of the building*.
4 I quite like supermarket pizza but I prefer to make *my own* / *mine own*.
5 I can't remember *the name of the book* / *the book's name*.
6 **A** Who's Sarah?
B She's *my husband's sister* / *my sister's husband*.
7 Every Christmas we go to *my wife's parents'* / *my wife's parent's*.
8 I've known him for years – he's a very good *my friend* / *friend of mine*.
9 Not many people live in *the centre of London* / *London's centre*.
10 I'm always really tired at *the day's end* / *the end of the day*.

3A

past simple, past continuous, or *used to*?

Revise the basics

past simple

1 When I **was** young I **loved** playing outside.
2 We **didn't live** in a big city.
3 Where **did** you **go** to school?

past continuous

4 I **was watching** TV when you arrived.
5 She **wasn't studying** when I called her.
6 What **were** you **doing** at 9.00 this morning?

used to

7 He **used to have** long hair.
8 They **didn't use to live** in London.
9 What music **did** you **use to like** when you were young?

past simple and past continuous

2 3

1 I **saw** him two minutes ago.
Humans **didn't live** in cities until about 8,000 years ago.
Where **did** you **grow up**?
2 What **were** you **doing** at 7.00 o'clock this morning?
He **was texting** a friend when the accident **happened**.
Sorry, what **did** you **say**? I **wasn't listening**.

1 We use the past simple for finished past actions or states (when we say, ask, or know when they happened). We can use the past simple for things which happened at any time in the past – very recently, or a long time ago. The important thing is that we see them as finished.

➤ *For irregular past simple verbs see* **Irregular verbs** *p.165.*

2 We use the past continuous:
- to talk about an action in progress at a specific time in the past.
- to describe a past action which was interrupted by another action (expressed in the past simple).

used to

2 4

1 We **used to live** in Rome.
I **used to have** very long hair.
2 I **often went** to the cinema **when I lived in London**.
He **never wore** a suit and tie **when he was a student**.

1 We use *used to* (not the past continuous) to describe a habit or state that was true for a significant period in the past, and that has now finished.
- We *don't* say *We used to live in Rome* if:
  – we only lived in Rome for a short period of time, e.g. three months (= *We **lived** in Rome for three months*).
  – we still live in Rome. (= *We've **lived** / We've **been living** in Rome for the last three years*).

2 We can also often use the past simple with an adverb of frequency instead of *used to*.

a Circle the correct form of the verb. Tick (✓) if both are possible.

I grew up / *I was growing up* in a little village.
1 They *were having* / *used to have* dinner when I *phoned* / *was phoning* them.
2 When we were young our parents *took* / *used to take* us to the beach every weekend.
3 She *was still having* / *still had* breakfast when the taxi *arrived* / *used to arrive*.
4 *Did your brother teach* / *Was your brother teaching* you to play the guitar when you were young?
5 When I was younger I *used to love* / *was loving* helping my mum cook.
6 He *had* / *used to have* a beard when he *was* / *was being* at university.
7 We *used to spend* / *were spending* all day playing together when we were children.
8 He *was using* / *used* his mobile when the accident *happened* / *was happening*.
9 We *didn't go* / *didn't use to go* abroad last year.
10 They *didn't use to have* / *weren't having* a car when I *knew* / *was knowing* them.

b Are the highlighted forms right (✓) or wrong (✗)? Correct the wrong ones.

Where did you use to go on holiday last year? ✗
Where did you go on holiday last year?
1 This time last week I was sitting on a beach.
2 When did they use to get married?
3 I used to find it very hard to get a job when I left university.
4 We used to love going to concerts when we were students.
5 Were you seeing anything good on TV last night?
6 My brother and I didn't use to get on very well when we were young.
7 He was never studying much at school.
8 Where did you grow up?
9 Sorry, I didn't hear what you said, I listened to the radio.
10 We were moving to Manchester when my father got a job there.

prepositions

prepositions of place

She sat **in** the square and watched the tourists. 2 20
There's a box **under** your bed.
You'll find some cash **inside** my purse.
The cups are **on** that shelf there.
There's a man standing **in front of** the gate.

- Prepositions that describe place, like *in* and *on*, have an independent meaning. They can be used with different verbs and places and the meaning doesn't change.

prepositions of movement

They flew **over** the city. 2 21
He ran **across** the road.
He walked **through** the door.
Go **along** the street, **past** the supermarket.
Don't run **down** the steps. You'll fall.

- Prepositions that describe movement, like *over* and *through*, have an independent meaning. They can be used with different verbs of movement and the meaning doesn't change.

dependent prepositions after verbs and adjectives

1 We **waited for** the film to start. 2 22
They all **laughed at** me.
2 I'm **worried about** my camera – the flash isn't working.
She's **interested in** astrology.
3 He's **good at spending** other people's money.
She **believes in taking** lots of pictures and then **choosing** the best.

1 Some verbs are always followed by the same preposition.
2 Some adjectives are always followed by the same preposition.
3 If there is a verb after the preposition, we use the *-ing* form, not the infinitive.

The verbs *ask*, *discuss*, *enter*, *marry*, and *tell* have no preposition, e.g.
I **asked Jack** for directions. NOT ~~asked to~~
We **discussed the situation**. NOT ~~discussed about~~
The police officers **entered the building**. NOT ~~entered in~~
She **married her personal trainer**. NOT ~~married with~~
The photographer **told everyone** to smile. NOT ~~told to~~

➤ *For a list of prepositions after verbs and adjectives see p.164.*

a Complete the story with the correct prepositions.

across onto under into ~~down~~ off towards
next to round on between in along

The mouse ran *down* the stairs, [1] ___ the corridor, and [2] ___ the kitchen. It jumped [3] ___ the table, and ran [4] ___ the salt and pepper and [5] ___ the coffee pot. There was some cheese [6] ___ a plate. The mouse stole a piece, jumped [7] ___ the table, and disappeared [8] ___ the door. Then it ran [9] ___ the garden and stopped [10] ___ the gate. But unfortunately two cats were hiding [11] ___ the grass, and they started to creep [12] ___ the mouse…

b Complete the sentences with the correct preposition.

She paid *for* my flight home.
1 I'm tired ___ all this work – I'm ready ___ a holiday!
2 I'm not looking forward ___ apologizing ___ what happened.
3 He's very proud ___ his new camera.
4 Mum! Josh won't share his sweets ___ me!
5 You can't always rely ___ the trains here – they're often late.
6 What are you talking ___?
7 The pilot told us not to worry ___ the turbulence.
8 Who's responsible ___ updating the website?
9 There's no point arguing ___ it now – let's wait ___ the boss to get here.
10 I'm interested ___ photography, but I'm not very good ___ taking photographs!

4A

future forms: *will / shall* and *going to*

will / shall

1 **Predictions** 2 38
Who do you think **will win** tomorrow's game?
The climate probably **won't change** much in the next five or ten years.

2 **Future facts**
I'**ll be** at work on Monday.
The election **will be** on 6 May.

3 **Instant decisions**
A Is that the phone ringing?
B Yes, I think so. I'**ll get** it.

4 **Promises**
A Have you been using my laptop? You didn't switch it off.
B Oh sorry. I'**ll remember** next time.
A The battery's almost run down!
B Sorry. I promise I **won't do** it again.

5 **Offers and suggestions**
I'**ll cook** dinner tonight.
Shall I **throw away** this bread?
What **shall** I **do** with my old phone?
Where **shall** we **go** for lunch today?

We use *will* / *won't* + infinitive:

1 to ask for or make predictions about what we think or believe will happen.
2 for future facts.
3 for instant decisions.
4 to make promises.
5 to offer to do something. If the offer is a question, we use *Shall I / we...?*
We also use *shall* with *I* and *we* to ask for suggestions.

going to

1 **Plans** 2 39
I'**m going to buy** a new phone this weekend.
He's **going to make** pizza for dinner.

2 **Predictions**
England **aren't going to win** – they're 3–0 down and there are only ten minutes left.
It's getting cloudy – the weather forecast says it'**s going to rain** this afternoon.

We use *going to* + infinitive:

1 when there is a plan to do something – a decision has been made.
2 to make predictions when we feel more sure of the future, for example if we can see what's going to happen.

We can often use either *will* or *going to* for predictions.

Present continuous for future arrangements
We use the present continuous when there is an arrangement to do something – something has been organized.
We're having Liz and Nick round for dinner tonight.
I'm meeting my bank manager tomorrow.
There is sometimes very little difference between a plan and an arrangement, and we can often use either *going to* or the present continuous.

a Are the highlighted forms right (✓) or wrong (✗)? Correct the wrong ones.

Shall I take the rubbish out? ✓
That's the phone – I'm going to get it. ✗ *I'll get*

1 A What are your plans for the weekend?
B I'm going to do lots of gardening, and we're going to see a film on Sunday.
2 A These cardboard boxes are all empty. Will I put them in the bin?
B No, I spoke to David and he's going to use them.
3 A I've decided to buy a new camera. I'll get one with a good zoom.
B Do I help you choose one? I know a bit about cameras.
4 A Is Katie going to be at the party?
B I don't know. Pass me my phone and I'm going to text her.
5 A Did you finish all the biscuits?
B Yes, I'm really sorry. I'm going to leave you some next time.

b Complete with the correct form of *will*, *shall*, or *going to* and the verbs in brackets.

We've decided that we *'re going to stay* in the UK for our holiday this year. (stay)

1 A It's really hot in here!
B I ______ the air conditioning. (turn on)
2 Can I borrow £10? I ______ you back tomorrow. (pay)
3 A What are you planning to do with these old clothes?
B I ______ them to the charity shop. (take)
4 A ______ I ______ some more bread when I go out? (buy)
B Yes, please. I've decided I ______ sandwiches for lunch. (make)
5 Are you going home by bus? I ______ you a lift if you like. (give)
6 A Let's go to the cinema.
B OK. What film ______ we ______? (see)
7 A What ______ you ______ with all those old bottles and jars? (do)
B I ______ them to the bottle bank for recycling. (take)
8 A I told you not to use my laptop without asking!
B Sorry, I ______ it again. (not do)

first and second conditionals

first conditional

1 If I **have** time, **I'll write** my CV tonight. 2 45
If you **don't work** hard, you **won't get** promoted.
2 If he **does** well at school, he **can go** to a good university.
I **might (may) go back** to college if I **can't find** a job.
If you **apply** for that job, you **must prepare** an up-to-date CV.
If they **fail** their exams, they **should take** them again.
3 If you **get** an interview, **think** carefully about what to wear.

We use the first conditional to talk about a possible future situation and its consequence.

1 The first conditional normally uses *if* + present simple, *will* | *won't* + infinitive.
2 We can also use other modal verbs instead of *will*, e.g. *can*, *might*, *may*, *must*, or *should*.
3 We can also use an imperative instead of *will*.

Unless

We can use *unless* instead of *if... not* in conditional sentences.
I won't come unless you come too. (= I won't come if you don't come too.)

second conditional

1 If I **had** more money, I **wouldn't need** evening work. 2 46
If they **offered** you a part-time job, **would** you **accept** it?
2 I **might meet** more people if I **lived** in a hall of residence.
You **could apply** for a scholarship if you **got** a place to study in the US.
3 If he **was (were)** here, he**'d know** what to do.
I'd take it back to the shop if I **were** you.

We use the second conditional to talk about a hypothetical or imaginary situation, or one that we *don't* think is a possibility.

1 The second conditional normally uses *if* + past simple, *would* | *wouldn't* + infinitive.
2 We can use *might* or *could* instead of *would*.
3 When we use *be* in the *if* clause, we can use *was* or *were* after *I* | *he* | *she* | *it*.
However, in the phrase *if I were you*, which is often used to give advice, only *were* is used. NOT ~~*If I was you*~~.

First or second conditional

The conditional we use depends on how likely the condition is. Compare:
If I have more time, I'll do it. (I think it's a real possibility that I'll have time.)
If I had more time, I'd do it. (I think it's unlikely or impossible that I'll have more time.)

a Circle the correct form.

If I go to university, *I'd study* | *I'll study* engineering.

1 If she had her own car, she *doesn't* | *wouldn't* need to borrow yours.
2 If I *had* | *have* a good degree, I'll get a better job.
3 You wouldn't always be late for work if you *get* | *got* an earlier bus.
4 We can't help you unless you *tell* | *told* us what the problem is.
5 If you *find* | *found* your phone, you can send me a text later.
6 *You'd* | *You'll* save time if you did your shopping online.
7 I *won't* | *wouldn't* go there unless I really had to.
8 They'd enjoy life more if they *didn't* | *don't* study all the time.
9 If you *can't* | *couldn't* find the street, just give me a ring.
10 If I *earned* | *earn* more, I could afford to go on an exotic holiday.

b Complete the sentences with the verbs in brackets.

I *wouldn't want* to do research if I didn't enjoy working on my own. (not want)

1 If I ______ to stay at university, I'll probably do a PhD or a master's degree. (decide)
2 If you didn't spend so much on clothes, you ______ borrow money all the time. (not have to)
3 I think my sister and her boyfriend ______ soon, if they can afford to pay for the wedding. (get married)
4 If I have time over the summer, I ______ for an internship. (apply)
5 I think Andy might get a scholarship if he ______ on working hard. (keep)
6 If we ______ a bigger house, we could rent a couple of rooms to students. (buy)
7 I might enjoy my job more if I ______ such awful colleagues. (not have)
8 If I ______ get a job, I won't retake my exams. (can)
9 My tutor says I must attend all the seminars if I ______ to fail. (not want)
10 I'd get more job offers if I ______ better qualified. (be)

5A

present perfect simple

Revise the basics

+		–	past participle
I **have** You **have** He / She / It **has** We **have** They **have**	I**'ve** You**'ve** He / She / It**'s** We**'ve** They**'ve**	I **haven't** You **haven't** He / She / It **hasn't** We **haven't** They **haven't**	**seen** the news.
Have you **seen** the news? **Has** he **seen** the news?		Yes, I **have**. / No, I **haven't**. Yes, he **has**. / No , he **hasn't**.	

1 I**'ve been** to Brazil but I **haven't been** to Argentina. **3 10**
Have you **ever lost** your suitcase?
She**'s never liked** skiing.
2 I don't believe it! We**'ve won** £500 on the lottery!
He**'s just sent** me a text – I'll tell you what it says.
3 **Have / Haven't** you **had** breakfast **yet**?
I **haven't talked** to her **yet** – I'm calling her later.
4 **A Have** you **painted** the kitchen?
B Yes, and I**'ve already done** the bathroom too.
5 She**'s known** him **for 20 years**.
I**'ve** only **worked** here **since last week**.
He**'s been** out **all morning**.

1 We use the present perfect for past experiences when we don't say when they happened. If we say when they happened (*five minutes ago, yesterday, last week*, etc.) we use the past simple, e.g. *I've been to Brazil a few times. I **went** to Rio in 2013.*
2 We use the present perfect to give news. If something has happened very recently, we often use *just*.
3 We use the present perfect with *yet* to ask if something has happened, or to say that it hasn't happened but that it will.
4 We use the present perfect with *already* to say that something has happened earlier than expected.
5 We can use the present perfect to talk about situations that started in the past and have continued to the present. We don't use the present simple or the present continuous, e.g.
I've lived here for three months. NOT ~~*I live here for three months*~~ / ~~*I'm living here for three months.*~~

- To express a period of time we often use *for* or *since*.
We use *for* + a period of time, e.g. *for two minutes / ten years / ages / a long time.*
We use *since* + a time in the past, e.g. *since this morning / 5.00 / September / 2004 / I was a child.*
- We can use phrases with *all* to express a period of time, e.g. *all my life, all day, all year*, etc. We don't use *for* with *all*, e.g. *I've been here all day.* NOT ~~*I've been here for all day.*~~

➤ *For irregular past participles see* ***Irregular Verbs*** *p.165.*

a Circle the correct form.

We're late – the film *has already started* / *hasn't started yet*.
1 This programme's been on for *an hour* / *10.30*.
2 I'm not really hungry because *I've already had* / *I haven't had* breakfast.
3 I've been to Canada but *I never went* / *I've never been* to the US.
4 We've known them since *we were at university* / *five years*.
5 I've only been at work for an hour but I've *just* / *already* done a lot.
6 They got married in May so *they're* / *they've been* married for six months.
7 You'll love New York – *have you been* / *did you go* there before?
8 He's lived here *since all his life* / *all his life*.
9 We've never been to Sweden but *we went* / *we've been* to Norway last year.
10 I moved to Paris 11 months ago so *I've lived* / *I live* here for nearly a year.

b Complete the sentences with the present perfect or past simple form of the verbs in brackets.

Have you *ever been* to the Edinburgh Festival? (ever / be)
1 **A** When ________ you ________ here? (get)
B I arrived at the weekend, so I ________ here for a few days. (only / be)
2 **A** ________ you ________ the weather forecast yet? (hear)
B No, I ________ the radio. (just / turn on)
3 **A** Bad news – Ben ________ a bike accident. (have)
B Oh no! When ________ that ________? (happen)
4 **A** Where's Linda?
B I think she ________ for lunch. (just / go)
5 **A** ________ you ________ him at tennis? (ever / beat)
B No, but I ________ a set the last time we played. (win)
6 **A** ________ he ________ his new job? (already / start)
B Yes, his first day ________ last Monday. (be)
7 **A** How long ________ you ________ a motorbike? (have)
B I ________ my first one 20 years ago. (buy)
8 **A** ________ you ________ that amazing documentary last night? (see)
B No, I ________ it. (miss)

5B

present perfect continuous

Revise the basics

+		–	
I **have** You **have** He / She / It **has** We **have** They **have**	I**'ve** You**'ve** He / She / It**'s** We**'ve** They**'ve**	I **haven't** You **haven't** He / She / It **hasn't** We **haven't** They **haven't**	**been living** here all year.

Have you **been playing** much tennis? Yes, I **have**. / No, I **haven't**.
Has he **been playing** much tennis? Yes, he **has**. / No, he **hasn't**.

3 16

1 **A** What **have** you **been doing** lately?
B I**'ve been playing** a lot of tennis.
She**'s been going** for a walk every morning this week.
My friends **have been coming round** a lot recently.

2 **A** You look tired.
B I**'ve been working** in the garden.
A You're covered in paint.
B Yes, I**'ve been decorating** the kitchen all day.

3 How long **have** you **been looking for** a new house?
We**'ve been living** here since last year.
It**'s been raining** all day.

1 We use the present perfect continuous with 'action verbs' for repeated actions that started in the past and have continued till now. We often use time expressions like *recently* / *lately*.

2 We use the present perfect continuous for continuous actions which have present results.

3 We use the present perfect continuous to ask or talk about situations which started in the past and are still happening now. We often use *for* / *since* or time expressions like *all day* / *all morning* / *all week*. We don't use the present continuous or the present simple, e.g.
I've been waiting since ten o'clock.
NOT ~~*I'm waiting since ten o'clock.*~~
~~*I wait since ten o'clock.*~~

- If you say *when* something happened, use the past simple, not the present perfect continuous, e.g.
I've been watching a lot of TV lately. I ***saw*** *a great programme* ***last night***. NOT ~~*I've been seeing a great programme last night.*~~

a Match the questions and answers, and complete the answers with the present perfect continuous.

Why are your clothes so wet? E
1 Why are you so late? ☐
2 It's hot in here, isn't it? ☐
3 Do you want a coffee? ☐
4 Are you going to move to London? ☐
5 Are you hungry? ☐
6 Is her English good? ☐
7 How's your new camera? ☐
8 Why are your hands all red? ☐
9 Do you think it's safe to drive? ☐
10 Have you lost a bit of weight? ☐

A I ________ strawberries. (pick)
B No, thanks. I ________ too much lately. (drink)
C Yes, I ________ to fix the air-conditioning. (try)
D I don't think so. It ________ very heavily. (snow)
E I *'ve been cleaning* the car. (clean)
F Not really. I ________ biscuits all afternoon. (eat)
G I hope so. We ________ a flat we can afford. (look for)
H Yes, she ________ it for a long time. (learn)
I Brilliant – I ________ pictures all day. (take)
J Yes, I ________ a lot of exercise. (do)
K I ________ in a traffic jam for two hours. (sit)

b Circle the correct form.

I've been working / *I'm working* too hard lately.
1 *I've been living* / *I'm living* in a small village for five years.
2 *She's travelling* / *She's been travelling* a lot for work at the moment.
3 *I haven't been sleeping* / *I'm not sleeping* well lately.
4 I arrived yesterday and *I've been staying* / *I'm staying* for two weeks.
5 He's not answering his phone – maybe *he's driving* / *he's been driving*.
6 At last! *I'm waiting* / *I've been waiting* for you for ages.

7 I can't stand this weather – *it's raining* / *it's been raining* all week.
8 Be quiet! *I've been trying* / *I'm trying* to concentrate.
9 *I've been seeing* / *I'm seeing* a lot of my family recently.
10 I need a rest. *I'm cooking* / *I've been cooking* all day.

6A

obligation, necessity, prohibition, advice

obligation and necessity

3 33

1 I **have to** fix the kitchen tap.
Do you **have to** do it yourself?
She **had to** buy new curtains.
2 You **must** be more careful.
Must I go to bed now?
You **must** pay him back as soon as possible.
3 I **need to** buy an extra tin of paint.
Did they **need to** ask someone to help them?

1 We use *have to* to talk about all kinds of obligation. *Have to* can be used in all tenses.

> **have got to**
> We often use *have got to* instead of *have to*, e.g. *I've got to phone him tomorrow.*

2 We also use *must* to talk about obligation. The meaning is similar to *have to*, but *must* is usually used when the speaker sees something as a personal obligation.
Compare:
*I **have to** start work at 9.00.* (A general obligation, the company rule.)
*I **must** remember to buy some batteries.* (A personal obligation, one that the speaker imposes.)
3 We can use *need to* to talk about things that are necessary. *Need to* can be used in all tenses.

no obligation / no necessity

3 34

1 You **don't have to** pay me now.
2 She **won't need to** paint the bathroom – it looks fine.
3 You **needn't** hurry. We have plenty of time.

1 We use (*not*) *have to* when there is no obligation to do something.
2 We use (*not*) *need to* when it is not necessary to do something.
3 We can also use *needn't* + infinitive without *to* to say that it is not necessary to do something.

prohibition

3 35

You **mustn't** change the bulb with the electricity switched on.
You **mustn't** touch that door. The paint's wet.

We use *mustn't* when there is an obligation *not* to do something. *Mustn't* and *don't have to* are completely different.
Compare:
*You **mustn't** come tomorrow. = Don't come.* (An obligation not to do something.)
*You **don't have to** come tomorrow. = It's not necessary to come.* (No obligation.)

advice

3 36

1 You **should** sell your car.
They **shouldn't** pay him before he's done the work.
2 You **ought to** get a smartphone.
She **oughtn't to** spend so much on clothes.
3 If you feel really ill, you **must** go to the doctor's.
When you're in Venice, you **have to** have a drink at Harry's Bar!

1 We use *should* / *shouldn't* to give someone advice, or to say what we think is the right thing for ourselves or for someone else to do.
2 We can also use *ought to* / *oughtn't to* to give advice.
The meaning is the same as *should*.
3 We can use *must* and *have to* to give strong advice when we think it's very important that someone does something.

a Circle the correct form. Tick (✓) if both are possible.

She *had to* / *must* buy some tools last week.
1 They *don't have to* / *mustn't* drive. There's a bus that goes there.
2 You *needn't* / *don't have to* worry about getting a ticket in advance – you can pay on the train.
3 He *shouldn't* / *doesn't have to* put a nail in the wall. It'll leave a mark.
4 *You'll have to* / *You'll need to* read the instructions before you try to assemble the table.
5 We *should* / *ought to* turn off the electricity when we go.
6 I *don't need to* / *mustn't* leave yet. I have plenty of time.
7 You *mustn't* / *don't have to* spill anything on the sofa – it's leather.
8 She *mustn't* / *didn't have to* go to work yesterday.
9 They *don't need to* / *needn't* phone us unless their train is delayed.
10 You *oughtn't to* / *don't have to* arrive late on your first day at work.

b Complete the sentences with one word.

I definitely think you *should* sell your house. It would be a really good idea.
1 You ______ remove light bulbs with wet hands. It's really dangerous.
2 Here's the form. You ______ to sign it at the bottom.
3 I think perhaps you ______ to buy a new table, and maybe you could get some chairs as well.
4 We ______ have to leave until 2.30. It'll only take an hour to get there.
5 She ______ come if she doesn't want to. Nobody will mind.
6 Our journey back was a nightmare. We ______ to wait hours for the bus.
7 You ______ read his new book! You'll love it.
8 You ______ to drink so much coffee. It's really not good for you.
9 Do I ______ to write a letter or can I just send an email?

6B

can, could, and *be able to*

ability, possibility, and permission

1 He **can** cook really well. 3 37
I **can't** come to class next week. I have an exam.
You **can't** park here. It's a no-parking zone.
2 **Can** I try this on?
Could I try it in a large?
3 **I've been able to** drive since I was 18.
You'**ll be able to** get it cheaper if you wait for the sales.
I'd love **to be able to** afford that jacket.
I like **being able to** try clothes on, so I never buy things online.
I'm afraid I **wasn't able to** speak to the manager about the new project.
4 She **could** ski when she was three years old.
They **couldn't** come to the concert last night.
He **was able to** read at a very young age.
5 I **couldn't** find it in the shops but I **was able to** buy it online.
The current was very strong, but he **was able to** swim to the shore.

1 We use *can* to talk about ability, possibility, and permission. *Can* is a modal verb, and it only has a present form (which can be used to talk about the future) and a past / conditional form (*could*).
2 We often use *Can I...?* or *Could I...?* to make requests. *Could I...?* is more polite.
3 For all other tenses and forms, we use *be able to* + infinitive. We also sometimes use *be able to* in the present and past if we want to be more formal.
4 We use *could* / *couldn't* to talk about general ability or possibility in the past. We can also use *was* / *were able to* but it is more formal.
5 If we want to talk about ability on **one specific occasion** in the past, we can use *couldn't* but not *could*. Instead we use *was* / *were able to*.
- We can also use *managed to* instead of *was* / *were able to*, e.g. *I managed to buy it online.*

deduction

The supermarket **can't** be closed – it's only 4.00 o'clock. 3 38
They **can't** be back yet. They said they were coming home on Sunday.

- We use *can't* to say we are sure that something is impossible / not true.
- In this sense the opposite of *can't* is *must*. Compare:
She can't be at work now. It's only 7.30 a.m. (= I'm sure it's not true.)
She must be at work now. It's 9.30 a.m. (= I'm sure it's true.)

a Are the highlighted forms right (✓) or wrong (✗)? Correct the wrong ones.

I'm afraid I won't can go to the meeting. ✗ *I won't be able to*
1 He can to speak French really well.
2 The office is closed now, but you should can phone them on Monday.
3 He loves music – he could play the violin when he was four!
4 You couldn't be serious! The ball was definitely out.

5 I love this shopping centre. It's great to be able to buy everything in one place.
6 There's a shop assistant – she might can help you.
7 I tried to phone the bank but I wasn't able to get through.
8 Will I can use my UK credit card when I'm in the US?
9 I bought a new bike yesterday – I could get 10% off by paying cash.
10 This camera's really cheap – it can't be very good.

b Complete the sentences with the correct form of *can, could,* or *be able to.*

The chemist's was closed, but I *was able to* get some aspirin at the supermarket.
1 I prefer real clothes shops to shopping online. I hate not __________ try things on.
2 If we __________ afford it, we'd eat out every week.
3 This shirt is much too small for me. It __________ be an extra large.
4 __________ you see if they have these jeans in my size?
5 If it doesn't fit you, you should __________ change it.
6 They __________ find the book anywhere in the UK, so they ordered it from a US website.
7 I've never __________ pronounce her name correctly.
8 £50 for two pairs of socks? They __________ cost that much!
9 I spent ages looking for the right shoes, and in the end I __________ find the perfect pair.
10 She's got a beautiful voice. I'd love __________ sing like that.

7A

phrasal verbs

Type 1 – phrasal verbs with no object

4 4

I **get up** at 6.00 o'clock.
They **went away** last weekend.
What time are you **coming back** tonight?
They **set off** early in the morning.
My sister and her boyfriend have **split up**.

- Some phrasal verbs have no object. The verb and the particle are never separated. NOT ~~*I get at 6.00 up.*~~

Type 2 – phrasal verbs with an object – separable

4 5

1 I **looked** the word **up** in the dictionary.
I **looked up** the word in the dictionary.
Can you **fill** this form **in**?
Can you **fill in** this form?
Did you **switch** the computer **off**?
Did you **switch off** the computer?

2 I **looked** it **up**.
Can you **fill** it **in**?
Did you **switch** it **off**?

1 Some phrasal verbs have an object and can be separated – we can put the object before or after the particle.

2 If the object is a pronoun (*it*, *them*, etc.), it *always* goes between the verb and the particle.
I put it on. NOT ~~*I put on it.*~~

Type 3 – phrasal verbs with an object – inseparable

4 6

1 My husband **looks after** the children.
A Where's your book?
B I don't know. I'm **looking for** it.
A Shall we ask for the bill?
B I've already **asked for** it.

2 He **doesn't get on with** his parents.
She's **looking forward to** her holiday.
You should **look out for** job vacancies.

1 Some phrasal verbs have an object but can't be separated – the verb and the particle must stay together, even if the object is a pronoun.
He looks after the children. He looks after them.
NOT ~~*He looks the children after. He looks them after.*~~

2 Some phrasal verbs have two particles – they are never separated.

Some common phrasal verbs

Type 1
be on, end up, grow up, move in, set off

Type 2
check out, close down, give away, give up, open up, pay back, pick up, put away, put on, put up, send back, set up, switch off, take back, take out, throw away, try on, turn up / down / on / off

Type 3
ask for, be out of, fall out with, fit in with, get away from, get out of, look after, look for, look forward to, look out for, look round, move back to

a Circle the correct form. Tick (✓) if both are possible.

Shall I *switch off my laptop* | *switch my laptop off*? ✓

1. The pasta was cold so I *sent back it* | *sent it back*.
2. I went to the cashpoint and *took out €100* | *took €100 out*.
3. Could you *turn down the music* | *turn the music down*?
4. They *set off at 7.00* | *set at 7.00 off*.
5. I decided I didn't like my new coat so I *took back it* | *took it back* to the shop.
6. I *picked up his wallet* | *picked his wallet up* for him.
7. She lent me some money but I haven't *paid back her* | *paid her back* yet.
8. I *set up our new computer* | *set our new computer up* at the weekend.
9. I *grew up in Wales* | *grew in Wales up*.
10. Can you *put those clothes away* | *put away those clothes*?

b Complete the sentences using a pronoun and the correct form of the phrasal verb in brackets.

Your phone's ringing. Please *turn it off*. (turn off)

1. My parents are arriving at 11.15. Could you ______ at the airport? (pick up)
2. **A** When do you leave on your trip to China?
   B Next Saturday. I'm really ______ (look forward to)
3. **A** Do they still have their website?
   B No, they ______ a month ago. (close down)
4. **A** Is she still with her boyfriend?
   B No, she's ______. (fall out with)
5. **A** Have you found your glasses yet?
   B No, and I've been ______ for half an hour! (look for)
6. **A** Did he buy the trousers?
   B No, he ______ but they didn't fit. (try on)
7. This cheese is past its sell-by date. I'm going to ______. (throw away)
8. She was with her husband for 20 years, and she ______ during his final illness. (look after)
9. **A** Have they brought the bill?
   B No, but I've ______. (ask for)
10. **A** Is the TV loud enough?
    B No. Could you ______ a bit? (turn up)

verb patterns

Revise the basics

infinitive with *to*

1 It's very difficult **to read** his writing. NOT ~~*It's very difficult read…*~~
2 I need **to go** to the supermarket. NOT ~~*I need go…*~~
3 I went to the cinema **to see** the new James Bond film. NOT ~~*I went to the cinema for to see…*~~
4 Be careful **not to stay** in the sun too long. NOT ~~*Be careful to not stay…*~~

infinitive without *to*

5 He can **speak** English very well. NOT ~~*He can to speak English…*~~
6 We mustn't **be** late. NOT ~~*We mustn't to be late.*~~

gerund (verb + *-ing*)

7 **Watching** TV helps me to relax in the evening. NOT ~~*Watch TV helps me…*~~
8 I'm not very good at **remembering** names. NOT ~~*I'm not very good at remember…*~~
9 I love **lying** in the sun. NOT ~~*I love lie…*~~
10 I hate **not seeing** the children at bathtime. NOT ~~*I hate not see the children…*~~

➤ *For a list of verb patterns see p.164.*

verbs + infinitive (with or without *to*)

4 18)))

1 She **agreed to come** with me.
They **decided to go** home early.
We **wanted to visit** the Tate Gallery.
2 We **can't buy** tickets till tomorrow.
Hurry up – we **might be** late!
You **shouldn't drink** so much coffee.

1 We use the infinitive with *to* after many verbs.
2 We use the infinitive without *to* after all modal verbs (except *ought*).

verbs + gerund (verb + *-ing*)

4 19)))

1 They **enjoy watching** DVDs at home.
I've finished reading the paper if you want it.
I **hate being** late for school.
2 She**'s given up working** on Saturdays.
I'm looking forward to hearing from you.
I'm going to **keep on studying** Italian for a few more years.

1 We use the gerund after some verbs, e.g. *enjoy*, *finish*, *hate*.
2 We use the gerund after phrasal verbs.

verbs + object + infinitive (with or without *to*)

4 20)))

1 They **want us to go** with them.
He **told me to get** an e-reader.
She **allowed me to leave** work early.
2 His parents **let him go** to the concert.
Our boss **makes us work** late on Fridays.

1 We use an object + the infinitive with *to* after some verbs. NOT ~~*They want that we go with them.*~~
2 We use an object + the infinitive without *to* after *let* and *make*.

a Complete the sentences with the correct form of the verbs in brackets.

We really enjoy *going* to concerts. (go)
1 We went to the box office ________ the tickets we'd booked. (pick up)
2 ________ to a live sporting event is much more exciting than ________ it on TV. (go, watch)
3 I hate ________ to visit my family more often, but they live so far away. (not be able)
4 I tried ________ tickets for the Olympics, but I didn't manage ________ any. (buy, get)
5 It's cheaper ________ tickets for the theatre than for a football match. (get)
6 She moved to a small village and she really misses ________ to plays and exhibitions. (go)
7 They told me ________ in the front row. (not sit)
8 They love ________ which film to see. (choose)
9 I can't afford ________ in this area. (live)
10 It's difficult ________ ________ a mobile phone. (imagine, not have)

b Rewrite the sentences to mean the same thing.

I didn't remember to turn my mobile off.
I forgot *to turn my mobile off*.
1 He said he wouldn't help her.
He refused ________.
2 Her teacher allowed her to leave school early.
Her teacher let ________.
3 They told me I should go to the cinema with them.
They persuaded ________.
4 My husband thinks I should go to the dentist.
My husband wants ________.
5 The police ordered him to move his car.
The police made ________.
6 He said that he'd help us.
He agreed ________.
7 I practise the piano for 20 minutes a day.
I spend 20 minutes a day ________.
8 They asked if we wanted to have dinner with them.
They invited ________.
9 We don't go to concerts any more.
We've given up ________.
10 It's going to continue to rain this afternoon.
It's going to carry on ________.

8A

have something done

I'm having my hair **cut** tomorrow. 4 29
She **has** her house **repainted** every year.
We**'ve had** a new bathroom **put in**.
You ought to **have** your roof **repaired**.
How often **do** you **have** your car **serviced**?
I **don't have** the flat **cleaned**. I clean it myself.
The flat was in good condition, so we **didn't have** it **redecorated**.
When **did** you **have** those photos **taken**?

- We use *have* + object + past participle when we arrange (and usually pay) for someone to do something for us, either because we can't or don't want to do it ourselves. Compare:
  I cleaned my car yesterday. (= I did it myself.) *I had my car cleaned yesterday.* (= I paid someone to clean it for me.)

- We can use *have something done* in any tense and with modal verbs.
- *Have* is the main verb, and is stressed. We use auxiliary verbs (*do*, *did*, etc.) to make questions and negatives.
- If we want to say who did the work, we use *by*, e.g.
  We had our wedding photos taken ***by the same photographer you used****.*
  I had the central heating checked ***by British Gas****.*

a Put the words in the correct order to make sentences.

I… my hair had yesterday cut
I had my hair cut yesterday.

1. Have… eyes your tested had ever you?
2. We… to repaired don't have roof the need
3. I… never whitened teeth have my would
4. She… hair to dyed not advised my me have
5. It's… expensive the to have too replaced carpets
6. He's… professionally have to passport his taken going photo
7. My… faces at children had festival the their painted
8. We… have need oil to checked the
9. I… while shopping had cleaned my was doing car I the
10. I… have before legs going want waxed holiday on to my

b Write sentences about the people.

He / hair / cut *He's having his hair cut.*

1. She / need / car / service
2. He / front door / replace
3. He / new battery / put in
4. They / should / windows / clean
5. She / ought to / eyes / check
6. He / not want / photo / take
7. She / portrait / paint
8. He / want / suit / dry clean

the passive; impersonal *you*

the passive

4 38

present simple	Some historical films **aren't based** on the facts.
present continuous	The election **is being held** in May.
present perfect	**Has** the village **been changed** by tourism?
past simple	10,000 soldiers **were killed** in an hour at Gettysburg.
past continuous	The castle **was being renovated** so we couldn't go in.
past perfect	The hospital **had been opened** by the Queen three years before.
will and *going to*	When **will** the new museum **be built**? We**'re going to be given** the exam results tomorrow.
infinitive with *to*	Does the city centre have **to be closed** to all traffic?
infinitive without *to*	The President must **be elected** by a clear majority.
gerund	I hate **being woken up** by a mosquito.

- We often use the passive when it's not said, known, or important who does an action.
  My phone has been stolen. (= Somebody has stolen my phone, but we don't know who.)
- If we want to say who did an action, we use *by*.
  Westminster Abbey was started by Henry III in 1245.
- We can often say things in two ways, in the active or the passive. Compare:
  Bill Bryson wrote *The Lost Continent*. (The focus is more on Bryson.)
  The Lost Continent was written by Bill Bryson. (The focus is more on the book.)
- We often use the passive to talk about processes, for example scientific processes, and in formal writing, such as newspaper reports.
  The chemicals are combined at very high temperatures.
  Parts of Windsor Castle have been damaged in a fire.

impersonal *you*

4 39

1 **You** can't learn English in three weeks.
You never know what the weather's going to do.
2 Exercise is good for **you**.

1 We can use *you* as an impersonal subject to mean *people in general*.
2 We can use *you* as an impersonal object.

a Complete the sentences with the correct passive form of the verb in brackets.

The Guggenheim Museum in Bilbao *was opened* in 1997. (open)

1 Many roads ________ to traffic for the royal wedding last month. (close)
2 In recent years many books ________ about the American Civil War. (write)
3 A new shopping centre ________ in the town centre at the moment. (build)
4 I think you should ________ to take photographs if you don't use flash. (allow)
5 The last battle on British soil ________ at Culloden in 1746. (fight)
6 Washington DC ________ by nearly 20 million people every year. (visit)
7 I love ________ round a city by someone who knows it well. (show)
8 The gallery was closed because a TV series ________ inside. (film)
9 I ________ by the neighbour's noisy dog three times already this week. (wake up)
10 The monarchy ought not ________ public money. (give)

b Rewrite the sentences to mean the same thing.

Someone's stolen my bike!
My bike *'s been stolen*.

1 They had to close the palace for renovations.
The palace ________.
2 You can find instructions on the internet.
Instructions ________.
3 Lincoln gave the Gettysburg Address in 1863.
The Gettysburg Address ________.
4 A seat belt must be worn at all times.
You ________.
5 Do you think they're going to offer you the job?
Do you think you're ________?
6 Has your sister ever beaten you at chess?
Have you ever ________?
7 Phones have to be switched off during take-off and landing.
You ________.
8 They're going to open a new visitor centre next year.
A new visitor centre ________.
9 The government should pay for new hospitals.
New hospitals ________.
10 Thousands of people visit the castle every day.
The castle ________.

9A

reported speech

Revise the basics

direct statements	reported statements
'**I have** a good memory.'	She said (that) **she had** a good memory.
'**I'm not leaving.**'	He told me (that) **he wasn't leaving**.
'**We'll never forget** you.'	They said (that) **they'd never forget** me.
'**I can't** remember.'	He said (that) **he couldn't** remember.
'**We might** / **may** be a bit late.'	They told us (that) **they might** be a bit late.
'**I must** go.'	She said (that) **she had to** go.

word changes in reported speech

5 4

1 '**I** love **your** bag.' — She said (that) **she** loved **my** bag.
'**I** think **you** told **me**.' — He said (that) **he** thought **we**'d told **him**.
2 'I'm leaving **now**.' — He said (that) he was leaving (**then**).
'See you **tomorrow**.' — He said (that) he'd see me **the next day**.
'I did it **yesterday**.' — She told me (that) she'd done it **the day before**.
'I went skiing **last week**.' — He said (that) he'd been skiing **the week before**.
3 'We don't like it **here**.' — She told us (that) they didn't like it **there**.
'**This** is your station.' — She said (that) **that** was our station.

- Remember that in reported speech as well as the verbs we often need to change other words or parts of the original sentence. We may need to change:
  1 pronouns 2 time expressions 3 *here* and *this*

reported questions

5 5

1 'Where **did you live** before?' — She asked (me) where **I'd lived** before.
2 '**Have you been** to Australia?' — He asked (us) **if / whether we'd been** to Australia.
'**Are you coming** with me?' — She **asked (him)** if / whether **he was going** with **her**.

1 Reported questions use normal word order with no question mark:
She asked me where I'd lived before. NOT ~~*She asked me where had I lived before?*~~
- The verb *ask* in reported questions can be used with or without a person or object pronoun.

2 We use *if* or *whether* to report questions which start with an auxiliary verb.

reported imperatives and requests

5 6

1 '**Don't forget**.'
He **told me not to forget**.
'**Wait** in the car.'
She **told me to wait** in the car.
'**Buy** six oranges.'
He **told me to buy** six oranges.
2 '**Could you close** the window?'
She **asked me to close** the window.
'**Can you wait** here, please?'
He **asked us to wait** there.

1 We can use *tell* + object pronoun + infinitive to report imperatives and instructions.
- The verb *tell* can mean *give information* or *give an instruction*. Compare:
  He told me (that) his name was Rob. (= information)
  He told me to close the door. (= instruction)

2 We can use *ask* + object pronoun + infinitive to report requests. We must use an object pronoun, e.g. *me, us*.
- The verb *ask* can mean *ask a question* or *make a request*. Compare:
  He asked (me) what I was doing. (= question)
  He asked me to close the door. (= request)

a Complete the sentences using reported speech.

'I don't know your email.'
He said… *he didn't know my email.*

1 'I can't remember which exit it is.' She said…
2 'I can't find my mobile.' He said…
3 'We probably won't get the message.' They said…
4 'I've finished my exams!' She said…
5 'The film will be on tomorrow.' They told us…
6 'I can't stay here very long.' He told me…
7 'I must leave at 6.30.' She said…
8 'We've never forgotten our visit.' They told me…
9 'I saw a man hiding in the bushes.' He said…
10 'I don't really want to see him.' She told me…

b Complete the sentences using reported speech.

'Where do you live?'
He asked me… *where I lived.*

1 'How many children do you have?' She asked him…
2 'Could you take a photo of us?' They asked the woman…
3 'Will you be able to visit us?' They asked us…
4 'Please fill in the application form.' He told me…
5 'Did you arrive on time?' He asked her…
6 'Make sure you buy enough food.' She told us…
7 'Can you help me with the cooking?' She asked me…
8 'How long have you been waiting?' He asked them…
9 'Can you confirm your date of birth?' He asked her…
10 'Don't forget to bring your laptops.' They told us…

uses of the past perfect

past perfect in narratives

5 13

He ran to the departure gate but the flight **had** already **closed**.
She didn't know where he'**d gone**.
We still **hadn't had** breakfast when the taxi arrived.
How long **had** they **been** engaged before they got married?

- We use the past perfect when we are talking about the past and we want to talk about an earlier past action.

past perfect in reported speech

5 14

1 'We haven't been married long.'
They said (that) they **hadn't been** married long.
'My boyfriend proposed to me in Paris.'
She told me (that) her boyfriend **had proposed** to her in Paris.
2 'I'd already seen the film.'
He said (that) he'**d** already **seen** the film.

1 We use the past perfect in reported speech when the original speech uses the present perfect or the past simple.
2 If the original speech is past perfect, there is no change in reported speech.

past perfect in third conditionals

5 15

If I'**d known** his number, I would have called him.
They'd have been much happier if they'**d** never **met**.
If I **hadn't gone** to university, I wouldn't have met my wife.
What would they have done if we'**d been** late?

- We use the past perfect in the *if* clause of a third conditional. We use third conditional sentences to talk about how things could have been different in the past, i.e. for hypothetical / imaginary situations and their consequences.

'd
In third conditionals, *'d* is the contraction of both *had* and *would*, e.g.
If I'd known your number, I'd have called you.
had would

a Complete the sentences with the past simple or past perfect form of the verbs in brackets.

When she woke up the house was empty – he 'd gone. (wake up, go)

1 I ________ that film very much, even though I ________ it three times before. (enjoy, see)
2 He ________ he ________ there for six months. (say, work)
3 She still ________ at 10.00, so I ________ the house without her. (not get up, leave)
4 We ________ an hour looking for my phone, but it ________. (spend, disappear)
5 He ________ across the road, but the taxi ________ by someone else. (run, already / take)
6 I ________ get on the flight because I ________ a ticket. (not can, not book)
7 I ________ in Sydney for a week when I first ________ Sally. (only / be, meet)
8 She ________ me if I ________ China before. (ask, visit)
9 They ________ me they ________ engaged. (tell, just / get)
10 The plane ________ yet, but I ________ to board. (not take off, not allowed)

b Complete the third conditional sentences with the correct form of the verbs in brackets.

If we 'd missed the bus, we wouldn't have got home till midnight. (miss, not get)

1 She ________ in love if he ________ her laugh. (not fall, not make)
2 If they ________ to the wedding, they ________. (invite, go)
3 I ________ our anniversary if you ________ me. (forget, not remind)
4 If we ________ earlier, we ________ our flight. (leave, not miss)
5 If you ________ in advance, you ________ your money. (not pay, not lose)
6 She ________ a wedding dress made if her grandmother's ________ perfectly. (have, not fit)
7 I ________ sleep if I ________ so much coffee. (be able to, not drink)
8 We ________ touch if I ________ your email address. (lose, not find)
9 If he ________ we were lost, he ________ to help. (know, offer)
10 If he ________ at the policeman, he ________. (not shout, not arrest)

10A

be, do, and *have*: auxiliary and main verbs

be – main verb and auxiliary

5 25

1 His name **was** David.
They haven't **been** here before.
2 **I'm** sitting on the bus.
They **aren't** coming to the party.
I **was** cycling to work when I saw him.
Were they watching TV when you phoned?
She**'s been** learning Japanese for two years.
They **haven't been** working here long.
Lots of clothes **are** now **being** made in the Far East.
Millions of books **have been** digitized.

1 We can use *be* as the main verb in a sentence.
2 *be* is also an auxiliary verb.
- We use *am* | *is* | *are* as auxiliaries in the present continuous.
- We use *was* | *were* as auxiliaries in the past continuous.
- We use *has been* | *have been* as auxiliaries in the present perfect continuous.
- We use *had been* as an auxiliary in the past perfect continuous.
- We use all tenses of *be* as auxiliaries in passives.

do – main verb and auxiliary

5 26

1 What do you **do**?
I **did** my homework last night.
2 She **doesn't** speak English.
Where **do** they live?
They **didn't** go to the theatre.
Did you enjoy the film?

1 We can use *do* as the main verb in a sentence.
2 We use *do* | *don't* | *does* | *doesn't* as auxiliaries in the present simple, and *did* | *didn't* as auxiliaries in the past simple.

have – main verb and auxiliary

5 27

1 I **have** two brothers and a sister.
He's **having** a shower at the moment.
What did you **have** for dinner?
2 I **have to** be at the airport at 11.00.
We **had** our computer repaired last week.
3 They**'ve** bought a new car.
I **haven't** seen him recently.
Has he ever been to Spain?
4 I was sure **I'd** seen him before.
We were hungry because we **hadn't** had breakfast.
Had she tried to phone you before she arrived?

1 We can use *have* as the main verb in a sentence. It can be an action or non-action verb – see Grammar Bank 2A *p.134*.
2 With *have to* and *have something done*, *have* is also a main verb.
3 We use *have* | *haven't* | *has* | *hasn't* as auxiliaries in the present perfect.
4 We use *had* | *hadn't* as auxiliaries in the past perfect.

a Put the words in the correct order to make sentences.

I... my hair had yesterday cut
I had my hair cut yesterday.
1 What... doing have been you ?
2 She... Africa because heat been to the hasn't like doesn't she
3 Why... had lunch yet you haven't ?
4 She... hair isn't today done her to going have
5 We... time do have enough shopping to the didn't
6 What... the at did do weekend you ?
7 Nothing... solve to being problem is done the
8 He... Boston be to until in tomorrow have doesn't
9 I... to soon passport have have my renewed
10 She... her when homework her doing was friend phoned

b Complete the sentences with the auxiliary verbs *be, do,* or *have*.

Does he like living in the UK, or *is* he feeling homesick?
1 **A** ________ you ever been to the States?
B No, my husband ________ like flying.
2 **A** ________ they miss the beginning of the film?
B No, luckily it ________ started yet.
3 ________ he know we ________ coming, or ________ we need to give him a ring?
4 **A** I'm sorry I ________ answer the phone when you called.
B That's OK. What ________ you doing?
5 We ________ often travel outside Europe, but we ________ been to Egypt twice.
6 I ________ working since 7.00 this morning, and now I ________ going home.
7 **A** Where ________ she going on holiday this year?
B Rome, I think. She ________ never been before.
8 They ________ only staying in New York for two days – they ________ have much time for sightseeing.

revision of verb forms

a Complete the conversation with the correct form of the verbs in brackets.

Tina Hi, Roger, how *are* (be) you?
Roger Hi, Tina. I'm exhausted – I [1] ________________ (work) really hard all week.
Tina Is that why you [2] ________________ (not come) out with us last night?
Roger Yes, I [3] ________________ (not can) come – I [4] ________________ (study). My last exam [5] ________________ (start) at 9.00 tomorrow morning.
Tina Really? I [6] ________________ (finish) all my exams!
Roger Lucky you! What [7] ________________ you ________________ (plan) to do next?
Tina I [8] ________________ (fly) to Australia in three days. I [9] ________________ (want) to go since my aunt and uncle [10] ________________ (move) there five years ago, but I [11] ________________ (never / be able to) afford it till now.
Roger Fantastic – I'm sure you [12] ________________ (love) it.
Tina I hope so! What about you? I [13] ________________ (speak) to Mary yesterday and she [14] ________________ (say) you [15] ________________ (invite) her to go to France.
Roger Yes, but unfortunately she [16] ________________ (already / make) other plans.
Tina And what about tomorrow evening? [17] ________________ you ________________ (celebrate)?
Roger Yes, I [18] ________________ (think) of going to that new pizzeria. [19] ________________ you ________________ (want) to come along?
Tina Yes, that would be great – I [20] ________________ (see) you tomorrow. And good luck with the exam!

b Complete the sentences to mean the same thing. Use the correct form of the verbs in brackets.

He cleaned the windows and earned £20. (pay)
He *was paid* £20 for cleaning the windows.

1 She first met him 20 years ago. (know)
She ________________ him for 20 years.
2 It's not necessary for you to bring any money. (need)
You ________________ to bring any money.
3 I can't repair the chair because I don't have any glue. (have)
If I ________________ some glue, I could repair the chair.
4 I learnt to swim when I was five. (able, swim)
I ________________ since I was five.
5 What are your plans after you graduate? (go)
What ________________ to do after you graduate?
6 He says it would be good to include a covering letter. (suggest, include)
He ________________ a covering letter.
7 The Queen opened the concert hall in 2009. (open)
The concert hall ________________ in 2009.
8 I had much longer hair when I was younger. (used, have)
I ________________ longer hair when I was younger.
9 You can pay me back tomorrow. (not have to)
You ________________ pay me back now.
10 She started learning Russian two months ago. (learn)
She ________________ Russian for two months.
11 Somebody had stolen his car so he phoned the police. (steal)
He phoned the police because his car ________________.
12 My boss said I could leave work early. (allow, leave)
My boss ________________ me ________________ work early.
13 She agreed to come to the wedding. (say, can)
She ________________ come to the wedding.
14 The photo was out of focus because I didn't use flash. (use)
The photo would have been in focus if I ________________ flash.
15 They shouldn't be so careless. (ought, be)
They ________________ more careful.

Adjective suffixes

1 DESCRIBING PEOPLE

a Add an ending to the nouns and verbs below to form adjectives. Write them in the correct column.

~~act~~ /ækt/ assert /ə'sɜːt/ attract /ə'trækt/ boss /bɒs/ cheer /tʃɪə/ create /kri'eɪt/ envy /'envi/ glamour /'glæmə(r)/ help /help/ impulse /'ɪmpʌls/ mood /muːd/ possess /pə'zes/ power /paʊə/ rebel /rɪ'bel/ rely /rɪ'laɪ/ self /self/ sense /sens/ style /staɪl/

> **Word endings for adjectives**
> Many adjectives are formed by adding suffixes (= endings) such as *-able / -ible*, *-y*, *-ive*, *-ous*, and *-ful* to a noun or verb. Sometimes another small spelling change is required, e.g. losing a final *e* (*fame – famous*). Check the spelling changes in your dictionary.
> Knowing typical suffixes will help you to recognise that a new word is an adjective.

-able / -ible	-y	-ive	-ous	-ful	-ish
sociable	lucky	aggressive	ambitious	beautiful	childish
responsible		sensitive			
		active			

b 1 10 Listen and check.

2 DESCRIBING PLACES AND THINGS

a Add an ending to the nouns and verbs on the right to form adjectives. Write them in the correct column.

~~afford~~ /ə'fɔːd/ comfort /'kʌmfət/ desire /dɪ'zaɪə/ dirt /dɜːt/ expense /ɪk'spens/ health /helθ/ impress /ɪm'pres/ luxury /'lʌkʃəri/ noise /nɔɪz/ profit /'prɒfɪt/ risk /rɪsk/ space /speɪs/ stress /stres/ success /sək'ses/ suit /suːt/ use /juːs/

-able / -ible	-y	-ive	-ous	-ful
recognizable	easy	addictive	delicious	colourful
incredible			dangerous	
affordable				

b 1 11 Listen and check.

3 *-FUL* AND *-LESS*

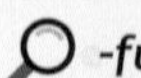

> ***-ful* and *-less***
> *-ful* and *-less* are suffixes which add the meaning 'with' or 'without' to the base word, e.g. *careful* = with care, *careless* = without care, *hopeful* = with hope, *hopeless* = without hope.
> However, not all words which can form an adjective with *-ful* can also form one with *-less*, e.g. we can say *successful* but NOT ~~*successless*~~, and not all words which can form an adjective with *-less* can also form one with *-ful*, e.g. we can say *endless* but NOT ~~*endful*~~.

a Look at the *-ful* adjectives in the charts in 1 and 2. Tick the ones that *can* form an adjective with *-less*.

b 1 12 Listen and check.

4 DESCRIBING COLOURS

a Match the phrases to the four shades of blue.

- dark blue (also navy blue)
- greyish blue
- light blue (also pale blue)
- bright blue

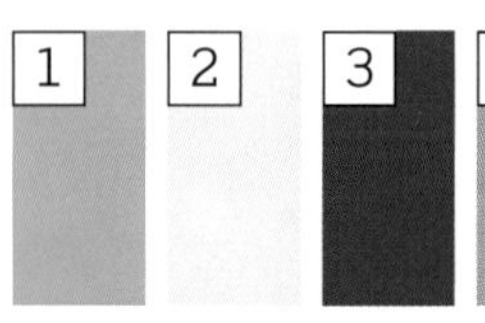

b 1 13 Listen and check. What does the suffix *-ish* means when you add it to another adjective, e.g. a colour?

c With a partner, say exactly what colour the things you are wearing are.

◀ p.8

Holidays

1 THINGS TO PACK

a Match the words and pictures.

- adaptor /ə'dæptə/
- brush /brʌʃ/
- comb /kəʊm/
- flip flops /'flɪp flɒps/
- guidebook /'gaɪdbʊk/
- hairdryer /'heədraɪə/
- insect repellent /'ɪnsekt rɪ'pelənt/
- make-up /'meɪkʌp/
- memory card /'meməri kɑːd/
- nail scissors /'neɪl sɪzəz/
- (phone) charger /'tʃɑːdʒə/
- pyjamas /pə'dʒɑːməz/
- raincoat /'reɪnkəʊt/
- razor /'reɪzə(r)/
- *1* sunscreen /'sʌnskriːn/
- swimming trunks /'swɪmɪŋ trʌŋks/
- swimsuit /'swɪmsuːt/
- toothbrush /'tuːθbrʌʃ/
- toothpaste /'tuːθpeɪst/
- towel /'taʊəl/
- wash bag /'wɒʃ bæg/ (also sponge bag) /'spʌndʒ bæg/

1 

2 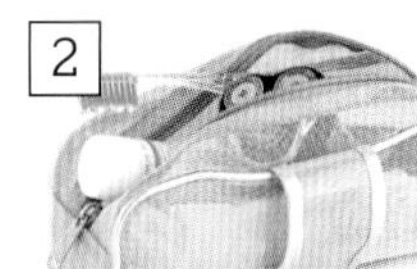

3 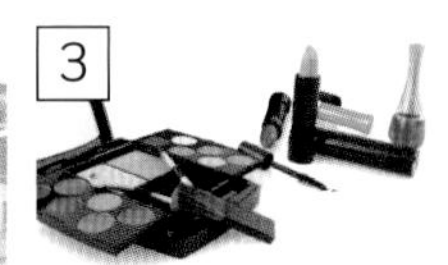

4 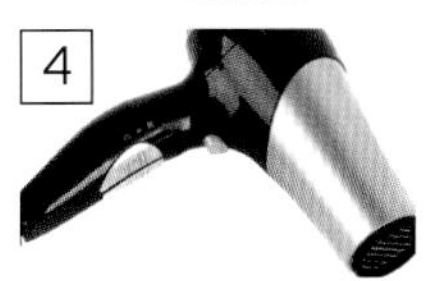

5 

6 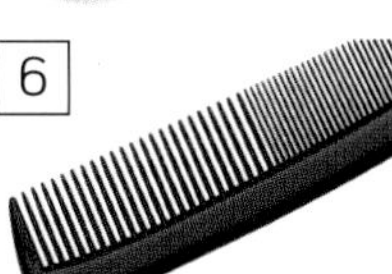

7 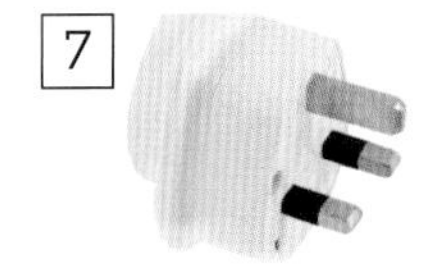

8 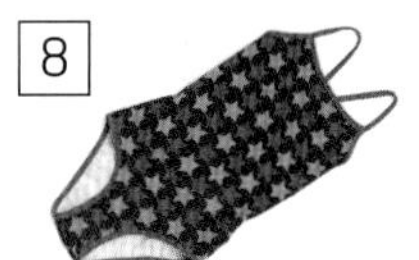

9 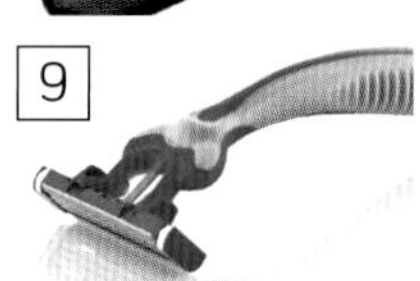

10 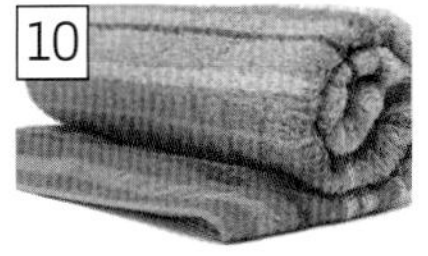

11 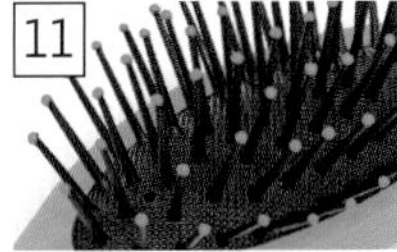

12 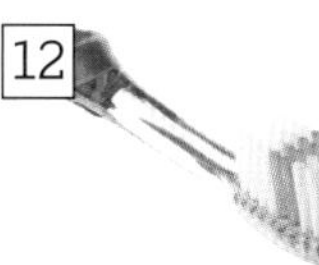

13 

14 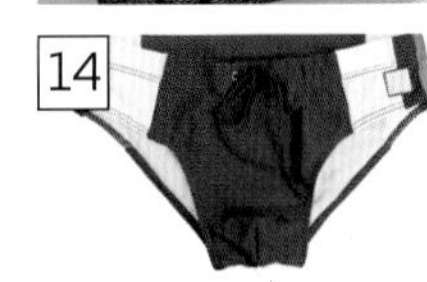

15 

16 

17 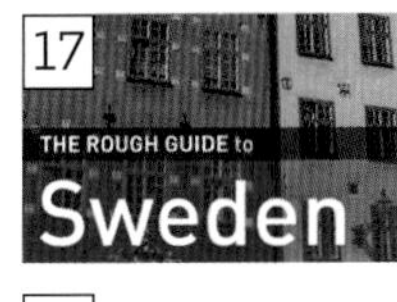

18 

19 

20 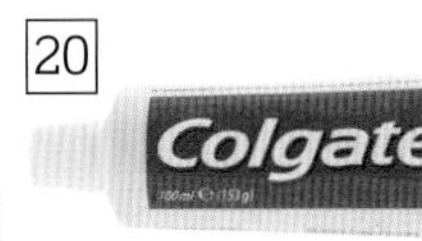

21 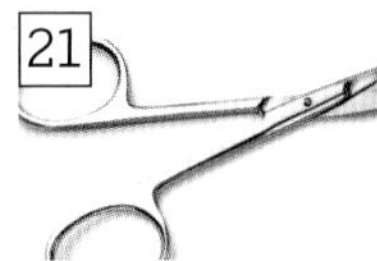

b 1 24 Listen and check.

c With a partner, say which things in **a** you always pack when you go on holiday. Are there any other things that you always pack?

2 VERB PHRASES WITH *GO*

a Match the phrases and pictures.

go* + verb + *-ing

- camping
- hiking
- sailing
- *1* scuba diving
- sightseeing
- snorkelling
- waterskiing
- windsurfing

1 

2 

3 

4 

5 

6 

7 

8 

b Match the phrases.

***go on* + noun**

1 go on a cruise
2 go on a (guided) tour
3 go on a safari
4 go on a boat trip
5 go on a package holiday

a of a city or a building
b with everything included
c on a lake
d round the Mediterranean
e to see wildlife

c 1 25 Listen and check your answers to **a** and **b**.

d With a partner, ask and answer about each phrase.

Have you ever been camping?

Yes, I have. I went camping last summer. Have you ever...?

3 MORE VERB PHRASES

a Complete the verb phrases.

climb do get have pack see ~~sunbathe~~ unpack watch

1 *sunbathe* on the beach
2 ________ sunburnt (bitten by insects)
3 ________ the sights (a show)
4 ________ the sunset (sunrise)
5 ________ voluntary work (a course)
6 ________ a mountain (a hill)
7 ________ and ________ your bags
8 ________ a massage (spa treatments)

b 1 26 Listen and check.

◀ p.14

Shops and services

1 PLACES

a Match the words and pictures.

- baker's /ˈbeɪkəz/
- butcher's /ˈbʊtʃəz/
- chain store /ˈtʃeɪn stɔː/
- chemist's /ˈkemɪsts/
- delicatessen /delɪkəˈtesn/ (also deli /ˈdeli/)
- DIY store /diː aɪ ˈwaɪ stɔː/ (also hardware store /ˈhɑːdweə stɔː/)
- dry cleaner's /draɪ ˈkliːnəz/
- estate agent's /ɪsˈteɪt eɪdʒənts/
- fishmonger's /ˈfɪʃmʌŋgəz/
- florist's /ˈflɒrɪsts/
- greengrocer's /ˈgriːŋgrəʊsəz/
- health food store /ˈhelθ fuːd stɔː/
- hypermarket /ˈhaɪpəmɑːkɪt/
- jeweller's /ˈdʒuːələz/
- launderette /lɔːnˈdret/
- market stall /ˈmɑːkɪt stɔːl/
- newsagent's /ˈnjuːzeɪdʒənts/
- off-licence /ˈɒf laɪsns/
- 1 stationer's /ˈsteɪʃənəz/
- travel agent's /ˈtrævl eɪdʒənts/

b 1 38 Listen and check.

1

2

3

4

5

6

7

8

9
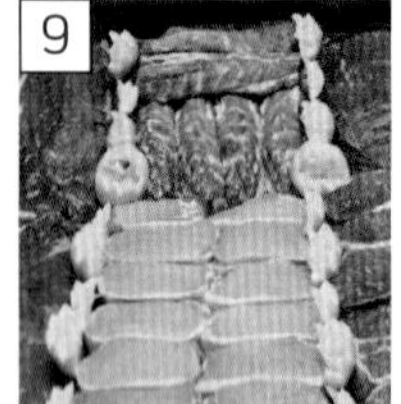

10

11

12

13

14

15

16
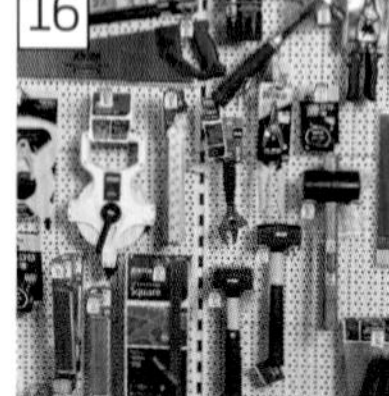

17

18

19

20

2 PHRASAL VERBS RELATED TO SHOPS AND SHOPPING

a Match the highlighted phrasal verbs and the definitions.

1 A lot of local shops and businesses have closed down because of the recession.

2 **A** Do you need any help?
B No thanks, I just want to look round.

3 Did you know they're opening up a new Thai restaurant where that old French one used to be?

4 **A** Is there somewhere where I can try on this sweater?
B Yes, the changing rooms are over there.

5 Excuse me, can you help me? I'm looking for a butcher's. Someone told me that there was one near here.

6 **A** Do you have these in a medium?
B I'm sorry, we're out of mediums at the moment, but we should be getting some in soon.

a not have in stock
b put something on to see if it fits
c start trading or doing business
d stop trading or doing business
e try to find something
f walk round a place to see what there is

b 1 39 Listen and check.

◄ p.18

Shop names with 's

- The names for many sorts of shops end in 's, which is short for 's *shop*, e.g. *baker's* = *baker's shop*, *chemist's* = *chemist's shop*.
- In the plural of these shops there is no apostrophe, e.g. *There are several bakers here.*
- Nowadays some shops sometimes use another word, e.g. *bakery* instead of *baker's*.

Other places to buy things in the UK

Charity shops sell second-hand items (especially clothes) which have been given to them by people to raise money for charity.

Pound shops sell a variety of cheap goods which cost one pound.

Craft fairs are events where you can buy handmade things, often made by local people.

Photography

1 DESCRIBING A PHOTO

a Look at the photos and compete the sentences with a word or phrase from the list. Use capital letters where necessary.

behind /bɪˈhaɪnd/ in front of /ɪn ˈfrʌnt əv/ in the background /ˈbækgraʊnd/
in the bottom right-hand corner /ˈbɒtəm raɪt hænd ˈkɔːnə/ in the centre /ˈsentə/
in the distance /ˈdɪstəns/ in the foreground /ˈfɔːgraʊnd/
in the top right-hand corner /tɒp raɪt hænd ˈkɔːnə/ on top of /ɒn ˈtɒp əv/ opposite /ˈɒpəzɪt/

b 2 14))) Listen and check.

Photo 1

1 *In the background* there's a mountain, and some low cloud.
2 __________ there's a grandmother and three children.
3 The boy in an orange T-shirt is standing __________ his grandmother.
4 __________ of the photo there's a building with lots of steps.
5 There's a small building that looks like a temple __________ a small hill.

Photo 2

6 __________ there's a woman standing on a terrace looking at the view.
7 The woman is standing __________ a low wall looking at the view.
8 __________ the woman there's a building with a tower that looks like a church.
9 __________ on the left you can just see an old building which looks like a ruin.
10 __________ there are two cypress trees.

on top of* or *at the top of

The bird is **on top of** the photo.

The bird is **at the top of** the photo.

2 TAKING PHOTOS

a Match the sentences halves.

1 *e* You **use flash** when…
2 You **zoom in** when…
3 A photo can be **out of focus** if…
4 Many cameras have a **portrait setting** to use when…
5 A photo can be **blurred** if…
6 With good cameras you can use different **lenses**, e.g. a wide-angle lens, when…
7 You **enlarge** a photo when…

a you are far away from something and you want to take a close-up of it.
b you can't step far away from your subject, but you want to get all of it in the picture.
c you move when you are taking it.
d you want to take a photo of a person.
e you want to take a photo somewhere dark, e.g. indoors or at night.
f your camera isn't automatic and you haven't used the right settings.
g you want to make it bigger.

b 2 15))) Listen and check.

◀ p.28

Rubbish and recycling

1 RUBBISH: NOUNS AND PHRASAL VERBS

a Read the definitions for *rubbish* and *waste*. Then match the other nouns to their definitions.

nouns

bin /bɪn/ bin bag /ˈbɪn bæg/
dustman /ˈdʌstmən/
landfill site /ˈlændfɪl saɪt/
~~rubbish~~ /ˈrʌbɪʃ/ ~~waste~~ /weɪst/
waste-paper basket /weɪst ˈpeɪpə bɑːskɪt/

1 *rubbish* things that you throw away because you don't want them any more (NAmE *garbage* or *trash*)
2 *waste* materials that are not needed, and thrown away, e.g. *industrial ~, toxic ~*
3 ______ a container kept outside that you put rubbish in (also *dustbin*)
4 ______ a plastic bag which you put rubbish in and then throw away
5 ______ a small basket kept in a room where people throw away paper and small things
6 ______ the person whose job it is to take away the rubbish (also *refuse collector*, NAmE *garbage collector*)
7 ______ an area of land where large amounts of waste are covered with earth

b 2 32 Listen and check.

c Complete the sentences with a phrasal verb from the list.

phrasal verbs

give away /gɪv əˈweɪ/ take away /teɪk əˈweɪ/
take out /teɪk ˈaʊt/ throw away /θrəʊ əˈweɪ/

1 If that pen doesn't work, just ______ it ______. I hate having pens around that don't work.
2 Please could you ______ ______ the rubbish? I did it yesterday.
3 I'm moving house in a few weeks, and I've decided to ______ ______ a lot of books and clothes to a charity shop.
4 In many countries there are special containers for used glass and cardboard. People then come and ______ it ______ to be recycled.

d 2 33 Listen and check.

2 PACKAGING

a Match the words and pictures.

bottle /ˈbɒtl/
can /kæn/
cardboard box /kɑːdbɔːd ˈbɒks/
carton /ˈkɑːtn/
jar /dʒɑː(r)/
lid /lɪd/
packet /ˈpækɪt/
plastic bag /plæstɪk ˈbæg/
polystyrene tray /pɒliˈstaɪriːn treɪ/
pot /ˈpɒt/
sell-by date /ˈsel baɪ deɪt/
tin /tɪn/
tub /tʌb/
wrapper /ˈræpə/

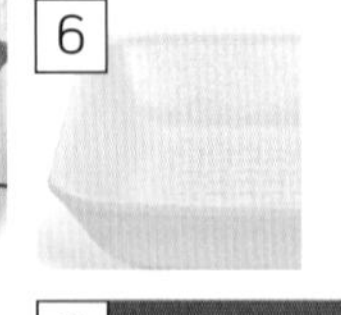

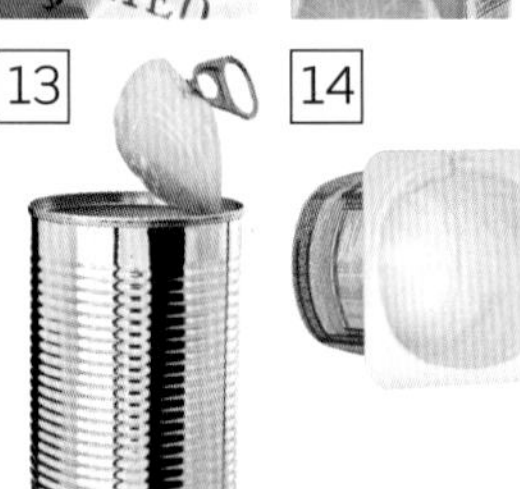

b 2 34 Listen and check.

c What kind of packaging is normally used for...?

yoghurt biscuits olives soft drinks
sardines a washing machine
ice cream milk

3 THE PREFIX *RE-*

a Complete the sentences with a verb from the list.

reapply /riːəˈplaɪ/ ~~recycle~~ /riːˈsaɪkl/ reheat /riːˈhiːt/
replay /riːˈpleɪ/ rethink /riːˈθɪŋk/ reuse /riːˈjuːz/

1 There's a bottle bank at the local supermarket where you can *recycle* all your glass bottles and jars.
2 Many supermarkets now charge extra for plastic bags. They prefer customers to have shopping bags which they can ______.
3 If you're not sure about the project, you should ______ the whole thing.
4 You can ______ your dinner in the microwave.
5 They'll have to ______ the match next Saturday.
6 You should ______ sunscreen every hour if you have fair skin.

b 2 35 Listen and check.

◄ p.35

Study and work

1 HIGHER EDUCATION

a Read the text about University College London (UCL) and complete it with words from the list.

~~campus~~ /ˈkæmpəs/ dissertation /dɪsəˈteɪʃn/ faculties /ˈfækltiz/ halls of residence /ˈhɔːlz əv ˈrezɪdəns/ lectures /ˈlektʃəz/ postgraduates /pəʊstˈɡrædʒuəts/ professors /prəˈfesəz/ seminars /ˈsemɪnɑːz/ thesis /ˈθiːsɪs/ tutor /ˈtjuːtə/ undergraduates /ʌndəˈɡrædʒuəts/ webinars /ˈwebɪnɑːz/

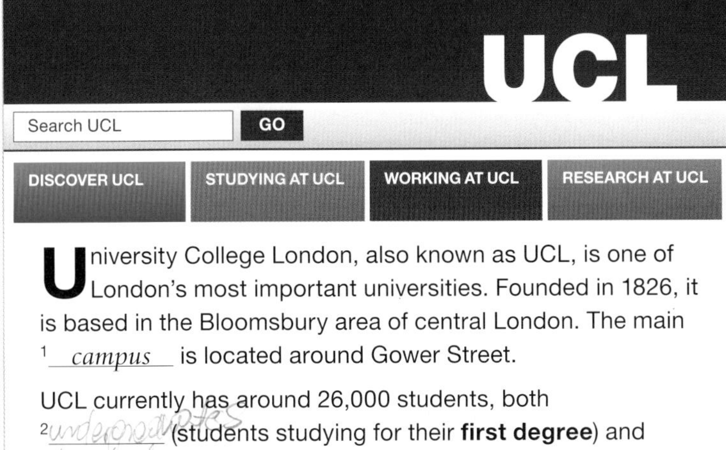

UCL

Search UCL GO

DISCOVER UCL | STUDYING AT UCL | WORKING AT UCL | RESEARCH AT UCL

University College London, also known as UCL, is one of London's most important universities. Founded in 1826, it is based in the Bloomsbury area of central London. The main [1] *campus* is located around Gower Street.

UCL currently has around 26,000 students, both [2] ___ (students studying for their **first degree**) and [3] ___ (students studying for **further degrees**). Further degrees include a **master's degree**, usually a one-year course at the end of which students have to write a [4] ___, or a **PhD** (doctorate), during which students have to write a doctoral [5] ___.

UCL has around 4,000 **academic and research staff**, and 650 [6] ___ (the highest ranked university teacher), which is more than any other British university. The research and teaching is divided into ten [7] ___, e.g. Arts and Humanities, Engineering Sciences, Medical Sciences, etc.

Many students, particularly first year undergraduates and **overseas students**, live in [8] ___. The majority of others find their own accommodation. Students are taught in **tutorials** (small groups of students with a [9] ___), or through [10] ___ (larger classes where students discuss or study with their teacher) or [11] ___ (where a large group of students listen to a talk but do not participate). Some teaching may also be in the form of [12] ___ (seminars conducted over the internet).

Famous past students range from Alexander Graham Bell, the inventor of the telephone, and Mahatma Gandhi, to all the members of the pop group Coldplay, who met while at university there.

b 2 40 Listen and check. What do the **bold** phrases mean?

c With a partner, say three things which are the same and three which are different about universities in your country.

2 APPLYING FOR A JOB OR COURSE

a Complete the gaps with a noun or verb from the list.

apply attend experience get look ~~qualifications~~ a referee skills work write

What you may need to have

- [1] *qualifications* (e.g. a degree, a diploma)
- [2] ___ (having done some work before)
- [3] ___ (e.g. languages, IT)
- [4] ___ (a person who would be prepared to recommend you) and their contact details

What you may need to do

- [5] ___ out for **job vacancies** or **courses**
- [6] ___ for a job (**a work permit**, a place on a course, **a grant / scholarship** = money that an organization gives sb to help pay for education)
- [7] ___ a **CV** and a **covering letter**
- [8] ___ an interview
- [9] ___ a **job offer** or an offer for a place on a course
- [10] ___ as an **intern** or a **trainee**

b 2 41 Listen and check. What do the **bold** phrases mean?

attend* or *assist

attend = to be present at an event

Students must attend at least 95% of lectures to pass the course.

assist = to help sb to do sth

Jack was happy to assist Peter with gathering information for the report.

apprenticeship* or *trial period

apprenticeship = a period of time working for an employer to learn the particular skills needed for a job

The apprenticeship to be an electrician lasts three years and there is an exam you must pass at the end.

trial period = a fixed period of time which tests the ability or performance of sb before they are offered the job permanently

They agreed to employ me for a trial period of three months.

p.38

Television

1 TV AND PHRASAL VERBS

a Label the picture with words from the list.

re<u>mote</u> (con<u>trol</u>) /rɪ'məʊt (kən'trəʊl)/
screen /skriːn/ stand /stænd/
<u>spea</u>kers /'spiːkəz/

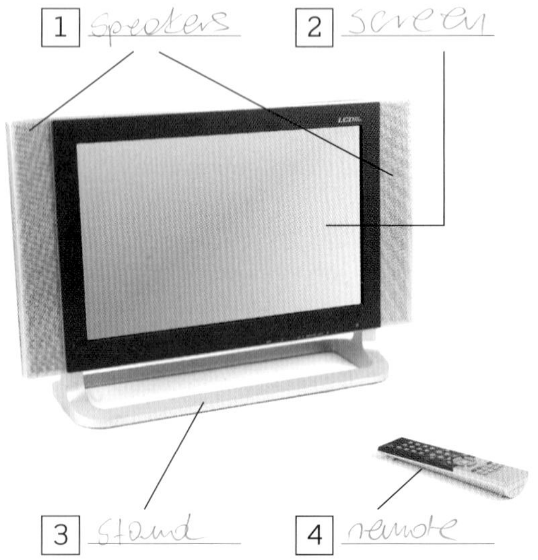

b Complete the sentences with a phrasal verb from the list.

be on /biː ɒn/
switch <u>o</u>ver /swɪtʃ 'əʊvə/
turn down /tɜːn 'daʊn/
turn off /tɜːn 'ɒf/
turn on /tɜːn 'ɒn/
turn up /tɜːn 'ʌp/

1 Please ______ the TV = press a button to start it working (also *switch on*)
2 Please ______ the TV = press a button to stop it working (also *switch off*)
3 Please ______ the TV = make the volume louder
4 Please ______ the TV = make the volume quieter
5 The programme ______ now = it is being shown on TV now
6 Let's ______ to another channel = press a button to move to another channel

c 3.3 Listen and check your answers to **a** and **b**.

2 TYPES OF PROGRAMME

a Match the TV screens with the types of programmes.

car<u>toons</u> /kɑː'tuːnz/ (or ani<u>ma</u>tion /ænɪ'meɪʃn/)
<u>chat</u> shows /'tʃæt ʃəʊz/
com<u>mer</u>cials /kə'mɜːʃlz/ (or <u>ad</u>verts /'ædvɜːts/)
<u>coo</u>kery <u>pro</u>grammes /'kʊkəri 'prəʊgræmz/
current <u>af</u>fairs <u>pro</u>grammes /'kʌrənt ə'feəz 'prəʊgræmz/
docu<u>men</u>taries /dɒkju'mentriz/
<u>dra</u>ma <u>se</u>ries /'drɑːmə 'sɪəriːz/
live sport /laɪv 'spɔːt/
<u>pe</u>riod <u>dra</u>mas /'pɪəriəd 'drɑːməz/
<u>quiz</u> shows /'kwɪz ʃəʊz/
re<u>a</u>lity shows /ri'æləti ʃəʊz/
<u>sit</u>coms /'sɪtkɒmz/
1 soaps /səʊps/
the news /ðə njuːz/
the <u>wea</u>ther <u>fore</u>cast /'weðə 'fɔːkɑːst/

b 3.4 Listen and check.

c Answer the questions with a partner.

1 What kind of programmes do you usually watch?
2 What do you never watch?
3 What's your favourite television programme of all time? What kind of programme was / is it?
4 What's the worst programme you have ever seen?

◀ p.44

The country

1 NATURE

a Match the words and pictures.

- bush /bʊʃ/
- cliff /klɪf/
- fence /fens/
- field /fiːld/
- gate /ɡeɪt/
- grass /ɡrɑːs/
- hedge /hedʒ/
- hill /hɪl/
- 1 leaf (plural *leaves*) /liːf/ /liːvz/
- mud /mʌd/
- path /pɑːθ/
- pond /pɒnd/
- rocks /rɒks/
- sticks /stɪks/
- stones /stəʊnz/
- stream /striːm/
- valley /ˈvæli/
- wood /wʊd/

1

2

3

4

5

6

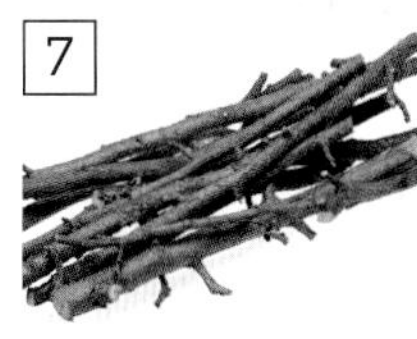

7

8

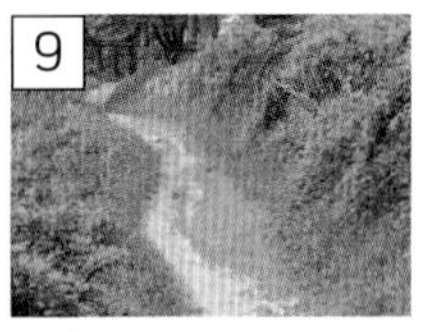

9

10

11

12

13

14

15

16

17

18

b 3 11 Listen and check.

> **the country and the countryside**
> We normally use *the country* to talk about any area that is not a town or city, e.g. *I live in the country.* We use *the countryside* when we are talking about the scenery in the country, e.g. fields, woods, etc., usually in a positive way, e.g. *We stayed in a little village surrounded by beautiful countryside.*

2 ON A FARM

a Match the words and pictures.

- barn /bɑːn/
- cockerel /ˈkɒkərəl/
- cow /kaʊ/
- farmhouse /ˈfɑːmhaʊs/
- hens /henz/
- lambs /læmz/
- sheep /ʃiːp/

b 3 12 Listen and check.

c Complete the text with a verb or past participle from the list.

In the UK, especially in the east of England, a lot of farmers [1] ______ cereals (for example, **wheat**), vegetables, and fruit. Most **crops** are [2] ______ in the early spring and are [3] ______ in the summer. For example wheat is [4] ______ in August, and most potatoes from June onwards. Soft fruits like strawberries are usually **ripe** in June and July, and many farms invite people to come and [5] ______ their own fruit.

d 3 13 Listen and check. What do you think the bold words mean?

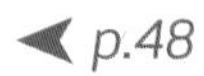
p.48

DIY and repairs

1 IN A SHED: TOOLS AND OTHER THINGS FOR REPAIRS

a Match the words and pictures.

- bricks /brɪks/
- bucket /ˈbʌkɪt/
- drill /drɪl/
- hammer /ˈhæmə/
- ladder /ˈlædə/
- nails /neɪlz/
- padlock /ˈpædlɒk/
- *1* paintbrush /ˈpeɪntbrʌʃ/
- pieces of wood /ˈpiːsɪz ɒv wʊd/
- rope /rəʊp/
- screwdriver /ˈskruːdraɪvə/
- screws /skruːz/
- string /strɪŋ/
- tap /tæp/
- tiles /taɪlz/
- wire /ˈwaɪə/

b 3 27 Listen and check.

2 IN A DRAWER: USEFUL THINGS AROUND THE HOUSE

a Match the words and pictures.

- batteries /ˈbætriz/
- glue /gluː/
- handle /ˈhændl/
- light bulb /ˈlaɪt bʌlb/
- matches /ˈmætʃɪz/
- needle and thread /ˈniːdl ən ˈθred/
- penknife /ˈpennaɪf/
- Sellotape™ /ˈselәteɪp/
- torch /tɔːtʃ/

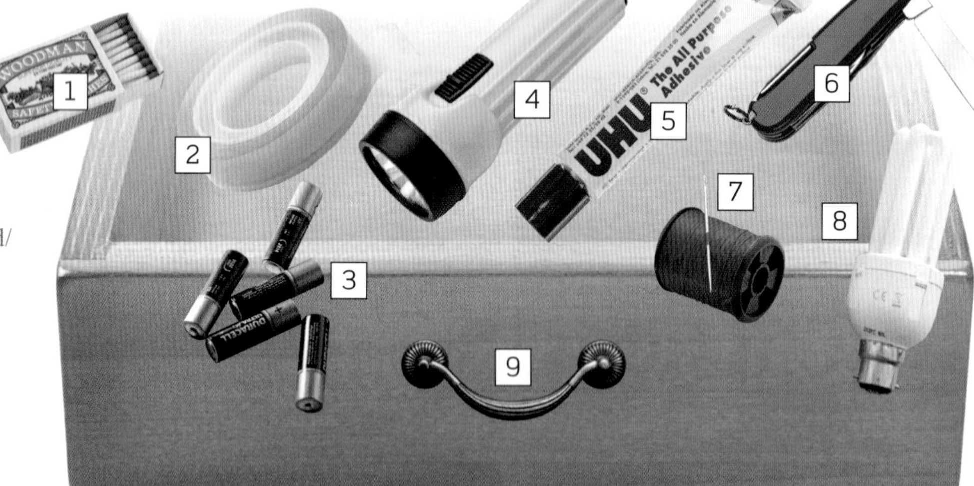

b 3 28 Listen and check.

3 VERB PHRASES

a Match verbs **1–7** with phrases **a–g**.

1 change
2 drill
3 put up
4 set up
5 sew
6 stick
7 tie

a something together that's broken with glue or Sellotape™
b a button on a shirt
c a light bulb or a tyre
d two things together, e.g. shoelaces or two pieces of string
e a new Wi-fi network or a home cinema system
f shelves or curtains
g a hole in the wall or in a piece of wood

b 3 29 Listen and check.

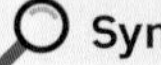

Synonyms

Synonyms are words with a very similar meaning, which are often interchangeable.
We can use *mend*, *repair*, or *fix* to talk about making something broken OK again.

◄ p.54

At a restaurant

1 THINGS ON THE TABLE

a Match the words and pictures.

- bowl /bəʊl/
- <u>cork</u>screw /ˈkɔːkskruː/
- cup /kʌp/
- fork /fɔːk/
- glass /ɡlɑːs/
- jug /dʒʌɡ/
- knife /naɪf/
- mug /mʌɡ/
- <u>nap</u>kin /ˈnæpkɪn/ (also servi<u>ette</u> /sɜːviˈet/)
- oil and <u>vin</u>egar /ɔɪl ən ˈvɪnɪɡə/
- plate /pleɪt/
- salt and <u>pep</u>per /sɒlt ən ˈpepə/
- <u>sau</u>cer /ˈsɔːsə/
- <u>ser</u>ving dish /ˈsɜːvɪŋ dɪʃ/
- spoon /spuːn/
- <u>ta</u>blecloth /ˈteɪblklɒθ/
- <u>tea</u>pot /ˈtiːpɒt/
- <u>tea</u>spoon /ˈtiːspuːn/
- tray /treɪ/
- 1 <u>wine</u> glass /ˈwaɪn ɡlɑːs/

b 3 40 Listen and check.

> **Plate, dish, meal, and course**
> ***plate*** = a round flat object that you put food on when you eat it.
> ***dish*** = 1 a flat container for serving food from; 2 food prepared in a particular way, e.g. *the dish of the day, a vegetarian dish.*
> ***meal*** = an occasion when people eat food, e.g. lunch, breakfast, dinner.
> ***course*** = a separate part of a meal, e.g. *the main course, a four-course meal.*

c What would you expect to find on a restaurant table in your country? What do you put on the table when you lay it for lunch or dinner?

2 THINGS PEOPLE DO IN RESTAURANTS

a Match the verb phrases and pictures.

waiters

- lay the table (opp. *clear*)
- take an <u>or</u>der
- recom<u>mend</u> a dish
- <u>car</u>ry a tray
- serve a table
- pour the wine

b 3 41 Listen and check.

p.60

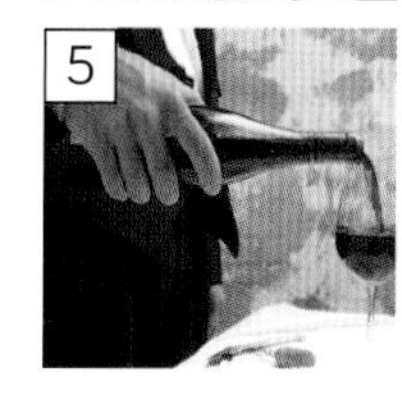

customers

- book a table
- <u>or</u>der food
- try the wine
- send something back
- ask for the bill
- leave a tip

Phrasal verbs

1 NEW PHRASAL VERBS

a Match the phrasal verbs with the definitions a–l.

1 ☐ **A** You have ten more seconds…
B I **give up**. What's the answer?

2 ☐ Hello? Is that the AA? I'm afraid my car's **broken down**. I'm on the A451…

3 ☐ If you **keep on** making such a noise I won't read you a story.

4 ☐ I waited for ten minutes and just when I was going to go, he **turned up**.

5 ☐ I've **come up with** a really good idea.

6 ☐ Sorry, I can't come tonight. I'm **taking** my girlfriend **out** for dinner.

7 ☐ They're **taking on** ten new interns at Radio London. Why don't we apply?

8 ☐ It's not true. I just **made** it **up**.

9 ☐ When I've finished **giving out** the exam papers, you can start.

10 ☐ Why don't you **come round** after class? We could watch the film together.

11 ☐ I asked my brother to help me **carry out** the repairs on my roof.

12 ☐ My aunt **passed on** all of her special recipes to her nieces and nephews.

a appear
b continue
c invent
d distribute
e employ
f go somewhere with someone you have invited
g come to someone's home
h stop something because you can't do it
i stop working
j think of
k give something to someone
l do

b 4 10 Listen and check.

Phrasal verbs

Type 1 = no object
The verb and particle(s) are never separated.
Type 2 = + object (separable)
The verb and the particle can be separated.
Type 3 = + object (non-separable)
The verb and the particle(s) are never separated.

2 PHRASAL VERBS WITH *AWAY* AND *BACK*

The meaning of the particle

With some phrasal verbs, the meaning of the particle (the preposition or adverb after the verb) can help you to understand the phrasal verb, e.g. *away* often means *to a different place, out of sight*, and *back* often means to *return* an action.

a Complete the gaps with a verb from the list.

be (x2) call get give (x2) pay put run take

away

1 If you don't want those clothes, *give* them away. I'm sure the charity shop would like them.
2 Don't ______ away! I won't hurt you.
3 The boss will ______ away until the end of next week. He's at a conference in Mexico.
4 Please ______ your toys away. They're all over the floor.
5 If you take a paracetamol, it'll ______ the pain away!

back

6 I can only lend you the money if you promise to ______ me back next month.
7 That's my book. ______ it back.
8 I'm sorry, but I'm confiscating your phone. You'll ______ it back at the end of the day.
9 He's out, I'm afraid. Could you ______ back in about half an hour?
10 **A** Where are you going?
B Just to the shops. I'll ______ back in ten minutes.

b 4 11 Listen and check.

3 REVISION OF PHRASAL VERBS

Look at some other phrasal verbs from Files 1–6. Can you remember what they mean?

Type 1
be on (*TV or at the cinema*), end up (*all right after a bad start*), grow up (*on a farm in Sweden*), move in (*someone with a new house*), zoom in (*with a camera*)

Type 2
check out (*a website that sounds interesting*), close down (*a business that's doing badly*), give away (*old clothes*), give up (*a bad habit*), open up (*a new shop*), pick up (*a newspaper to read*), put on (*a show*), put up (*shelves*), send back (*a dish that you don't like*), set up (*a Wi-fi network*), switch off (*a boring TV programme*), take back (*something that was broken*), take out (*the rubbish*), throw away (*food that's past its sell-by date*), try on (*some jeans*), turn up / down / on / off (*the TV*)

Type 3
ask for (*the bill*), be out of (*a product that's sold out*), fit in with (*a new group of people*), get away from (*the noise*), get out of (*a car*), look after (*children or a pet*), look for (*your glasses*), look forward to (*a holiday next month*), look out for (*job vacancies*), look round (*a new city*), move back to (*your home town*)

◄ p.67

Looking after yourself

1 KEEPING FIT

a Match the words and pictures for equipment and exercises.

Equipment

- (use) an exercise bike
- (go on) a running machine (also treadmill)
- (do / lift) weights
- (use) a rowing machine
- (use) a cross-trainer
- (use) a yoga mat

Exercises

- do sit-ups
- do press-ups
- stretch
- do aerobics
- do spinning
- *10* do Pilates (or yoga)

b **4 27** Listen and check.

c What equipment or exercises are good if you…?

- want to lose weight
- want to tone your muscles
- want to do cardio exercises
- have a bad back
- want to improve your flexibility

2 BEAUTY TREATMENTS

a Match the words and pictures.

- manicure /ˈmænɪkjʊə/
- pedicure /ˈpedɪkjʊə/
- facial /ˈfeɪʃl/
- massage /ˈmæsɑːʒ/
- waxing /ˈwæksɪŋ/
- fake tan /feɪk ˈtæn/

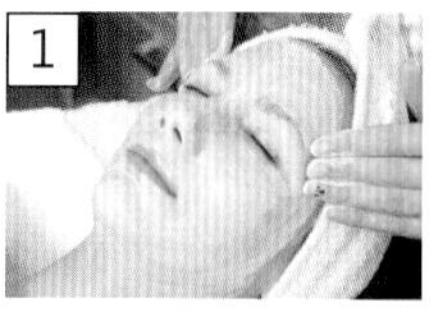

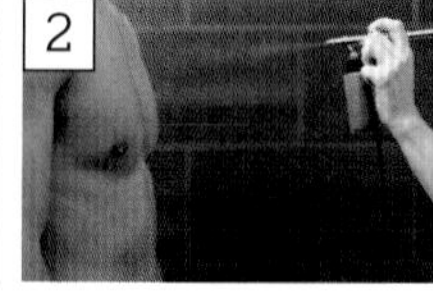

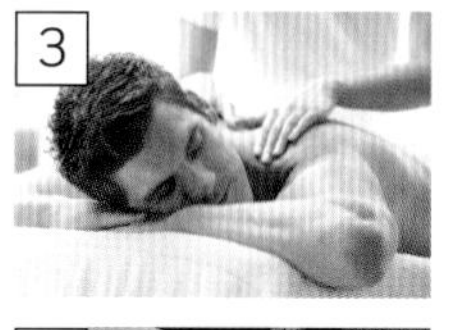

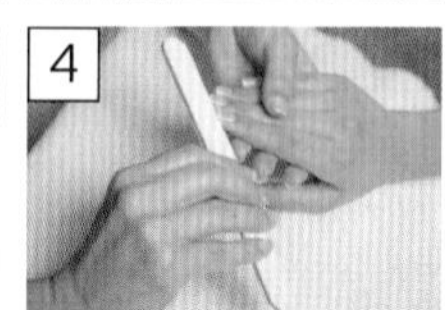

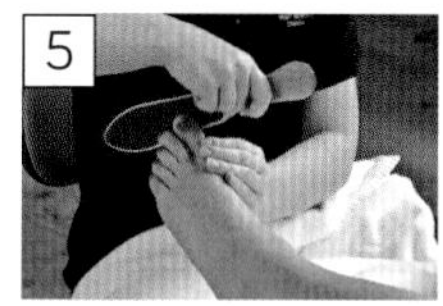

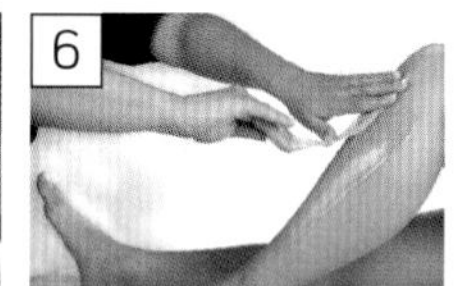

b **4 28** Listen and check.

c Have you ever had any of these treatments?

◄ p.74

3 AT THE HAIRDRESSER'S OR BARBER'S

a Match the words and pictures.

- bunches /ˈbʌntʃɪz/
- a buzz cut /ˈbʌz kʌt/ (also crew cut /ˈkruː kʌt/)
- a fringe /frɪndʒ/
- *6* a parting /ˈpɑːtɪŋ/
- a ponytail /ˈpəʊniteɪl/
- plaits /plæts/

have your hair…

- curled /kɜːld/
- cut /kʌt/
- dyed /daɪd/
- put up /pʊt ʌp/
- straightened /ˈstreɪtnd/

have…

- a blow dry /ˈbləʊ draɪ/
- a shave /ʃeɪv/
- a trim (or have your hair trimmed) /trɪm/
- highlights /ˈhaɪlaɪts/

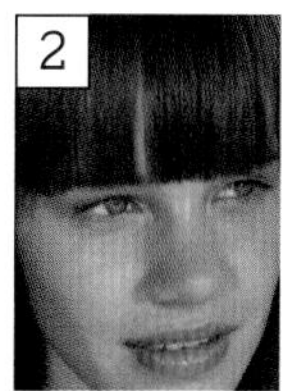

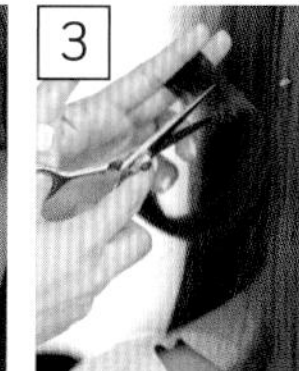

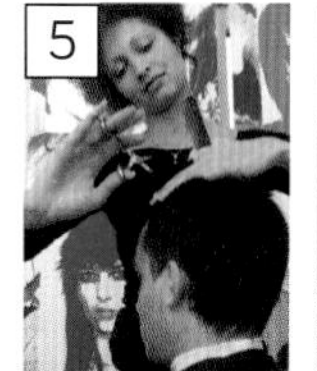

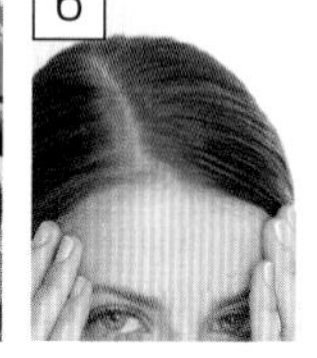

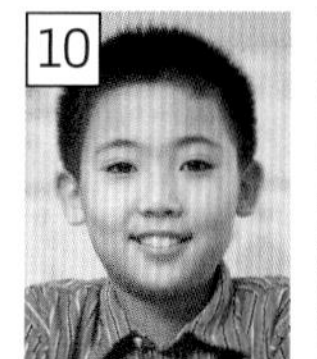

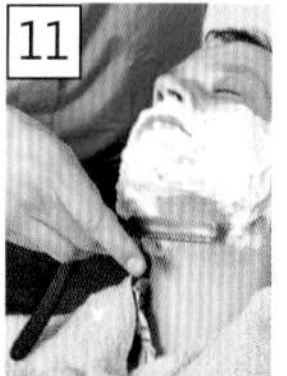

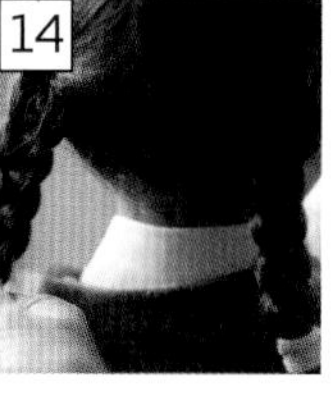

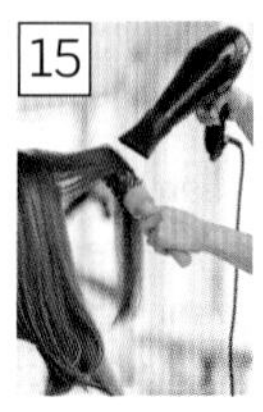

b **4 31** Listen and check.

◄ p.77

Appendix

Dependent prepositions

prepositions after verbs

I **agree with** my boss **about** the problem.
He **apologized for** being late.
She **applied for** the job.
We always **argue about** money.
I used to **argue with** my sister a lot.
We **arrived at** the airport at 6.00 a.m.
We **arrived in** Paris in the evening.
I don't **believe in** ghosts.
That bag **belongs to** me.
I can't **choose between** these two shirts.
Our weekend plans **depend on** the weather.
I **dreamt about** my grandfather last night.
They all **laughed at** me when I fell over.
I'm **looking forward to** my holiday.
I'll **pay for** your coffee.
We all **posed for** a photograph.
I **prefer** taking the train **to** flying.
You can always **rely on** your parents.
He **reminds** me **of** an old school friend.
She **shared** her sweets **with** my son.
They **smiled at** me.
I love **spending** money **on** clothes.
They **succeeded in** climbing the mountain.
I **talked to** the hotel manager **about** my room.
Are you **waiting for** someone?
Don't **worry about** it, it's not a problem.

prepositions after adjectives

She's **angry about** her salary.
She's **angry with** her boss.
He's very **close to** his father.
The film is **different from** the book.
I'm really **disappointed with** these photos.
She's **excited about** her new job.
Oxford is **famous for** its university.
I'm **fed up with** waiting. Let's go!
He's very **fond of** his teacher.
I'm **frightened** / **afraid** / **scared of** snakes.
He's **good** / **bad at** remembering names.
Vegetables are **good for** you.
She's **interested in** French literature.
I'm not very **keen on** fast food.
They were very **kind to** me.
He's **married to** my best friend.
I'm very **pleased with** my progress.
I'm **proud of** my children.
I'm **ready for** a holiday.
He's **responsible for** the sales team.
Don't be **rude to** him.
We're **sorry about** what happened.
They're **tired of** working every day.
She's **worried about** her car.

Verb patterns

verb + infinitive with *to*

be able (*to swim*)
afford (*to buy a flat*)
agree (*to help someone*)
arrange (*to meet*)
choose (*to do something*)
decide (*to buy a new computer*)
expect (*to fail an exam*)
forget (*to lock the door*)
help (*to cook dinner*)
hope (*to go to university*)
learn (*to swim*)
manage (*to escape*)
need (*to leave early*)
offer (*to do the washing-up*)
plan (*to start a family*)
pretend (*to be someone else*)
promise (*to pay someone back*)
refuse (*to cooperate*)
remember (*to buy a present*)
seem (*to be broken*)
try (*to repair the car*)
want (*to go on holiday*)
would like (*to travel abroad*)

verb + gerund (*-ing*)

admit (*stealing the money*)
avoid (*driving in the city centre*)
can't stand (*queueing*)
deny (*being involved*)
dislike (*going shopping*)
enjoy (*playing tennis*)
feel like (*going home early*)
finish (*having breakfast*)
hate (*being late*)
imagine (*living without the internet*)
keep (*forgetting his name*)
like (*cooking for friends*)
love (*reading*)
mind (*working in the evenings*)
miss (*living in Spain*)
practise (*playing a difficult piece*)
prefer (*running to swimming*)
recommend (*opening a bank account*)
spend (*a long time practising*)
stop (*raining*)
suggest (*seeing a doctor*)

verb + object + infinitive with *to*

advise (*me to pay cash*)
allow (*us to leave early*)
ask (*her to help*)
invite (*us to go away for the weekend*)
need (*you to fill in a form*)
order (*him to sit down*)
persuade (*me to come to the party*)
teach (*me to play the piano*)
tell (*them to be quiet*)
want (*you to explain*)

verb + object + infinitive without *to*

let (*me stay up late*)
make (*me tidy my room*)

Irregular verbs

5 39

Infinitive	Past simple	Past participle
be /bi/	was /wɒz/	been /biːn/
beat /biːt/	beat	beaten /'biːtn/
become /bɪ'kʌm/	became /bɪ'keɪm/	become
begin /bɪ'gɪn/	began /bɪ'gæn/	begun /bɪ'gʌn/
bite /baɪt/	bit /bɪt/	bitten /'bɪtn/
break /breɪk/	broke /brəʊk/	broken /'brəʊkən/
bring /brɪŋ/	brought /brɔːt/	brought
build /bɪld/	built /bɪlt/	built
buy /baɪ/	bought /bɔːt/	bought
can /kæn/	could /kʊd/	–
catch /kætʃ/	caught /kɔːt/	caught
choose /tʃuːz/	chose /tʃəʊz/	chosen /'tʃəʊzn/
come /kʌm/	came /keɪm/	come
cost /kɒst/	cost	cost
cut /kʌt/	cut	cut
do /duː/	did /dɪd/	done /dʌn/
draw /drɔː/	drew /druː/	drawn /drɔːn/
dream /driːm/	dreamt /dremt/ / dreamed /driːmd/	dreamt / dreamed
drink /drɪŋk/	drank /dræŋk/	drunk /drʌŋk/
drive /draɪv/	drove /drəʊv/	driven /'drɪvn/
eat /iːt/	ate /eɪt/	eaten /'iːtn/
fall /fɔːl/	fell /fel/	fallen /'fɔːlən/
feel /fiːl/	felt /felt/	felt
find /faɪnd/	found /faʊnd/	found
fly /flaɪ/	flew /fluː/	flown /fləʊn/
forget /fə'get/	forgot /fə'gɒt/	forgotten /fə'gɒtn/
get /get/	got /gɒt/	got
give /gɪv/	gave /geɪv/	given /'gɪvn/
go /gəʊ/	went /went/	gone /gɒn/
grow /grəʊ/	grew /gruː/	grown /grəʊn/
hang /hæŋ/	hung /hʌŋ/	hung
have /hæv/	had /hæd/	had
hear /hɪə/	heard /hɜːd/	heard
hide /haɪd/	hid /hɪd/	hidden /'hɪdn/
hit /hɪt/	hit	hit
hurt /hɜːt/	hurt	hurt
keep /kiːp/	kept /kept/	kept
know /nəʊ/	knew /njuː/	known /nəʊn/

Infinitive	Past simple	Past participle
lay /leɪ/	laid /leɪd/	laid
learn /lɜːn/	learnt /lɜːnt/	learnt
leave /liːv/	left /left/	left
lend /lend/	lent /lent/	lent
let /let/	let	let
lie /laɪ/	lay /leɪ/	lain /leɪn/
lose /luːz/	lost /lɒst/	lost
make /meɪk/	made /meɪd/	made
mean /miːn/	meant /ment/	meant
meet /miːt/	met /met/	met
pay /peɪ/	paid /peɪd/	paid
put /pʊt/	put	put
read /riːd/	read /red/	read /red/
ride /raɪd/	rode /rəʊd/	ridden /'rɪdn/
ring /rɪŋ/	rang /ræŋ/	rung /rʌŋ/
run /rʌn/	ran /ræn/	run
say /seɪ/	said /sed/	said
see /siː/	saw /sɔː/	seen /siːn/
sell /sel/	sold /səʊld/	sold
send /send/	sent /sent/	sent
set /set/	set	set
sew /səʊ/	sewed /səʊd/	sewn /səʊn/
shine /ʃaɪn/	shone /ʃɒn/	shone
shut /ʃʌt/	shut	shut
sing /sɪŋ/	sang /sæŋ/	sung /sʌŋ/
sit /sɪt/	sat /sæt/	sat
sleep /sliːp/	slept /slept/	slept
speak /spiːk/	spoke /spəʊk/	spoken /'spəʊkən/
spend /spend/	spent /spent/	spent
stand /stænd/	stood /stʊd/	stood
steal /stiːl/	stole /stəʊl/	stolen /'stəʊlən/
swim /swɪm/	swam /swæm/	swum /swʌm/
take /teɪk/	took /tʊk/	taken /'teɪkən/
teach /tiːtʃ/	taught /tɔːt/	taught
tell /tel/	told /təʊld/	told
think /θɪŋk/	thought /θɔːt/	thought
throw /θrəʊ/	threw /θruː/	thrown /θrəʊn/
understand /ʌndə'stænd/	understood /ʌndə'stʊd/	understood
wake /weɪk/	woke /wəʊk/	woken /'wəʊkən/
wear /weə/	wore /wɔː/	worn /wɔːn/
win /wɪn/	won /wʌn/	won
write /raɪt/	wrote /rəʊt/	written /'rɪtn/

Vowel sounds

	usual spelling	! but also
fish	i risky bin lid tin sitcom since	pretty women busy decided village physics
tree	ee sheep screen ea stream leaf e recycle thesis	people machine key field receipt
cat	a pack campus active cash packet stand	plaits
car	ar carton charger starter jar a craft drama grass	aunt laugh heart
clock	o bossy rock top bottom off on	watch want wash sausage because
horse	(o)or torch corkscrew al stall fall aw awful saw	war quarter pour fought saucer caught audience board
bull	u bush butcher's oo wood cookery look good	could should would woman
boot	oo spoon zoom u* glue true ew screw crew	suitcase cruise shoe move soup through queue
computer	Many different spellings. /ə/ is always unstressed. speaker spacious around contain professor	
bird	er serve prefer ir dirty circle ur turn blurred	research work world worse journey
egg	e pet hen lens sell fence selfish	friendly already healthy jealous many said

	usual spelling	! but also
up	u brush dustman mug mud bucket jug	money front someone enough touch couple
train	a* gate baker's ai nail waiter ay replay tray	break great weight straighten they grey
phone	o* remote stone tone rope oa boat soap	grow show bowl although sew
bike	i* tie wire y dry recycle igh light bright	buy eyes height
owl	ou round out found foreground ow towel crowd	
boy	oi noisy avoid oil join oy enjoy employ	
ear	eer cheerful volunteer ere here we're ear clear hear	really idea period theatre series
chair	air airport repair fair hairdresser are careful square	their there wear area
tourist	A very unusual sound. euro tour sure manicure luxurious	
/i/	A sound between /ɪ/ and /iː/. Consonant + *y* at the end of words is pronounced /i/. happy angry thirsty	
/u/	An unusual sound between /ʊ/ and /uː/. education usually situation	

* especially before consonant + *e*

short vowels   long vowels   diphthongs

Consonant sounds

	usual spelling		! but also
parrot	p pp	plate packet adaptor trip opposite apply	
bag	b bb	bulb bin bag probably tub rubbish robbed	
key	c k ck	comb score keep trekking brick padlock	chemist's scholarship qualifications account
girl	g gg	greengrocer's guidebook forgetful vinegar aggressive luggage	
flower	f ph ff	florist's safari pharmacy photography cliff affairs	enough laugh
vase	v	valley vacancy travel envious CV shave	of
tie	t tt	tutor teapot stick start batteries bottle	asked passed
dog	d dd	drill handle comedy hairdryer addictive middle	planted bored
snake	s ss ce/ci	swimsuit likes bossy dissertation fence cinema	science scene cycle
zebra	z s	quiz razor easy newsagent's loves reuse	
shower	sh ti (+ vowel) ci (+ vowel)	shop toothbrush childish cash ambitious stationer's delicious facial	sugar sure machine chef
television	An unusual sound. revision decision massage usually		

	usual spelling		! but also
thumb	th	throw rethink thread path tablecloth maths toothpaste	
mother	th	the that with weather sunbathe together	
chess	ch tch t (+ure)	chat chicken stretch match lecture future	
jazz	j g dge	jeweller's pyjamas dangerous package hedge bridge	
leg	l ll	lay lucky until reliable skill rebellious	
right	r rr	result referee profitable story current carry	written wrong
witch	w wh	war waste webinar switch whistle which	one once DIY
yacht	y before u	yet yellow yoga yourself university argue	
monkey	m mm	memory stream mountain moody hammer swimming	lamb climb
nose	n nn	needle pond intern barn spinning thinner	knife know
singer	ng before k	unpacking flying string bring thanks pink	
house	h	hill hiking behind farmhouse unhappy perhaps	who whose whole

voiced unvoiced

OXFORD

UNIVERSITY PRESS

Great Clarendon Street, Oxford, OX2 6DP,
United Kingdom

Oxford University Press is a department of the University of Oxford. It furthers the University's objective of excellence in research, scholarship, and education by publishing worldwide. Oxford is a registered trade mark of Oxford University Press in the UK and in certain other countries

First published in 2014
2018 2017 2016 2015
10 9 8 7 6 5 4

ISBN: 978 0 19 455809 9
ISBN: 978 0 19 455808 2 (with Oxford Online Skills)

Printed in China

This book is printed on paper from certified and well-managed sources.

ACKNOWLEDGEMENTS

The authors would like to thank all the teachers and students round the world whose feedback has helped us to shape English File.

The authors would also like to thank: all those at Oxford University Press (both in Oxford and around the world) and the design team who have contributed their skills and ideas to producing this course.

A very special thanks from Clive to Maria Angeles, Lucia, and Eric, and from Christina to Cristina, for all their support and encouragement. Christina would also like to thank her children Joaquin, Marco, and Krysia for their constant inspiration.

Mike Boyle would like to thank his wife Christine for her support, as well as Christina and Clive for their invaluable assistance.

The publisher and authors would also like to thank the following for their invaluable feedback on the materials: David Silles McLaney, Alfredo Ramos Benedito, Juan J. Lago Leis, Enrique Pilar Narros, Jonathan Grimes, Asunción Calderón González, Ignacio Bermejo, Isabel Corral Prieto, Marta del Arco, Beatriz Martin Garcia, Brian Brennan, Gill Hamilton, Jane Hudson, Lucie Cotterill, Marcus Mattia, Sophie Rogers, Donna Hutchinson, Rachel Buttery-Graciani, Lenka Slunečková, Ivona Cindlerová.

The Publisher and Authors are very grateful to the following who have provided information, personal stories, and/or photographs: Debbie Kuan, (p.4), Wendy Woodward (p.9), Catherine Ball, Emi Kinoshita, (p.19), Brian Voce (pp.28–29), Samantha Richter (pp.31, 113), Krysia Cogollos (p.31), Steve and Joan Boyle (pp.31, 48, 117), Joe Kenyon (p.39), Wendy and Lizzie Molyneux (pp.44–45), Tim Bentinck (p.51), Dino Karveli (p.77), Anna Kenyon (p.90), Kate Chomacki (p.99)

We would also like to thank all the friends, colleagues and people in the street who have constantly answered surveys and questions for us.

The authors and publisher are grateful to those who have given permission to reproduce the following extracts and adaptations of copyright material: p.34 Adapted extract from "Freegans: The bin scavengers" by Liz Scarff, www.independent.co.uk, 20 February 2006. Reproduced by permission of The Independent. p.38 Adapted extract from "What price your first step?" by Jane Phillimore, You Magazine, 27 March 2011. Reproduced by permission of Solo Syndication. p.40 Adapted extract from "The best Saturday job I ever had …", The Times, 4 July 2012. Reproduced by permission of News Syndication. p.43 Adapted extract from "Recycling facts and figures", www.recycling-guide.org.uk, accessed 23 October 2013. Reproduced by permission of Fubra Limited. p.46 Adapted extract from "House of Cards: what I learned by watching the whole series in one sitting" by Gennady Kolker, www.guardian.co.uk, 5 February 2013. Copyright Guardian News & Media Ltd 2013. p.49 Adapted extract from "Goodbye... and good riddance!" by Liz Jones, The Mail on Sunday, 11 November 2012. Reproduced by permission of Solo Syndication. p.58 Adapted extract from "My 10 worst customer service crimes" by Mary Portas, www.telegraph.co.uk, 18 January 2011. © Telegraph Media Group Limited 2011. Reproduced by permission. p.63 Adapted extract from "United Kingdom: Tipping & Etiquette", www.tripadvisor.co.uk, accessed 23 October 2013. Reproduced by permission of TripAdvisor LLC. p.66 Adapted extract from "When luck comes to town" by Sonia Zhuravlyova, The Times, 5 July 2012. Reproduced by permission of News Syndication. p.71 Adapted extract from "Welcome to the new gold mines" by Rowenna Davis, The Guardian, 5 March 2009. Copyright Guardian News & Media Ltd 2009. Reproduced by permission. p.111 Adapted extract from "Big chill: the hidden medical benefits of cryotherapy" by Anna Moore, www.telegraph.co.uk, 9 February 2009. © Telegraph Media Group Limited 2009. Reproduced by permission. p.79 Extract from The Lost Continent: Travels in Small Town America by Bill Bryson, published by Secker & Warburg, 1989. © 1989 by Bill Bryson. Reprinted by permission of The Random House Group Limited and Bill Bryson. p.83 Adapted extract from "Event cinema: live screenings of opera and ballet are the British new wave" by Jonathan Owen, www.independent.co.uk, 27 January 2013. Reproduced by permission of The Independent. p.84 Adapted extract from "I always have a notecard in my pocket that tells me what the date is" by Gweneviere Mann and Yasir Salem, http://storycorps.org, accessed 4 July 2013. Reproduced by permission of StoryCorps. p.86 Adapted extract from "Jill Price, the woman who remembers everything", The Sunday Times, 21 September 2008. Reproduced by permission of News Syndication. p.88 Extract from "Mabel" by W. Somerset Maugham, *The Complete Short Stories of Somerset Maugham*, William Heinemann Ltd, 1952. Reprinted by permission of United Agents on behalf of: The Literary Fund. p.96 Extracts from "10 Things Brits Do That Drive Americans Nuts" by Ruth Margolis, www.bbcamerica.com, 17 May 2012. Reproduced by permission of BBC News. p.97 Extracts from "10 Things Americans Do That Drive Brits Nuts" by Ruth Margolis, www.bbcamerica.com, 15 May 2012. Reproduced by permission of BBC News. p.100 Adapted extract from "The dreaded gaokao looms" by Patti Waldmeir, Notebook, 5 June 2012. Reproduced by permission of Financial Times. p.103 Adapted extract from "How Do I Choose?" by Anthony Nemecek, Uni in the USA...and Beyond (www.uniintheusa.com), accessed 23 October 2013. Copyright Lucas Publications Ltd. Reproduced by permission.

Sources: www.houseofcolour.co.uk, www.marketresearchworld.net, http://blog.notonthehighstreet.com, www.dailymail.co.uk, www.techradar.com, www.guardian.co.uk, www.nypost.com, http://online.wsj.com, http://nymag.com

The Publisher would like to thank the following for their kind permission to reproduce photographs: Alamy pp.6 (Sony logo/© Business), (Nike logo/ Dorling Kindersley), 10 (shop/Julian Eales), 18 (ticket/shinypix), (apples/ incamerastock), (Adele cd/Studio 101), (book/CBW), (iphone/Adrian Lyon), 21 (firehose/Imagebroker), 24 (Nick/I love images), 26 (teen girl/ Flickr Open), 28 (tower/Rebecca Johnson), 30 (Andes/Friedrich Smeier), 43 (recycling/Alex Segre), 48 (Spanish village/Robert Harding Picture Library), (English village/nagelestock.com), 54 (bulb/Construction photography), 55 (Ikea/D Burke), 58 (cash register/Justin Kase) (customer/Kumar Sriskandan), 59 (receipt/Plinthpics), 60 (sign/Michael Neelon), 63 (Ben Molyneux food and drinks), 71 (still/Zuma Press, Inc), 72 (Ecover/shinypix), 76 (woman cutting hair/BSIP SA), 77 (shaved head/ Bubbles Photolibrary), 78 (Spartan soldier/Hercules Milas), 80 (exterior Westminster/A.p.S (UK), 85 (gray-haired woman/Bubbles photolibrary), (man in red T shirt.Buzzshotz), 88 (Diana Memorial/Gianni Muratore), 90 (Eygptian wedding/Andrew Holt), 95 (starbucks mugs/Erkan Mehmet), (cupcakes/Corey Vidler), 98 (oral exam/Angela Hampton), 105 (Lauren/juanmonino), 109 (handsaw/Image Farm Inc), (broom/ Derek Croucher), (pins and pegs/incamerastock), (washers/Anton Starikov), 110 (mop/Olmarmar) , (saw/Image Farm Inc.), 113 (pink and blue cushion/Yay Media), (pink fluffy cushion/photonic 14), (plain pink cushion/Yongyut Khasawaong), 114 (Sheila/David J Green/Lifestyle), (Andrew/ONOKY/photononstop), 118 (Zoe/Image Source), (wishing column/LOOK Die Bildagentur der Fotografen GmbH), 153 (make-up bag/YAY Media AS), (pyjames/Creative Control), (swimsuit/Art Directors & TRIP), (toothbrush/Danny Smythe), (phone charger/Metta digital), (repellent/whiteboxmedia limited), (toothpaste/Richard Heyes), (dinghy sailing/Joel Douillet), (sightseeing/Caro), snorkelling/LOOK Die Bildagentur der Fotografen GmbH), (hiking/superclic), 154 (stationers/ Charles Stirling), (estate agent/Ian Masterton), (drugs/Bonkers AboutPictures), (travel agents/Radharc Images), newsagents/Gregory Wrona), (butchers/RGB Ventures LLC dba Superstock), (bakers/Noble Images), (fishmongers/Alex Segre), (craft stall/Steppenwolf), (hypermarket/Peter Bowater), (off-licence/Jack Sullivan), (GAP/Ben Molyeux Retail), (Zara/Lou- Foto), (health food store/Richard Levine), (laundrette/reppans), 156 (jar/RT images), (plastic bag/Mode Images), (tub/studiomode), (box/B.A.E Inc.), polystyrene tray/Metta digital), (lid/ RT Images), (wrapper/Chris Haye), (sell-by date/David J Green), (coke can/pumpkinpie), (packet/Carolyn Jenkins), (juice carton/Nikreates), (yoghurt carton/studiomode), 158 (advertising/Art Directors/TRIP), (weather/Mark Richardson), 159 (sticks/ncamerastock), (path/Derek Croucher), (stones/Peter Stone), (valley/Robert Harding World Imagery), (bush), (pond/Ana Stowe), (farmhouse/Stephen Dorey), 160 (a paintbrush/Jon Helgason), (rope/Derek Croucher), (tap/Milos Luzanin), (bucket/Judith Collins), (ladder/Hugh Threlfall), (tiles/Anton Starikov), (wood/Anatoliy Sadovskiy), (shed/macana), (matches/David J. Green), batteries/Oliver Leedham), (glue/whiteboxmedia), (penknife/Judith Collins), (thread/Helen Sessions), (lightbulb/Construction photography), 161 (carrying tray/Andrew Catterall), (recommending a dish/ViewStock), (serving/Kumar Sriskandan), (pouring wine/Bon Appetit), (laying table/David Levenson), (trying wine/UpperCut Images), (asking for bill/Beyond Fotomedia GmbH), (complaining/allesalltag), 163 (yoga mat/Wilawan Khasawong), (press-ups/Tetra Images), (running machine/Wilawan Khasawong), (tanning/ableimages), (massage/ stockbroker), (manicure/Mandy Godbehear), (pedicure/HP Canada), (waxing/Francis Vachon), (dying hair), (fringe/Latin Stock Collection), (ponytail/Ellen Isaacs), (trim/Caro), (parting/Emotive Images), (pigtails/ YAY Media AS/Alamy), (highlights/CandyBox Photography), (plaits/ RayArt Graphics); Mike Boyle pp.31 (all bar b), 117, 155; Dairygoodness. ca p.118 (cheese brochette); Arnos Design Ltd pp.18 (DVD cover), (laptop box), 30; The Bridgeman Art Library p.11 (*Woman Embroidering* 1812/Georg Friedrich Kerstin); Abigail Bryans pp.20 (jar and sign), 21 (mugshot and sign); Edwina Cooper pp.20 (cushions), 21 (mugshot), 74 (mamman/Paule Seux/Hemisemis), 78 (flag/Eduard Korniyenko), 95(GAP/Steve Vidler), 99 (driving/Ocean); Corbis pp.11 (butterfly/Horst Ossinger), 24 (Laura/Rick Gomez), 37 (bottles/Andrew Brookes), 40 (Kane/Robbie Jack), (Stafford/Colin Mc Pherson), 100 (Gaokao/ Imaginechina), 115 (grey haired woman/Janusz Kawa, 118 (restaurant/ Atlantide Phototravel), 120 (wedding), 154 (deli/cultura), (dry cleaners/ Ocean), 161 (taking orders/Wavebreak Media Ld), (ordering food/Hill Street Studios/Blend Images), 163 (put-up hair/Jutta Klee/ableimages), (buzz cut/Shannon Fagan); Bryce Duffy pp.86a (Jill Price); Drcap.co.uk pp.95 (cap); Elvis and Kresse pp.20 (firehouse bag); Endemol p.158 (Big Brother still); Eyevine pp.69 (all/Sara Krulwich/The New York Times); Fatface/PR Shots pp.18 (T shirt); Getty Images pp.6 (Google logo/ Bloomberg), (Steve Jobs/John G Mabanglo), 11 (dead salmon/Stockbyte), 16 (Caroline/Juanmonino), 18 (bread/stockbyte), 20 (wallet/Barcroft Media), 21 (Kresse and Elvis Wesling/Barcroft media), 24 (Sarah/Image Source), 26 (baby/photodisc/Leanne Temme), (toddler/Shunyu Fan), (woman 30's/OJO Images), (man at computer/Tara Moore), (noise/Don Bayley), 31 (blowing bubbles/Nathan Jones), 40 (Fiennes/Ton Shaw), 44 (all stills/Twentieth Century Fox televison), 45 (all stills/Twentieth Century Fox televison), 48 (alps/Brian Lawrence), 51 (corn/stockbyte), (recording b/w/Fox Fotos), 58 (Mary Portas/Neale Haynes), (supermarket checkouts/The Image Bank), 59 (clothes rail/thenakedsnail/Flick Open), 70 (World of Warcraft/Bloomberg), 71 (chinese game players/Liu Jin), 74 (pool/Ludovic), 76 (woman painting walls/Nadya Lukic), 77 (punk style/ Jame Evans), (dreadlocks/Lonely Planet Images), (blue streaked hair/ Jamie Evans), 78 (Danish queen/Antony Jones), 79 (cannon/John Moore), 80(chair/Oli Scarff), 81 (The Shard/Cultura Travel/Richard Seymour), 85 (man in brown shirt/stevecoleimages), (brunette with scarf/Rafael Elias/Flickr), 88 (Somerset Maughan/Michael Ochs Archive), (steamer/Buyenlarge), 98 (written exam/Chris Ryan), (cheating/Glow Images), (invigilator/Roy Mehta), 104 (imac/Handout), 105 (plane/Hans Neleman), 113 (pink room/gerenme), (glitterball/Buenavista Images), 114 (Caroline/Juanamonino), (Mark/Jena Ardell), (Haylee/Jay p. Morgan), (Michael/Laflor), (Danielle/Mint Images/Tim Robbins), Sam (Joshua Hodge Photography), 115 (child playing/thebang), 116 (Kate Lewis/Hero Images), 118 (Rafael/Arsela), 119 (Hagia Sofia/Marco Brivio), (mosaic// DEA/G. Dagli Orti), 154 (greengrocers/Jason Todd), 158 (wildlife documentary/Sylvain Cordier/hemis.fr), (chat show/CBS Photo Archive), 159 (rocks/Matthew p. Wicks), (gate/Anne C. Dowie), (cliffs/ David Henderson), (field/Image Source), (hedge/Francois de Heel), (stream/Peter Unger), (hill/Lok Photography), 163 (spinning/Yellow Dog Productions), (sit ups/Robert Daly), (curling hair/AAGAMIA), (straightened/Zero Creatives); House of Colour pp.9 (website); Ikea pp.6 (logo); Istockphoto pp.6 (Samsung logo/George Clerk), 11 (tree/ mb-fotos), 18 (trainers/Alec051), 26 (pensioner/Alex Raths), 85 (afro-american woman/digital skillet), (man with glasses/Suzana Profeta); Dino Karveli pp.77; Manchester News pp.49 (Liz Jones); Wendy Molyneux p.45 (script writers); McKittrick Hotel pp.69 (logo); NB Pictures ((Meryl Streep/Annie Liebowitz); New York Media pp.75 (King Spa sauna/Marvin Orellana); Chris O' Donovan pp.39 (Rosie and Lauren); Oxford University Press photobank pp.18 (jeans/Gareth Boden); Plain Picture p.77 (pink hair/fstop); Press Association Images pp.5, 6 (Jeff Bezos), 34 (freegan/Soeren Stache/DPA), 51 (Camilla/Arthur Edwards/The Sun), (Timothy Bentinck); Rex Features Ltd pp.40 (Ross/ Richard Gardner), (Parks/Geoffrey Swaine), 51 (Bentinck and cast/Denis Jones), 60 (restaurant), (Michel Roux cooking), 75 (cryotherapy/Paul Webb), 76 (man at hairdressers/I love images), 78 (Ataturk/Sipa Press), 80 (wedding). 81 (ceiling/Graham Wiltshire), (Taylor Swift), 101 (exam results/Skye Brackpool), 158 (cookery/Nils Jorgensen), (drama/MCT), (quiz) (sport/Back Pages Images), (sitcom/CBS/Everett), (soap/TNT/ Courtesy: Everett Collection), (period drama//Everett Collection), (news); Reuters pp.19 (high street/Luke MacGregor), (boarding up shop/ StefanWermuth), (closed down sign/Phil Noble); Riccochet pp.61 (Roux and trainees); Sam Richter p.113 (Ana); Roy Ritchie p.36; Shutterstock pp.18 (oranges/Hamik), (flowers/Kietr), 26 (boy on floor/Sergey Peterman), 54 (string/jocic), (nail/Yanas0, (screw driver/Oleg Golovnev), 74 yoga/Anna Furman), (crunches/Dmitry Kalinovsky), 76 (male painter/Tyler Olson), 91 (cake ornament/Gemenacom), 109 (spanner/ Kitch Bain), (stapler/domnitsky), (pliers/Paul Paladin), (tweezers/ Coprid), 110 (Velcro/Praisaeng), (a drill/Kitch Bain), 153 (sunscreen/ Konstantin Faraktinov), (wash bag/Carlos Yudica) (hairdryer/Nordlng), (comb/You Touch Pix of EuToch), (adaptor/exopixel), (razor/ canonzoom), (beach towel/sergign), (brush/Artur Synenko), (trunks/ Karkas), (memory card/Ilya Akinshin) (flip flops/dotshock), (nail scissors/Kostenko Maxim), (scuba diving/C.K. Ma), (waterskiing/Valery V Markov), (camping/Studio1 One), (windsurfing/Dima Fadeev), 154 (jewellers/Iakov Filimonov) (florists/Polia Shestakov), 156 (bottle/ design56), (tin/Sebastien Crocker), 158 (TV stand/Kitch Bain), (remote control/Andrzej Petelski), 159 (leaf/Iurii Konoval), (fence/GQ), (mud/ Matthijs Wetterauw), (grass/digitalvox), (wood/Piotr Krzeslak), (cow/ Supertrooper), (sheep/Eric Isselee), (chickens/Anna Stowe), (lambs/Eric Lam), (cockerel/Christian Musat), 160 (bricks/Elnur), (hammer/STILLFX), (screwdriver/Golovnev), (wire/Claudio Divizia), (nails/Yanas), (screws/ Boris Toshhev), (electric drill/RusGri), (padlock/koosen), (sellotape/ Coprid), (torch/Petr Malyshev), (handle/B Calkins), (drawer/Sfocato), 161 (leaving a tip/photowind), (woman on phone/Warren Goldswain), 163 (weights/STILLFX), (bike/Kitch bain), cross trainer/Dimitar Sotirov), (rowing machine/Kjpargeter), (stretches/Brocreative), (yoga/ Deklofenak), (aerobics/Andrey Popov), (facial/c12), (cut/Andresr), (shave/VOF), (blow dry/Andresr); Simon & Schuster p.86 (book cover); StoryCorps p.85 (women at mike), (Gweneviere and Yasir); The Picture Desk pp.45 (still/Media Rights Capital), 78 *Lincoln*/Dreamworks/20th Century Fox), (*300*/Warner Bros/legendary Pictures), (*Dr Zhivago*/MGM Ken Danvers), 95 (*Mad Men*/Radical Media), 158 (*The Simpsons*/20th Century Fox/Groeing, Matt); The Rough Guide pp.153 (Sweden); Philippe Tarbouriech p.115 (child in red); Brian Voce pp.29 (all bar Meryl Streep); WeareLucky.com pp.66,67 ; Wikipedia Commons p.11 (paint pot); www.curtainupevents.com pp.103 (short film still); Mari Yamazaki p.49 (Rob Penn).

Commissioned photography by: Gareth Boden pp.9 (Wendy), 50, 54, 154 (DIY), 161 (table and tray). *Practical English stills photography by*: Rob Judges

Photoshoot management and art editing by: Helen Reilly/Arnos Design Ltd

Although every effort has been made to trace and contact copyright holders before publication, this has not been possible in some cases. We apologise for any apparent infringement of copyright and if notified, the publisher will be pleased to rectify any errors or omissions at the earliest opportunity.